—————————— STATES OF NATURE ——————————

Support for this book comes from an endowment for environmental studies made possible by generous contributions from Richard C. Bartlett, Susan Aspinall Block, and the National Endowment for the Humanities.

STATES OF NATURE

Science, Agriculture, and Environment in the Spanish Caribbean, 1760–1940

STUART MCCOOK

UNIVERSITY OF TEXAS PRESS

AUSTIN

Requests for permission to reproduce material from this work should be sent to
Permissions, University of Texas Press, Box 7819, Austin, TX 78713-7819.

⊗ The paper used in this book meets the minimum requirements of ANSI/NISO
Z39.48-1992 (R1997) (Permanence of Paper).

Library of Congress Cataloging-in-Publication Data

McCook, Stuart George, 1965–
States of nature : science, agriculture, and environment in the Spanish
Caribbean, 1760 –1940 / Stuart George McCook—1st ed.
p.   cm.
Includes bibliographical references (p.   ).
ISBN 978-0-292-75257-3
1. Agriculture—Caribbean Area—History.   2. Agricultural innovations—
Caribbean Area—History.   3. Agriculture—Technology transfer—
Caribbean Area—History.   4. Agriculture—Environmental
aspects—Caribbean Area—History.   I. Title.
S477.A1 M33   2002
630′.9729—dc21   2001052228

Para Alicia, por todo

CONTENTS

ILLUSTRATIONS

FIGURES

TABLE

ACKNOWLEDGMENTS

So many people have helped along the way that it is hard to know where to begin my acknowledgments or where to end them. At Princeton, Jeremy Adelman and the late Gerry Geison supervised the dissertation on which this book is based. I received the news of Gerry's death just as the manuscript for this book was being copyedited. I regret that he will not see the book in its final form, since his counsel, insights, and advice are woven into its fabric. I, and many others, will sorely miss him. I first explored the ideas that appear here at the weekly meetings of the Program in History of Science. Special thanks to Michael Mahoney, Angela Creager, and Mary Voss and to my classmates, Jordan Kellman, Jim Strick, Paul Lucier, Kevin Downing, Teri Hopper, and Andrea Rusnock. Michael F. Jiménez, Ken Mills, Clara García Ayluardo, and Arcadio Díaz Quiñones helped me to learn the intricacies of Latin American history and culture. Peter T. Johnson, Latin America bibliographer at the Firestone Library, helped me to track down many obscure sources. The Program in History of Science, the History Department, the Program in Latin American Studies, the Association of Princeton Graduate Alumni, and the Council on Regional Studies provided essential funding for research and for language training.

Marcos Cueto, now of the Universidad Peruana Cayetano Heredia, introduced me to the small but lively world of the history of science in Latin America. My intellectual home in South America was the Science Studies Department of the Instituto Venezolano de Investigaciones Científicas. There, Hebe Vessuri and Yajaira Freites were my patient and generous mentors during my six months as a resident scholar and ever since. Yolanda Texera Arnal, of the Centro de Estudios del Desarrollo (CENDES) of the Central University of Venezuela, shared with me her research and thoughts on Henri Pittier and the history of botany in Venezuela. At the Jardín Botánico de Caracas, my research was speeded along by Lic. Rafael Ortiz and Lic. Alberto Rodríguez. The staffs of the libraries of the Biblioteca Nacional, the Hemeroteca Nacional, the Ministerio de Agricultura y Cría, the Ministerio de Relaciones Exteriores, the Ministerio de Fomento, and the Banco Central de Venezuela provided extensive help, often in the face of severe institutional limitations. The library of the Maracaibo branch of the Banco Central de Venezuela was also an important source for information on the economic history of Venezuela, as well as pleasantly air-conditioned.

In Puerto Rico, Carlos Domínguez Cristóbal, of the Institute of Tropical Forestry, introduced me to the research libraries of San Juan. I am particularly grateful to Carlos Chardón, Jr., who not only gave me access to his father's papers but also filled in many of the blanks that the letters and documents could not fully explain. His insights on Puerto Rico past and present were particularly helpful. In Río Piedras, I thank Dr. Henri Liogier and Dr. Frank Wadsworth. At the Colegio de Mayagüez, Rector Stuart J. Ramos and Professors Juan Rivero, Angel Berríos, and Inez Sastre helped me to develop a historical overview of the community of biologists who worked in early-twentieth-century Puerto Rico. The staffs at the libraries of the Institute of Tropical Forestry in Río Piedras, the Colección Puertorriqueña at the UPR–Río Piedras, and the Colección Puertorriqueña at the Colegio de Mayagüez were models of speed and efficiency.

Angel Ruíz Zuñiga of the University of Costa Rica introduced me to San José and, on two separate research trips, helped me to locate key resources at the university and elsewhere. Over the course of many dinners and outings, both he and his family taught me much about Costa Rica past and present. Luis Diego Gómez of the Organization of Tropical Studies helped me to clarify my picture of botany in late-nineteenth-century Costa Rica and kindly lent me copies of rare botanical and ecological maps. The staffs of the Archivo Nacional, the Biblioteca Nacional, and the Museo Nacional helped me to track down often obscure documents and publications, many of which were uncataloged and which I would not have found without their assistance.

A postdoctoral fellowship in 1996–1997 at the Program in History of Science and Technology at the University of Minnesota allowed me to do further research and writing and provided a lively intellectual home. Sally Kohlstedt's perceptive and incisive commentary helped me to rethink and reorganize several chapters. Thanks also to John Beatty, John Eyler, Sara Tjossem, Mark Largent, Erik Conway, Juliet Burba, and Karin Matchett. I am also grateful to the University of Minnesota's MacArthur Program in Peace and International Cooperation, which funded a research trip to Costa Rica in spring 1997.

The History Department at The College of New Jersey (TCNJ) has been home since fall 1997. It is a small yet vibrant intellectual community, whose members have introduced me to the history of other parts of the world. Through many conversations (and many meals) over the past few years, they have helped me to place this project in a global context. Tom Allsen, Cynthia Paces, honorary department member Jay Carter, and Derek Petersen have each brought sharp critical perspectives to various parts of this work. TCNJ's Faculty Institutional Research and Sabbatical Leave committee granted me alternate assignment time so as to complete the manuscript.

In addition to the people already mentioned, many others in Canada, the United States, and Latin America generously took time to read and comment on parts of the manuscript or helped me to work out some key ideas. Profuse thanks to John Soluri, Kate Christen, Sterling Evans, Reinaldo Funes, Catherine LeGrand, Christopher London, J. H. Galloway, J. C. Mutchler, Jon Earle, Leslie Tuttle, Eric Love, Robert E. Kohler, Henrika Kuklick, Helen Rozwadowski, Rebecca Scott, Judy Ewell, Elinor Melville, Juanita de Barros, and Pamela Henson. I have presented parts of this book at the Departmental Colloquium in the History of Science, Medicine, and Technology at Johns Hopkins University, at the Encuentro Bilateral Harvard University–Jardín Botánico de Cienfuegos in Cuba, the Minnesota Seminar in the History of Science and Technology, and the Institutes of Plant Botany and Systematics at the University of Zurich. The participants in these seminars did me the great favor of asking me tough but constructive questions.

It has been a great pleasure to work with the University of Texas Press. Bill Bishel has shepherded this project from raw manuscript to finished book with efficiency and good humor. Sheila Berg's careful copyediting has made this book much tighter and clearer. Allison Faust and Lynne Chapman oversaw the many steps involved in preparing the manuscript for publication and graciously allowed me extra time to complete the revisions. Meri Clark proofread the galleys with meticulous care. I am especially grateful to the two referees who read the original version of the manuscript, Marshall Eakin and Angus Wright, for their detailed and thoughtful comments and for forgoing their anonymity so that I could consult with them as I worked on the revisions.

I could not have done any of this without the support of family and friends. Special thanks to my parents, Monica and Buff McCook, to my sister Susan and my brother Douglas, and to my wonderful grandmothers, Edith McCook and Marion Sullivan. Edith McCook and my aunts Katherine and Sheila McCook devoted an entire afternoon to helping me come up with a pithy title for the book, which had eluded me for a long time. For me, the greatest reward of this project was meeting Alicia Viloria Petit. We have shared many journeys since we met in Caracas, and I look forward to sharing the journeys to come. Her love and her passion for life are my greatest inspirations.

Parts of this book originally appeared in the journals *Agricultural History* and *Americas: A Quarterly Review of Inter-American Cultural History.* I thank these journals for permission to reprint parts of this book that originally appeared in their pages and the Hunt Institute for Botanical Documentation for permission to reproduce the photograph of Henri Pittier at the herbarium of the Jardín Botánico de Caracas. Carlos Chardón kindly granted permission to quote from his father's papers.

$\backsim$

INTRODUCTION

Science, Nature, and Development
during the Export Boom, 1760–1940

$\backsim$

Т he process of nation building in Latin America transformed the relations among the state, the economy, and nature. As Latin America became integrated into the world economy between the late eighteenth century and the early twentieth century, nature took on new roles and meanings. It became the raw material for national economic and political development. Natural objects—plants, minerals, and even guano—were transformed into primary commodities to be exported to global markets. In the Caribbean basin, the most important export commodities were plants. Coffee and bananas fueled economic growth in Central America; sugar, tobacco, and coffee in Cuba, the Dominican Republic, and Puerto Rico; coffee, cacao, and bananas in Colombia and Venezuela. Nation, economy, and nature thus became deeply intertwined. The words of the Cuban sugar planter José Manuel Casanova, *"Sin azúcar, no hay país"* (Without sugar, there is no nation), succinctly capture the ideological, economic, and political roles of nature in forming nations.

This book traces the history of the intersections of nature, economy, and nation in the Spanish Caribbean through a history of the agricultural and botanical sciences. The power of governments, planters, and, later, scientists depended on their ability to control the natural world and shape it to their models of development. During the late eighteenth and early nineteenth centuries, governments and planters sponsored some research into the region's key crops and landscapes. The political and economic tumult of the wars of independence, however, stopped most scientific activity. Later in the nineteenth century, as the Spanish Caribbean entered the global economy, public and private sponsorship of the plant sciences revived and strengthened. During the liberal era (roughly 1870–1930), dozens of botanical gardens, natural history museums, and agricultural experiment stations were founded throughout the region. They were funded by state and national governments, by agricultural associations, by transnational corporations, and by affluent planters. The plant sciences offered these groups the tools to extend their control over the natural world and thereby consolidate their own political and economic power.[1]

In the aftermath of independence from Spain, the new governments sought to extend their power over corporate institutions and citizens. Their models of nation building reflected prevailing liberal ideologies, which advocated the regulation and standardization of all aspects of public and private life. They took censuses to measure the size and composition of the citizenry. They wrote constitutions that aimed to make all citizens—at least in theory— equally subject to the law. These efforts to regulate, standardize, and subjugate extended to the nations' wild and domesticated landscapes. Liberal governments used science and technology to subjugate all facets of the natural world, from mosquitoes to mountains. To eradicate the mosquitoes that carried yellow fever, malaria, and other tropical diseases, governments hired physicians and biologists. To overcome mountains and other geographic barriers, they hired engineers to build railroads. To bring their nations' plants under the control of the state, they turned to the plant sciences. They turned their gaze toward the seemingly limitless wild landscapes and wondered what kinds of timbers, fibers, and other potentially lucrative plants lay within. They hired botanists to nationalize landscapes by conducting botanical inventories and publishing floras. They hired agricultural scientists to ensure the continuing production of export crops.[2]

The control of nature through science also helped the region's agricultural elites to sustain their economic power, which depended on their ability to continue producing crops for export. During the eighteenth and early nineteenth centuries, planters first increased crop production through a strategy of extensification, of clearing new agricultural lands and improving the technologies of harvesting and transportation. Gradually, planters also began a strategy of intensification, of improving the yields per acre. In the latter half of the nineteenth century, however, the natural world began to slip from their control, thereby jeopardizing their power. Planters expressed mounting concern about impediments to cultivating their plants. They worried about deforestation and declining crop yields, about floods and drought, about insects and rodents and myriad other problems that threatened to reduce or put a stop to export growth. In their single-minded pursuit of increasing production, they created many of these problems themselves. They cleared extensive tracts of forest, which generated new environmental problems, such as declining soil fertility, widespread erosion, and even local climate change. Epidemic crop diseases also began to afflict many of the region's major export crops. Planters felt that it was essential to enlist scientists to bring these environmental problems under control. Agricultural chemists could advise them on the appropriate fertilizers; plant pathologists and entomologists could rid their fields of diseases and pests; plant breeders could find new ways to increase agricultural production.[3]

The control of nature was also important to the scientists themselves. Their ability to obtain public and private support for scientific institutions depended on their ability to produce results that their sponsors found "practical" or "useful." During the early nineteenth century, governments and agricultural interests had funded specific research projects but had been reluctant to provide sustained funding for research institutions. As the environmental problems of production became more acute, they began to fund more scientific research. In spite of the scientists' financial dependence, however, their views were not reducible to those of their sponsors. The plant scientists belonged to a broader "republic of rational agriculture," whose primary goal was to promote biologically sound agriculture everywhere. They were, therefore, sometimes critical of government policies and agricultural practices that they saw as environmentally destructive. The scientists also saw themselves as belonging to the international scientific community, dedicated to the universal pursuit of knowledge for its own sake. Unlike their counterparts in the United States in this period, however, no scientist in the Spanish Caribbean ever advanced a plea for "pure science," unsullied by practical considerations. They saw no incompatibility between the pursuit of scientific knowledge and the pursuit of practical goals.[4]

Planters, government officials, and scientists could all agree that science was necessary to solve the environmental problems of development, especially agricultural development. They often disagreed sharply, however, over who had the power to decide what the main agrarian problems were and how best to solve them. Each group perceived the relative importance of biological problems, and the role of science in solving them, quite differently. These debates were often couched in terms of what constituted "useful" or "practical" science. Planters wanted scientists to help them solve biological problems of production. Most often, they saw such problems as just one part of a wider array of agrarian problems, including shortages of labor and capital. For them, how the problems were solved was not terribly important. A good solution to a biological problem was one that allowed them to sustain or increase production, whether or not it involved scientific research. In contrast, scientists contended that the region's most pressing agrarian problems were biological and could best be solved through basic scientific research. They also tried to get planters to adopt more environmentally rational agricultural practices, although their success in this was mixed. At first, government officials were interested only in sponsoring scientific research projects. Their interest deepened during the 1920s, however. Many government officials saw the plant sciences as offering technocratic solutions to the region's increasingly acute agrarian problems, both in export agriculture and in food production.[5]

This story offers some insights into broader issues in Latin American history, the history of science, and environmental history. Combining these three historiographies offers new perspectives on key issues in each. For Latin American history, this story highlights the importance of nature as an analytical category: as a variable that requires explanation rather than as a constant that does not. The natural world has often appeared in Latin American historical writing as land, as property, as commodity. Yet each nation's nature shaped its path of development, although it did not strictly determine it. The particular configurations of nature in each nation (which economic historians describe as the "commodity lottery") presented a distinct set of economic opportunities. This process was further complicated by the fact that the natural world itself was constantly changing. The introduction of new economic systems could transform nature, which in turn transformed the economic systems. Elinor Melville has shown, for example, how the introduction of sheep in central Mexico after the conquest dramatically transformed the landscapes and its subsequent patterns of development. In several articles and books, the late Warren Dean explained the constantly changing interactions between ecosystem and economy. Brazilian planters, for example, transformed many of Brazil's rich tropical forests into highly profitable coffee plantations. When the coffee trees and soil were exhausted, the land was abandoned by the planters and became impoverished pasture. Such dramatic changes could often occur within two generations. To fully understand *power* in these agrarian societies, then, it is essential to understand *nature*.[6]

The existing literature on the history of science provides few tools for understanding the transnational character of science in Latin America during this period. Recent works by Richard Grove and Richard Drayton have explored the role of the plant sciences in the development of formal or informal empires. They have presented—rightly, I think—the natural sciences as an essential tool for the construction of empires and for shaping how agents of the metropolitan powers understood nature. These and other works have studied scientific research in the tropics, but they have done so largely from the perspective of the metropole. Given the large role that the United States assumed in the Caribbean during this period, it might be tempting to tell this story in terms of U.S. imperialism. After all, most centers for plant research in the Spanish Caribbean were modeled after institutions in the United States. Moreover, many U.S. scientists worked at these institutions, and many Latin

American scientists at the same institutions had been trained in the United States. The United States was the primary market for most of the crops they studied. But even so, it is impossible to explain the growth of science in terms of the United States alone.[7]

Drawing on recent literature on the cultural history of U.S.–Latin American relations, I present an alternative way of speaking about transnational scientific activities in Latin America that seeks to dissolve the sharp distinction between "imperial" and "national" science. Scientists at research institutions in the Spanish Caribbean during the time I study developed a set of ideologies and practices that I call "creole science." I am building deliberately on the ambiguity and tensions between the English *creole*—a hybrid, like a creole language—and the Spanish *criollo*—which in contemporary Spanish describes things of local origin. Creole science was at once transnational or hybrid in its form and practice and distinctively local in its goals. The models for scientific institutions were selectively appropriated from abroad, primarily the United States, and adapted to local environmental, economic, and political conditions. Scientists in Latin America frequently drew on an international network of scientists and institutions in the pursuit of local goals. As Latin Americans had done with the doctrine of positivism, they appropriated foreign models and transformed them into something distinctively Latin American. Although the relations between the United States and the Spanish Caribbean nations were significantly unequal, scientists often found ways of using the formal and informal bonds of empire to pursue their own ends.[8]

Finally, many scholars have examined the environmental impacts of the Spanish conquest and colonial period and the years following World War II. But, for reasons that are not entirely clear, few historians have explored the environmental history of the liberal period or tried to measure the environmental impact of the export boom. Yet the liberal era saw what was arguably the largest environmental transformation of Latin America since the conquest. Economic historians have described this period as the "Second Conquest of Latin America"; this term applies equally to its environmental history. Prevailing liberal ideas about the state and economy produced new ways of imagining and representing the natural world. Elites in the liberal era tended to see the natural world in terms of economic production, particularly in terms of export commodities. They paid special attention to plants and landscapes that could somehow contribute to the production of export crops and comparatively little attention to those that did not. They also saw the natural world in terms of state building, seeking to "nationalize" the natural world by producing national botanical inventories and ecological maps.

Looking at Spanish Caribbean landscapes through the eyes of plant scientists highlights a hidden history of catastrophic environmental transformations. The planters' single-minded pursuit of profit generated a host of environmental changes. To expand export crop production, planters cleared extensive tracts of forest. Deforestation unleashed other environmental problems, including large-scale erosion. I devote particular attention to the widespread outbreak of epidemic crop diseases, some of which had originated on the other side of the globe, that assailed the region's export crops with increasing frequency and severity during the late nineteenth century. I contend that this phenomenon was a *consequence* of the way in which planters had organized their landscapes to maximize the production of export crops. The epidemic crop diseases also point to the limits of the power of governments, corporations, and scientists to control the natural world. Some stricken landscapes fell out of production entirely; others required constant care from scientists to remain productive. While scientists were able to control a viral epidemic in sugarcane, they could only watch helplessly as fungal diseases wiped out most of the region's commercial cacao plantations. Even the United Fruit Company, with its deep financial resources and large technical staff, could only manage the banana diseases; it could not eradicate them. In short, the export boom produced sick, deteriorated landscapes over large swaths of the Spanish Caribbean.[9]

The chapters in this book focus on particular episodes in the broader history of science, nature, and development in the Spanish Caribbean. My method has been to follow the migrations of specific people, plants, and pathogens from one country to another. I follow the Swiss botanist Henri Pittier in his wanderings between Costa Rica, the United States, and Venezuela. The national floras he produced in Costa Rica and Venezuela symbolically nationalized the natural world in each nation. I pursue varieties and hybrids of sugarcane in their slow journeys around the globe and the distressingly rapid journey of the sugar mosaic virus along the same routes. The former helped to increase the economic power of sugar planters everywhere; the latter threatened to undermine it completely. The Puerto Rican plant pathologist Carlos Chardón traveled through most of tropical Latin America; here I concentrate on his work in Puerto Rico and Colombia. His role in combating mosaic disease in Puerto Rico gave him and his Department of Agriculture considerable power on the island. His attempts to reproduce Puerto Rican institutional models in Colombia, however, were less successful. Following these migrants, large and small, allows me to compare the similarities (and differences) among nations more systematically. I concentrate on five nations in the Spanish Caribbean: Cuba, Puerto Rico, Venezuela, Colombia, and Costa Rica. But processes similar to those I describe here took place throughout the Spanish Caribbean.

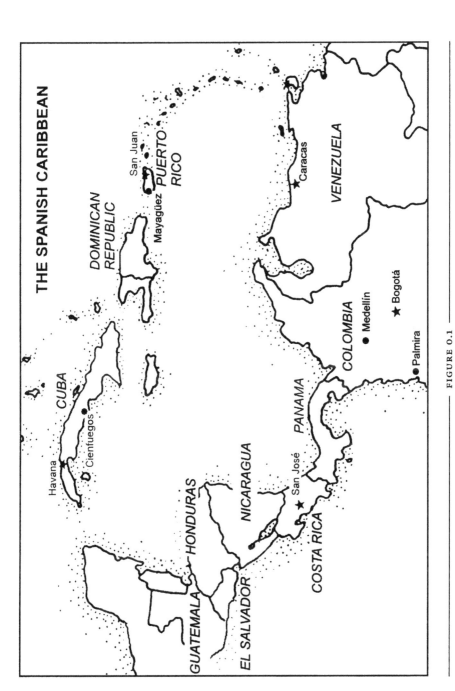

FIGURE 0.1

The Spanish Caribbean.

Latin America's elites began supporting the plant sciences for both practical and ideological reasons. Their interest can be traced to the loosening of trade restrictions and the rapid growth of Latin America's agricultural colonies in the late eighteenth century. Many governments embraced the philosophy of positivism, which, under the rhetorical banner of "order and progress," envisioned societies organized by the state along rational, scientific principles. These liberal ideologies were not simply abstractions; they were also fundamentally practical in character. Latin America's political elites enlisted science, technology, and medicine to promote liberal models of economic development and state formation. Engineers built railroads, which helped to speed tropical commodities from the countryside to the ports. Doctors carried out urban sanitation campaigns in the ports and the countryside. "Railroads, urban plazas, and public buildings, water and sewage systems, electricity, telegraph, and their ancillary services," argue Vincent Peloso and Barbara Tenenbaum, "meant quantitative changes in the Latin American economies and qualitative changes in the state-building debate." As planters in Latin America began to confront large-scale agricultural problems in the late nineteenth century, then, it is not surprising that they too turned to scientists for help.[10]

Liberal projects of state building included defining and controlling the national space. Agricultural and botanical research helped the states to nationalize and commodify the region's wild landscapes. Between 1880 and 1930, almost every country in Latin America undertook a national inventory of its plants. These floras sought to impose a rational order on the natural world by identifying plants and giving them standardized scientific names. Naming plants gave them a "civil status," in the telling words of Henri Pittier. In addition to this civil function, the floras also fulfilled an economic function. They commodified the nations' wild nature by identifying plants with potential commercial value. They also generated new representations of the nations' nature. For example, the late-nineteenth-century floras of Costa Rica represented it as a biologically singular place, with an unusually large diversity. The scientists who produced the floras also began to describe and measure the large-scale environmental destruction that had begun to plague the region. These floras were also fundamentally *nationalist*: botanists sought to repatriate the knowledge that foreign naturalists had extracted over the previous centuries. To do so, they had to develop innovative ways of working with foreign scientists and scientific institutions.[11]

The wave of institution building began in earnest after the turn of the twentieth century. In Cuba and Puerto Rico, as elsewhere in the Spanish Caribbean, most plant research institutions were modeled after the new nationally funded agricultural experiment stations in the United States. Nonetheless, neither the U.S. institutional model nor U.S. research agendas could simply be replicated in the tropics. All centers for plant research in the Spanish Caribbean had to adapt—to "creolize"—their research agendas and institutional forms to fit the local institutional and agricultural ecology. For example, scientific research agendas primarily reflected the prevailing elite ideas about economic and agricultural development. This meant that research in the Spanish Caribbean focused primarily on export crops even while some U.S. colonial officials and scientists tried unsuccessfully to promote the development of domestic food crops. Agricultural knowledge is also not as easily transportable as engineering knowledge. North American expertise on temperate crops was of little use in tropical Latin America. All scientists who worked in the region—be they Latin American or foreign—commented on how little was known about Latin American plants.

State building also entailed managing the region's agricultural landscapes. Plant scientists played a key role in this process, helping to address emergent environmental problems caused by the export boom. In the pursuit of economic growth, Latin America's planters and governments had promoted the transformation of wild forests into domesticated, homogeneous, and profitable "new forests" of export crops. They remade Latin American landscapes to reflect the prevailing ideologies of economic development.[12] Among the most apparent and dramatic environmental problems created by the radical simplification of nature into monocultures were epidemic crop diseases, which affected most of the region's major export crops—including bananas, cacao, rubber, and sugar—between 1880 and 1930. It is difficult to overstate the significance of these epidemics; one caused the collapse of Ecuador's cacao industry in the early 1920s, and another prevented Brazil from developing commercial rubber plantations. In the late 1910s, planters feared that a new epidemic of sugarcane, known as the mosaic disease, would wipe out Cuba's and Puerto Rico's cane industry. A small group of scientists working in Puerto Rico identified the vector of the disease and were able to bring it under control by introducing new, hybrid sugarcanes. These scientists, led by the young Carlos Chardón, celebrated their victory over the disease and proclaimed that science finally had a legitimate place in Latin America. Chardón began to promote Puerto Rico as a model for science-based agricultural development in tropical Latin America.

Transferring models of science-based agricultural development from one country to another within the Spanish Caribbean, however, proved to be just as difficult as transferring North American or European models had been. Agricultural organizations and governments throughout the Spanish Caribbean sought Chardón's help in organizing agricultural research centers of their own but often wound up disagreeing sharply with Chardón's plans. The reasons were ideological as well as agricultural. Chardón argued forcefully that the most pressing problems in Latin American agriculture were biological and could be solved through original scientific research. While this may have been true for Puerto Rico's sugar industry, it was less true of most other agricultural export regimes. For example, Colombia's agricultural associations wanted to rationalize their agriculture and make it more scientific, but they did not feel that basic research was as essential as Chardón claimed. Coffee growers were more interested in improving basic agricultural practices than they were in research. Colombia's politicians, on the other hand, were attracted to the technocratic aspects of Chardón's model, which appeared to address agricultural problems in a way that could avoid social conflict.

The Great Depression ended the export boom, and with it the liberal paradigm of economic development that had dominated the Spanish Caribbean for much of the previous century. By the early 1930s, the goal of increasing export crop production no longer dominated paradigms of national development. But the depression marked a transformation, not a rupture. Even though they did not enjoy the robust growth of previous decades, export crops remained important in most Spanish Caribbean economies. Governments continued consolidating and integrating their nations' citizens and territory. They used the tools of science and technology—the symbols of liberalism—to try to solve the problems left by the collapse of liberal models of development. Ideas about development—particularly the idea that Latin America's most pressing problems had scientific or technical solutions—had become firmly rooted in Latin American thought.

ONE

COMMODITY AND COUNTRY

The Rediscovery of Nature
in the Spanish Caribbean, 1760–1890

*[The] relation between plant and the land in which it lives, will be
constantly ruled by the quality of the knowledge about their behavior,
for the most advantageous execution of their vital acts. . . . [The]
knowledge of these elemental truths and their learned application to
the plant-individual, is the base of modern agricultural science.*

JOSÉ RAMÓN ABAD, *PUERTO RICO EN LA*
FERIA-EXPOSICIÓN DE PONCE EN 1882 (1885)

In the mid-eighteenth century, Spaniards and Creoles in the Caribbean began
to rediscover nature. There was much to learn: little had changed since the
sixteenth century, when the naturalist Gonzalo de Oviedo had remarked,
"[There are so many different kinds of plants that] not even the native Indians know them nor know how to give names to the majority, and the Chris-
tians much less, since they are so new, and not known or seen by them before.
And in this respect one could say that this is a GREAT AND DARK SEA; because though part is seen, much more is not, since their names and properties
are unknown." [1]

Government officials and planters in the Spanish Caribbean—and
throughout Latin America—began to take an interest in the plant sciences.
This new interest was motivated by significant political and economic transformations in the Spanish Caribbean over this period: Bourbon imperial reforms, independence, the age of liberalism, and the export boom. The Spanish imperial government, and the republican governments that succeeded it,
used science to nationalize nature, to extend state power over the natural
world. Over the next one hundred fifty years, they organized botanical gardens, natural history museums, and agricultural experiment stations through-

out the region. Governments funded plant inventories, botanical maps, and botanical gardens to define and control their political territory and to identify plants that might contribute to economic growth.

Planters began using science to rationalize nature, to manage crop plants and their ecosystems so as to maximize production. Latin America's economies grew explosively in these years, as trade restrictions of the imperial period gave way to liberal laissez-faire policies that promoted free trade and economic growth through the export of primary commodities. Export crop producers became more interested in the sciences during the nineteenth century, as the challenges of sustaining growth began to mount. Stagnant and declining agricultural productivity, the spread of biological problems such as crop diseases and soil exhaustion, and increased competition in the international commodity markets placed planters under considerable pressure to find new ways to increase production. The region's persistent economic and political turmoil meant that efforts to nationalize and rationalize nature fell short of expectations.[2]

IMPERIAL AND CREOLE BOTANY: FROM THE BOURBON REFORMS TO INDEPENDENCE, 1750–1830

Two processes spurred the systematic research into Latin American plants that began in the mid-eighteenth century: the imperial reforms begun during the reign of Charles III and the rapid growth of Latin America's agricultural export economy. The economies of Spain's Caribbean colonies had become stagnant after the mid-sixteenth century. The Crown had devoted most of its attention to the densely populated colonies of New Spain and Peru, both of which had rich deposits of silver. The Spanish Caribbean remained at the periphery of the empire until the eighteenth century, when the Bourbon dynasty assumed the Spanish throne. The Bourbon kings reorganized and centralized the administration of the empire. They also began to look for new sources of revenue and turned their attention to their neglected Caribbean colonies. In 1728, for example, King Philip V granted the Royal Guipúzcoana Company a commercial monopoly on Venezuelan cacao, hoping to increase imperial revenues while stemming smuggling. The company began an aggressive program to promote cacao cultivation. By midcentury cacao was the second most valuable export in Latin America, after precious metals. The Crown gradually began to open trade within the Spanish empire, prompted in part by external forces. When the British occupied Havana in 1762, they opened Cuba to free trade. British merchants and British goods flooded into the country during the eleven months of the occupation. Cuba's sugar planters were among the biggest beneficiaries of the occupation. They had access to cheap slaves, easy credit, and new sugar technology. The sugar industry continued to grow rapidly even after the British returned Cuba to Spain in 1763. Two years later the Crown allowed free trade within the Spanish empire. By the 1770s official Cuban sugar exports were thirty times greater than they had been in the 1750s.[3]

Reflecting this revitalization of its New World colonies, the Spanish Crown began to sponsor imperial botanical research. Botanical research was attractive to the Crown for several reasons. First, it offered the empire potentially valuable commercial information. Second, it helped to contribute to the growth of scientific knowledge within the empire, symbolizing the end of Spain's intellectual isolation from the rest of Europe. Third, it contributed to imperial prestige in an age when Spain's imperial rivals, France and Great Britain, were sponsoring scientific voyages around the world. The Crown reorganized and expanded the Royal Botanical Garden in Madrid. The garden's research agendas reflected the centralized policies and practices of the Bourbon state, directed primarily toward the enrichment of the metropolis. The garden developed a network of amateur collectors in the colonies—often military engineers, doctors, or priests—who would send specimens back to Spain. It also appointed naturalists to serve on voyages of exploration and boundary surveys in the New World. For example, the boundary survey of the Orinoco (1750–1767) included four Crown-appointed naturalists, one of whom was Pehr Löfling, a disciple of the great systematist Linnaeus. Their task was to map this borderland and identify any potentially useful natural products. Although the Crown was primarily interested in "useful" products—particularly medicinal plants—the expedition also produced many new discoveries of interest primarily to scientists.[4]

The Crown also sponsored several long-term botanical expeditions to the New World—the Royal Botanical Expedition to New Spain lasted from 1788 to 1803; the expedition to Peru, from 1777 to 1778—but none visited the Spanish Caribbean or the Río de la Plata, the peripheral regions where the most rapid agricultural innovations were taking place. Rather, they concentrated on the viceroyalties of New Spain and Peru, with smaller expeditions to Chile, New Granada (Colombia), and Cuba. Although the Royal Botanical Garden accumulated a significant collection of New World plants from these expeditions, its staff was overwhelmed by the sheer volume. Many rich collections of New World plants languished in the garden's herbarium, unstudied and unclassified. Some of these collections were not studied until the twentieth century, when Latin American botanists working on national floras began to take an interest in them.[5]

Interest in botanical research did not spring from Madrid alone. Royal officials in several of Spain's Caribbean colonies wished to use science to improve agriculture. They did so in part because the imperial government had given them the task of increasing colonial revenue. For example, one of the principal missions of Venezuela's Intendencia de Ejército y Real Hacienda, created in 1776, was to stimulate the province's agricultural production. The year after it was founded, the Intendencia sent twelve technicians to Guayana, Venezuela's easternmost province, to begin a project to grow linen. The Intendencia also promoted the diversification of Venezuela's export crops by introducing exotic plants. Encouraged by the Intendencia, farmers in Guayana planted experimental plots of exotic crops such as cinnamon, mangoes, and cloves. After the Crown established a tobacco monopoly in 1779, the Intendencia sponsored a soil survey of Venezuela to learn where tobacco could best be grown. Based on these results, it began to promote tobacco cultivation in the western province of Barinas. Later, the Intendencia provided agricultural technicians to advise the tobacco planters of Barinas on agricultural issues ranging from fertilizer to disease control.[6]

Latin America's Creole elites also began to sponsor botanical research. In Venezuela, Creole planters used the Creole-controlled Real Consulado of Caracas to promote systematic agricultural innovation. The Real Consulado was composed of Venezuela's leading merchants and planters, all of whom wanted to improve the country's productive infrastructure. Agustín de la Torre, head of the Real Consulado in the 1790s, had begun to advocate agricultural innovation since becoming rector of the Royal and Pontifical University of Caracas. He had argued then that "no nation has made significant progress in arms, arts, agriculture, or commerce until it has undertaken the necessary cultivation of science." As head of the province's Real Consulado, he had the chance to enact some of his ideas. In the 1790s, for example, the Consulado sponsored reports on the state of Venezuela's major export crops. The report on coffee criticized the colony's coffee industry for "stumbling along blindly" and proposed to remedy this by presenting a model of rational coffee cultivation. It is not clear how much of an impact these reports had, however, as Caracas did not have a printing press until the last years before independence. The report on coffee was probably written in the 1790s, but it was not published until 1809. The Real Consulado also lobbied the Crown for the creation of a chair of mathematics to help promote useful knowledge in the province. The Crown turned down the Consulado's request, having grown suspicious of Enlightenment ideas, which it associated with revolutionary France. In Venezuela, as elsewhere in Spanish America, growing tensions between the Creole elites and the Crown caused many Creole projects to founder.[7]

The visit of the German naturalist Alexander von Humboldt also generated imperial and Creole interest in botany. Between 1799 and 1804 Humboldt traveled through much of the Spanish Caribbean, spending time in Venezuela, New Granada, Cuba, and New Spain. It was on this voyage that he began to articulate a new way of seeing the natural world. Like many naturalists before him, Humboldt collected plants. Unlike many of his predecessors, however, Humboldt also measured natural phenomena. He traveled with a large collection of scientific instruments, including a chronometer, a telescope, a sextant, a theodolite, a quadrant, a compass, a graphometer, a magnetometer, thermometers, and barometers. He collected thousands of measurements and thousands of plants. This mountain of observations, he hoped, would help him to discover broad patterns in the natural world. His principal goal was to develop a unified science of the environment that could explain the complex relations between the organic and inorganic worlds.

Although Humboldt's principal goal remained elusive, his ideas and innovations helped to shape the course of natural history in the decades that followed. Based on his travels in South America, he sketched out a new theory of plant geography in his 1807 *Essai sur la géographie des plantes*. Central to this new theory was the concept of botanical provinces, which drew on late-eighteenth-century ideas of the nation. Just as European intellectuals argued that each "nation" consisted of people who shared a common characteristic, Humboldt argued that plants formed natural assemblages defined by common characteristics. The goal of Humboldt's plant geography was to find the unifying characteristics of these plant groups. Doing so meant conducting detailed plant inventories, mapping plant distribution, and studying their relation to the inorganic environment. Plant geography thus blended the concepts of nature and nation. Humboldt, however, did not focus his attention on the natural world alone. His observations on South America included detailed commentaries on the structure of societies. He noticed the growing tensions between Creole colonists and Spanish officials and predicted that independence was not far off.[8]

The wars of independence Humboldt predicted broke out in 1808, when Napoleon's armies invaded Spain and deposed King Ferdinand VII, leaving a power vacuum at the center of the empire. Patriot forces seized the opportunity to declare autonomy and then independence from Spain. Independence, however, proved harder to achieve. The wars of independence raged through South America for almost twenty years, and they exacted a high cost on the nascent scientific communities and institutions in Spanish America and in Spain itself. The scientific communities in New Spain and New Granada had blossomed in the late colonial period, and small groups of naturalists could be found in most of the colonial capitals. These Creole naturalists had modeled their science after that of France; many of them were also inspired by France's radical politics. Most Creole naturalists, therefore, sided with the patriot forces, which supported independence from Spain. When royalist troops reconquered the viceroyalty of New Granada in 1816, they executed many of the viceroyalty's patriot naturalists, including six of the eleven members of the New Granada Botanical Expedition of 1806. After Ferdinand VII was restored to the Spanish throne in 1814, he began to purge Spain and what was left of his empire of any groups he suspected of being sympathetic to French and liberal thinking. He persecuted the scientific community in Spain itself, dissolving the Royal Academies because of their liberal tendencies. By 1823 most of Spain's top scientists had either emigrated or been forcibly exiled. By the mid-1820s, then, the imperial community of naturalists had been destroyed. Most of the valuable botanical knowledge about the Americas that they had accumulated over decades was lost.[9]

SURVEYING THE STATE: ECONOMIC SOCIETIES AND BOTANICAL INVENTORIES, 1820–1850

The decades following independence were ones of reconstruction, stagnation, and slow economic recovery for most of Latin America. Independence had spelled an end to the old imperial economic policy of mercantilism, and for the first time Latin American economies were open to the outside world. The new Latin American republics enjoyed free access to foreign capital and foreign markets. The wars had destroyed much of Latin America's productive infrastructure, however, and both foreign capital and domestic capital were scarce. The exceptions to this general rule were Cuba and Puerto Rico, which had remained within the Spanish empire. Seeking to ensure the continued loyalty of Cuba's planters, in 1817 the Spanish government abolished many old mercantilist policies and allowed the island to sell its products freely in foreign markets. Unscathed by the wars of independence and fueled by the rapidly growing demand for sugar in Europe and North America, Cuba's economy in these decades was the most dynamic in the Spanish Caribbean. The agricultural economies of the newly independent republics of the Spanish Caribbean began to recover at midcentury, and the pace of economic growth throughout the region accelerated (although often unsteadily) throughout the rest of the century.[10]

Although by midcentury most of Latin America's Creole elites were looking to Europe for models of national development, the first institutions to systematically sponsor botanical research were leftovers from the colonial period. In each country these organizations, known as economic societies (*sociedades económicas*), brought together local "enlightened citizens"—planters, politicians, doctors, and engineers. The societies promoted economic development by diagnosing the country's main problems and proposing concrete solutions to them. Economic societies had originated in Enlightenment Europe and had become especially popular in Spain and its colonies during the late eighteenth century. Many survived the wars of independence or were reconstituted in the new republics. All of these economic societies, whether in Spain's remaining colonies or in the independent republics, promoted agricultural modernization. The Economic Society of Havana, for example, revived plans to organize a botanical garden, which had first been proposed in 1793 but had stalled at the planning stage. With the support of the Economic Society, the Havana Botanical Garden opened in 1817. Puerto Rico's Economic Society, founded in 1811 by a decree of the Spanish government, included a permanent commission on agriculture. The commission was given responsibility for collecting seeds, instruments, and machines and for cultivating an experimental field. Several hundred miles to the south, the Creole elites of Caracas founded Venezuela's Economic Society in 1826, several years after the country had achieved independence from Spain. During the society's short life (1826–1839), its committee on agriculture encouraged the cultivation of wheat and coffee and sponsored the earliest statistical surveys of the country.[11]

The economic societies provided political and economic support for the first national scientific surveys. In this age of nation building, scientific surveys helped to define a nation's physical and natural characteristics. By producing maps and detailed descriptions of its topography, flora, and fauna, a nation extended its dominion over the natural world. These surveys also had economic value, as they listed and located potentially valuable new export commodities. From the perspective of the economic societies, the twin goals of enlightenment and economic development were part of the same enterprise. In 1833 one member of Venezuela's economic society wrote that "the links between botany and social life, agriculture, the arts, and commerce are so many and so indispensable that it would be impossible to do without it." In the same spirit, the Faculty of Medicine at the Central University of Venezuela proposed a bill that would specify the rights of the government over all the plants of the nation, particularly plants of medicinal and economic value.[12]

The natural history surveys of Venezuela typified the nation-building projects of the mid-nineteenth century. These surveys mapped the territorial boundaries and provided a rough overview of the main topographic features contained within them. When Venezuela split from Gran Colombia in 1830, one of the first actions of the new country's Constituent Congress was to convene the Corographic Commission to undertake a statistical and geographic survey of the nation. The commission's work was carried out almost entirely by one man, the Italian engineer Agustín Codazzi, a prominent member of Caracas's Economic Society who had been a colonel of engineers during the wars of independence. It took Codazzi nine years to complete the survey. Meanwhile, the Economic Society published aspects of his research, particularly those concerning the province of Caracas. The full project, the *Resumen de la geografía de Venezuela*, was completed in 1839 and published in 1841. Codazzi modeled the *Resumen* on the works of Humboldt, who had visited Venezuela three decades earlier. It described Venezuela's politics and economics, natural history, and agriculture. Following Humboldt, Codazzi described the vegetation of Venezuela by zones of altitude. The *Resumen* also included a list of the scientific names of Venezuela's most important economic plants, along with a description of their history, their habitats, and their economic potential.[13]

In Cuba, the Spanish naturalist Ramón de la Sagra produced a Humboldtean survey of the island and its natural resources. De la Sagra, a Spaniard from Galicia, had first arrived in Cuba in 1822, after the Crown had appointed him professor of botany at the Havana Botanical Garden. He began work on a natural history of the island. He enjoyed the help of Bishop Espada of Havana, who also happened to be the director of Havana's Economic Society. Bishop Espada called on the priests in parishes around the island to collect plants for de la Sagra. De la Sagra also drew on the help of amateur Cuban naturalists in the provinces. Unlike most earlier natural histories of Cuba, which had a regional focus, de la Sagra's ability to draw on both formal and informal networks of power to build his collections meant that he could cover the entire island. In 1831 de la Sagra published the *Historia económico-política y estadística de la Isla de Cuba*, followed in 1845 by the two-volume *Historia física, política, y natural de la isla de Cuba*. The latter work was Humboldtean in scale and ambition. The twelve-volume French-language edition included an inventory of Cuban plants, as well as surveys of the island's fauna, climate, agriculture, commerce, and population.[14]

Like many later Latin American floras, de la Sagra's *Historia física, política, y natural* aimed to be of both scientific interest and practical use. In addition to the French-language edition, intended for European naturalists, de la Sagra published a Spanish-language edition for the Cuban market. In the introduction to the latter, he explained the practical value of his natural history surveys, sketching out an argument that many later naturalists in Latin America would echo. He began by noting that the Cuban government was interested in scientific agriculture: it had supported the Havana Botanical Garden in order to "base the cultivation of crops in scientific principles, and to extend these principles to a great number of plants, both indigenous and exotic." But scientific cultivation was impossible, he argued, "because of the complete lack of data and preliminary observations indispensable for this end." The botany of Cuba, like that of many countries in Latin America, was only poorly under-

stood. The scientific study of Cuba's plants was also necessary because its tropical climate and vegetation meant that scientists could not use "scientific laws
discovered and only applicable to the temperate and cold regions of Europe."
The *Historia física, política, y natural* aimed to provide this baseline information. In spite of the work's quality and comprehensiveness, however, it is not
clear what impact it had on Cuba's scientific or agricultural communities.
The chronic wars that plagued Cuba for much of the second half of the nineteenth century made any further botanical explorations difficult, and the island's government—busy with other things—did little to disseminate de la
Sagra's findings.[15]

The works of Codazzi and de la Sagra were among the few comprehensive
natural history surveys produced by Creole naturalists in the mid-nineteenth
century. Governments throughout the Spanish Caribbean confronted political unrest and economic uncertainty and had few resources to support botanical research. In the decades following independence, therefore, natural
history in Latin America became primarily an extractive enterprise controlled
by foreigners. They continued to dominate botanical research in Latin America until the end of the nineteenth century. The collapse of the Spanish empire
opened the rich and poorly known natural worlds of Central and South America to foreign naturalists. They mined Latin America for information about
plants and animals the same way that foreign businessmen mined it for petroleum, copper, gold, and guano. Foreign naturalists tended, in fact, to visit
those areas where their home countries had political or economic interests.
Before midcentury, foreign naturalists, most of whom were British or French,
collected in Mexico or southern South America, particularly Argentina, Brazil, and Chile. The most famous of these visitors was Charles Darwin, who
came to the region in the 1830s with a Royal Navy surveying expedition. Darwin's collections and observations in Brazil, Argentina, and Ecuador's Galapa-
gos Islands helped to shape his theory of evolution.[16]

Few collectors visited the Spanish Caribbean until after midcentury, when
North American and German collectors, in particular, began to arrive in
greater numbers. Some of these left vivid narratives of their travels, such as the
British engineer Thomas Belt's 1874 book, *The Naturalist in Nicaragua.* Other
foreign naturalists worked on comprehensive surveys of regional flora. Late in
the century the German botanist Ignatius Urban began publishing the *Sym-
bollae Antillanae,* a study of the flora of the West Indies, while a group of British botanists worked on the *Biologia Centrali-Americana,* which covered Mexico and Central America. Most of these foreign naturalists, however, treated
Latin America simply as a source for plants. Their publications were aimed at
the international scientific community rather than at planters or naturalists in
Latin America itself. By the latter part of the nineteenth century, then, Latin

American naturalists found themselves in the strange position of having to travel to Europe or North America to learn about their country's native plants.[17]

LIBERAL STATES, THE EXPORT BOOM, AND AGRICULTURAL SCIENCE, 1850–1900

The midcentury emergence of liberalism as Latin America's dominant ideology of national development contributed both directly and indirectly to a modest resurgence of interest in the plant sciences. After independence, liberalism had been one among many competing ideologies. Liberals supported, among other things, laissez-faire state policies and free trade. With free trade, each nation could produce and sell the goods for which it had a comparative advantage. For the Spanish Caribbean, most of these goods were tropical crops. The export boom, which began during the 1870s, seemed to affirm the liberal model, and liberalism became the dominant ideology throughout Latin America in the 1870s.[18]

In this era of liberal governments, science, technology, and medicine began to play a more prominent role in the construction and maintenance of the state. Latin America's liberal elites were interested in science for both ideological and practical reasons. Earlier in the century, they had appropriated and adapted the French philosophy of positivism. Under the banner of order and progress, positivism articulated a model of social development supposedly based on scientific principles. This elite fascination with positivism helped to promote Latin American interest in the natural sciences. But this interest in science was rooted more strongly in Latin American ideologies of national development that emphasized the "practical" benefits of science and technology, with "practical" being defined as anything that supported the export economy. Governments hired foreign engineers to build roads and railways and foreign doctors to eradicate disease in the crowded cities. Local scientists, doctors, and engineers also began to play an important role in building and maintaining the productive structure of the new states. Not surprisingly, then, when planters in the Spanish Caribbean were confronted with growing competition from abroad and environmental problems at home, they turned to agricultural scientists for help. In spite of their newfound popularity, scientists did not always give the planters the solutions they wanted, and the place of the agricultural sciences in the liberal era remained uncertain.[19]

At first, however, planters could obtain significant results by bringing new land into production, by increasing their labor force, and by rationalizing the harvesting and processing of their crops. Cuba, for example, was already the world's largest exporter of sugar by 1820, producing some 43,000 tons. Venezuela, Costa Rica, and Puerto Rico slowly began exporting coffee in the 1830s and 1840s. The volume of Latin America's exports grew explosively after midcentury, increasing by 1,000 percent between 1850 and 1913. In 1850 Cuba produced 223,000 tons of sugar. By 1894 Cuban sugar production had quadrupled, reaching one million tons. Likewise, figures for land use in Puerto Rico reflect its increasing orientation to the export markets. In 1830 more than two-thirds of the island's cultivated lands had been devoted to subsistence crops; by 1899 only a third of the land was used for subsistence agriculture. In the same period, sugar production more than doubled and coffee production tripled. More than half of Puerto Rico's cultivated lands were devoted to coffee production alone. Coffee also drove economic growth in Central America. Costa Rica entered smoothly into the global coffee economy during the 1830s, while liberal governments in Guatemala and El Salvador initiated coffee expansion during the 1860s and 1870s. Coffee also accounted for more than 60 percent of Venezuela's exports by 1870.[20]

The absolute growth in the volume of exports, however, masks economic problems that became increasingly serious as time went on. Most commodities went through cycles of boom and bust, which could be caused by either external or domestic factors. Overseas demand often fluctuated significantly. For example, the British market—the most important one for many Latin American countries—was stagnant for much of the 1870s and 1880s. In addition, as more producers both in Latin America and elsewhere in the tropics increased production to meet the European demand, prices declined. Planters often responded by further increasing production, hoping to offset the drop in price with an increase in volume. This increased supply, however, forced prices even lower. Internally, civil unrest often disrupted economic production. In Cuba, for example, nationalist armies carried out a policy of economic warfare, destroying sugar mills and burning cane fields. Sugar production fell 80 percent between 1894 and 1897—from more than one million tons to just 212,000 tons.[21]

The rapid expansion of export agriculture also created unprecedented environmental problems, which in turn contributed to the cycles of boom and bust. Seeking to maximize production, planters devoted most of their lands to a single cash crop. In doing so, they unintentionally created an environment ideal for the spread of diseases and pests. Global crop epidemics became commonplace as the development of steamships and railroads accelerated the spread of pathogens and pests. Ironically, Latin America was an early beneficiary of these epidemic crop diseases. During the 1870s, a coffee fungus, *Hemileia vastatrix*, destroyed most of the commercial coffee plantations in the

Old World. *H. vastatrix* preferred the finer grades of coffee, particularly *Coffea arabica*. The devastation of the Old World coffee plantations contributed to the late-nineteenth-century coffee boom in Latin America, where the fungus was not present. Latin American planters were not so lucky with other crops. Epidemic crop diseases had appeared sporadically since the colonial period, often striking the most intensely cultivated areas. As early as 1653 a cacao blight, known locally as the *alhorra*, destroyed more than half the cacao trees in the province of Caracas, Venezuela's richest cacao zone. In the nineteenth century such outbreaks became more frequent. Sugar plantations were highly susceptible to epidemic disease. In the 1840s a sugar disease forced Cuban planters to abandon the traditional Creole cane variety and replace it with a new variety imported from Asia. In the 1870s a mysterious disease struck the cane fields in western Puerto Rico. Even if these diseases did not have as devastating an effect as did *H. vastatrix* on coffee, planters became alarmed.[22]

Other environmental problems also harmed agricultural production in the Spanish Caribbean. Soil exhaustion sharply reduced crop yields, often to the point where harvesting them was no longer economically viable. Soil exhaustion is not, of course, just a "natural" problem. Soils became exhausted because planters were unwilling or unable to devote the capital and labor necessary to fertilize their plantations. This problem was particularly evident farther to the south, in Brazil's coffee plantations. Once coffee yields had declined to the point where cultivation was no longer viable, Brazilian planters simply abandoned the exhausted plantations and moved on to establish new plantations in recently cleared areas. Such environmentally wasteful behavior was possible in late-nineteenth-century Brazil, which still had large areas of uncleared forest. Planters in the smaller countries of the Spanish Caribbean did not have this luxury. By the last decades of the nineteenth century, for example, Central American coffee growers had brought most of the viable coffee lands into production. Although Cuba still had a large agricultural frontier, Cuban planters were facing environmental problems of their own. Cane yields were declining, a decline that planters attributed to the "degeneration" of the cane plant. In retrospect, it appears more likely that the underlying cause was soil exhaustion.[23]

In spite of these growing economic and environmental problems caused by the pursuit of export-led growth, few people in Latin America questioned the model's viability. Planters and government officials alike tended to understand the boom-and-bust cycles as technical problems of production rather than as structural problems with the underlying model. For that reason, they pursued technical rather than structural reforms. Agricultural production was low, planters argued, because of the effects of the civil wars, or because of a shortage of capital or labor. When slavery was abolished in Cuba, for example, Cuban planters experimented with hiring Indian laborers from the Yucatan and, in the mid-1840s, indentured laborers from China. In Venezuela, agricultural associations asked the state to establish a bank that could give them credit at reasonable interest rates. Paradoxically, planters began to expect the state to support an economic order whose fundamental tenet was laissez-faire. As one Venezuelan planter wrote in 1870, the state should support agriculture by offering "the defense of property, security in the fields, freedom of work, safe and fast means of communication, peace, order, morality and respect; and this, is not requested as a favor, but as a demand for justice. Nothing more." And states throughout the Spanish Caribbean acquiesced to the planters' demands, providing agricultural credit, promoting immigration, and building infrastructure. The Costa Rican government, for example, built a road from the coffee regions of the central valley down to the Pacific port of Puntarenas. Most governments in the Spanish Caribbean also financed extensive modernization of port facilities and the construction of railroads, both of which would expedite shipping of crops to the markets overseas.[24]

Agricultural scientists and botanists had played only a small role until then, largely because they appeared to have little to offer that governments or planters considered practical. In Cuba, for example, early attempts to introduce scientific agriculture fell flat. Cuba was home to Alvaro Reynoso, perhaps the world's leading expert on sugar agriculture in the nineteenth century. Based on scientific principles, Reynoso developed a new system of cane agriculture, which he described in his *Ensayo sobre el cultivo de la caña de azúcar*, published in 1862. The "Reynoso system" involved carefully tilling and fertilizing the soils, planting the cane rows at precisely measured intervals, and then irrigating regularly. Reynoso also argued that the cane should be replanted annually. Traditionally, cane growers had harvested several crops of cane over three or four years from a single planting.[25]

In Cuba, however, economic rationality (even short-term economic rationality) trumped agricultural rationality. Although a few Cuban planters adopted the Reynoso system with great success, most Cuban planters continued their traditional methods. Reynoso reported that some planters objected to his system because they claimed that their slaves were not intelligent enough to carry out such sophisticated operations. Reynoso refuted this claim, pointing out that many slaves who worked in the sugar mills were intelligent enough to carry out highly complex technical operations. Other planters had technical objections to his system. They argued that if they followed Reynoso's recommendation and planted cane in widely spaced rows, the spaces would become choked with weeds. The task of clearing these weeds would make heavy demands on labor, which was in short supply. This shortage of labor, in particular, acted as a brake on many agricultural innovations. Most Cuban planters clearly felt that the costs of adopting Reynoso's system outweighed the benefits of continuing their traditional methods of planting. In an ironic twist, sugar planters in Java, where labor was plentiful and land scarce, almost universally adopted the Reynoso system. By the end of the century, Java had become one of the world's major sugar producers, in direct competition with Cuba.[26]

New research in Europe, however, showed that agricultural science could produce substantial practical benefits without making excessive demands on labor or capital. The chemical studies of Justus von Liebig demonstrated that chemical fertilizers could greatly increase crop yields. Liebig's discovery generated worldwide interest in agricultural science. The first national network of agricultural experiment stations was established in Germany during the 1850s. In 1855 there were 24 agricultural experiment stations worldwide. By 1900 the total had reached 590, most of which had been founded in the preceding two decades. At first, research at the agricultural experiment stations focused almost exclusively on fertilizer chemistry. Gradually, however, research missions expanded to include all biological aspects of crop production. Like Latin American crops, European and North American crops had been stricken with diseases and pests, and growers hoped that agricultural experiment stations could address these problems. They also hoped that plant breeders, using the new science of genetics, could breed higher-yielding crop varieties.[27]

Latin America's planters enthusiastically embraced the idea of agricultural experiment stations. In Latin America, as elsewhere in the tropics, agricultural research concentrated on export crops rather than on food crops. This emphasis reflected the political and economic power of the planters who grew the export crops and the relative weakness of those who grew food crops. Nonetheless, the planters did not always enjoy unlimited power, even in countries whose economy was driven by agricultural exports. Agricultural experiment stations were frequently used as political footballs in conflicts between planters and the government. Puerto Rico is a case in point. Beginning in 1882, Puerto Rican planters lobbied the island's government, which was dominated by bureaucrats from Spain, to establish an agricultural experiment station. The government finally relented in 1888 and established two agricultural experiment stations, one in Mayagüez, on the western end of the island, and the other in Río Piedras, just outside the capital city of San Juan. The two stations carried out a range of research programs, including studies of chemical fertilizers, of the white worm disease of sugarcane, and of coffee pests. Because of political infighting between the agricultural societies and the insular government, however, the government closed the stations in 1890. Since they had been in operation a for only a short time, their impact on Puerto Rican agriculture was limited.[28]

By the end of the nineteenth century, nature, in the guise of commodity and country, had become part of the liberal discourse of progress and development. Government officials, intellectuals, and naturalists argued that nationalizing the natural world was an essential part of nation building. Individual planters and organized agricultural associations began to explore ways to rationalize the biological aspects of crop production, as part of a broader program of rationalizing all aspects of agriculture. Emergent environmental and economic problems gave them further impetus to study crop ecology. At the same time, institutional and intellectual innovations in the plant sciences— the articulation of Humboldtean botany and plant geography, the emergence of agricultural chemistry, and the birth of agricultural experiment stations— offered new ways to carry out the liberal projects of domesticating nature. Yet few of these projects were ever begun, and even fewer were completed. In part, these projects were impeded by the persistent political and economic turmoil that plagued the Spanish Caribbean during this period. Other projects, such as Reynoso's work on sugar, had little impact because the solutions they offered did not seem workable. This was to remain a problem over the next half century: what scientists identified as a good biological solution to an agricultural problem was not always a viable economic solution. So while the Spanish Caribbean's political and economic elites had begun to rediscover nature, it was a rediscovery that was largely rhetorical. Over the next fifty years, they began more systematic efforts to put rhetoric into action.

〜

TWO

GIVING PLANTS A CIVIL STATUS

Scientific Representations of Nature and Nation in Venezuela and Costa Rica, 1885–1935

〜

*When a country directs its activities to the exact and direct knowledge
of the territory it encloses and of the appearances which nature presents
in both the inorganic and organic realms . . . , no effort will be wasted
if we are firmly persuaded that time will reveal material interest and
value to that which before had appeared to be mere curiosity or
entertainment for intellectuals.*

LISANDRO ALVARADO, INTRODUCTION TO
HENRI PITTIER'S *EXPLORACIONES, BOTÁNICAS Y OTRAS,
EN LA CUENCA DE MARACAIBO* (1923)

For much of the nineteenth century, botanical research in Latin America was dominated by foreign naturalists. They extracted botanically interesting plants in much the same way that foreign corporations such as Grace & Company extracted guano from Peru or the United Fruit Company extracted bananas from Central America. They contributed little to the development of local communities of botanists. The valuable collections acquired on their brief visits to the tropics were brought back to Europe or North America, where they were classified and stored. Their findings were published in European and North American journals. Later in the century, foreign naturalists began to synthesize these smaller studies into comprehensive botanical surveys. W. B. Hemsley's regional flora, *Biologia Centrali-Americana* (1879–1888), for example, was based on the extensive collections of Mexican and Central American plants at the Kew Botanical Gardens in London.

Building a flora involved three steps: collecting the plants, classifying them, and then, based on these classifications, producing a standardized representation. The heart of this process was the herbarium, a library of dried plant specimens classified systematically by genus and species [Figures 2.3 and 2.4]. Plants would be collected in the wild, where they were dried and pressed, and then forwarded to the herbarium. Specialists at the herbarium classified each new plant by comparing it to known plants. If the new plant did not match any known plants, the botanist would write a detailed description and assign it a Linnaean name, which denoted its genus and species (e.g., *Coffea arabica*). The individual plant on which this new description was based was known as the type specimen. Until the late nineteenth century, the most important herbaria of Latin American plants were to be found in Europe or North America, particularly at Berlin, Kew Gardens, the U.S. National Herbarium in Washington, D.C., and the New York Botanical Garden. During the same period, few Latin American countries had enough money or scientific expertise to maintain large herbaria.[1]

Late in the century this state of affairs began to change. In pursuit of rational, orderly programs of development, Latin America's liberal governments began to fund scientific research. Between 1885 and 1935, most countries in Latin America established or revived national centers for agricultural and botanical research. Costa Rica, one of the smallest countries in the Spanish Caribbean, supported two natural history research institutions in the late nineteenth century, the Museo Nacional and the Instituto Físico-Geográfico. Most other countries established at least one scientific institution whose research agenda included collecting plants at the national level, organizing national herbaria, and, most significantly, compiling national floras.[2]

To produce these national floras, Latin American botanists began to forge a new relationship with foreign botanists that emphasized the primacy of national interests. Latin American naturalists reversed the extractive flow of botanical information that had characterized much of the nineteenth century. Most Latin American countries had small communities of botanists, who had neither the expertise nor the manpower to classify all the plants they collected. Many type specimens of Latin American plants, likewise, remained in overseas herbaria. Collaboration with foreign botanists was therefore essential. But Latin American botanists began to ensure that this collaboration worked in the national interest. For example, they required that foreign collectors leave duplicate sets of the plants they collected in the national herbarium. In exchange for contributing Latin American plants to herbaria overseas, the foreign specialists would help Latin American botanists classify their collections. This collaboration was not always smooth, and it was sometimes a struggle for Latin American botanists to retain control over all facets of the project.

The floras reflected prevailing liberal ideas of nature and nation. They nationalized nature in three ways. First, they took the nation as the unit of analysis. A flora can survey the plants of any region, the size of which can be defined by a wide range of criteria. Before the mid-nineteenth century, the regions covered by most floras were defined according to geographic criteria. They focused on regions either substantially smaller than the nation (e.g., river valleys) or substantially larger (e.g., the isthmus of Central America). In contrast, the areas surveyed by national floras were defined according to political criteria. This meant that their primary purpose was to represent the *nation*, in naturalistic terms. Second, the floras provided the scientific equivalents for the welter of foreign, vernacular, and indigenous plant names. This standardization made nature legible to the state, a process that Pittier described as giving plants a "civil status." Third, they nationalized nature symbolically by repatriating foreign research on a nation's plants. They did so by translating foreign works and incorporating their findings and by compiling historical and bibliographic reviews of all previous botanical research conducted in a nation's territory. Some, but not all, floras nationalized nature in another way. These emphasized "useful" plants, many of which were the export crops that drove national development. They thus commodified the natural world by identifying plants of actual or potential commercial value.[3]

Between 1885 and 1935 two national floras were produced in Costa Rica—the *Primitiae Florae Costaricensis* (1891–1901) and the *Ensayo sobre las plantas usuales de Costa Rica* (1908)—and one was produced in Venezuela—the *Manual de las plantas usuales de Venezuela* (1926). All were done through the efforts of Henri Pittier, a Swiss-born naturalist who spent most of his career working for the Costa Rican and Venezuelan governments. These floras illustrate how scientists in Latin America began to develop institutional models distinct from those in Europe and North America. They also demonstrate how the dominant paradigms of economic and political development in each country shaped scientific representations of nation and nature.

CONSTRUCTING BIOLOGICAL DIVERSITY: BOTANY IN COSTA RICA, 1885–1935

Pittier's floras of Costa Rica, produced between 1885 and 1910, made that nation's plants among the best studied in tropical Latin America. The growth of botany in nineteenth-century Costa Rica reflected the country's increasing economic and intellectual ties with the outside world, driven primarily by the expanding coffee industry. Costa Rica had embarked on a program of modernization under the "progressive authoritarian" dictatorship of General Tomás Guardia (1870–1882). Guardia's government began building a railway from the coffee regions to the port of Limón on the Caribbean coast. Guardia's successor, President Bernardo Soto (1885–1889), continued his liberal reforms, focusing in particular on education. As part of these reforms, the government established two public high schools (*liceos*) in the capital, San José, and hired a group of European scholars to staff them.[4]

The foreign scholars provided the impetus for the formation of a small scientific research community in Costa Rica. Among them was Pittier, who would come to represent a new role for foreign naturalists in Latin America. Previously, most foreign naturalists had worked for foreign governments or foreign institutions and had pursued the agendas of their sponsors. Latin American governments had occasionally hired foreign scientists but usually for short-term projects. In contrast, Pittier and other scientists like him were employed by Latin American governments and organizations and acted on their behalf. This new generation of foreign scientists often made their careers in Latin America. Most also retained ties with scientists in their home countries, which often formed the basis of collaborative relationships. Their status as foreigners often conferred a degree of prestige. Pittier, for example, used his status and his considerable powers of persuasion to convince the Costa Rican government to finance the Instituto Físico-Geográfico Nacional (IFG) as a center for the study of the natural history of Costa Rica. The institute officially opened in 1887, with Pittier at its head. The relations between resident foreign scientists and locally born scientists could sometimes be tense. In 1887 the Costa Rican naturalist Anastasio Alfaro convinced the government to establish the National Museum, whose mandate was similar to that of the IFG. In spite of these tensions, Pittier and Alfaro maintained their working relationship.[5]

The small group of naturalists at the IFG and the National Museum began work on the first national flora of Costa Rica. They followed two strategies. First, they collected, collated, and translated European and North American publications on the plants of Central America and Costa Rica. The National Museum, for example, translated and published a list of Costa Rican plants excerpted from the *Biologia Centrali-Americana,* a catalog of the plants of Mexico, the Caribbean, and Central America that had been assembled by British naturalists from Kew Gardens. Sometimes they found it difficult to gain access to foreign research. For example, Anders Oersted, a Danish botanist, had made extensive collections of Costa Rican plants during the 1850s but had published only a small part of his findings. Pittier complained that Oersted's botanical collections "lay forgotten in various European herbaria." Second, Costa Rican naturalists amassed large plant collections of their own. They collected plants while on surveying expeditions for another of Pittier's pet projects, a national map of Costa Rica [Figures 2.1 and 2.2]. The translations of foreign research and the original Costa Rican research were published in a new national scientific journal, the *Anales* of the Instituto-Físico Geográfico Nacional.[6]

In the late 1880s Pittier began work on a comprehensive national flora. To produce the aptly named *Primitiae Florae Costaricensis* (First Flora of Costa Rica), he developed a new, typically Latin American way of organizing scientific research. Since neither the National Museum nor the IFG had the financial or intellectual resources to classify their rapidly growing collections of Costa Rican plants or to publish a large-scale flora, Pittier enlisted the help of botanists abroad. He sent the Costa Rican plant collections to Théophile Durand of the Brussels Botanical Garden, who in turn distributed them to specialists in Belgium, Switzerland, France, Germany, and the United States. Each specialist studied the plants and submitted the diagnoses (and sometimes an analytical essay on a particular genus or family of plants) to Durand and Pittier. The first parts of the *Primitiae Florae Costaricensis* were published in Brussels between 1891 and 1895. It was written primarily for professional botanists: the essays and commentary were in French, while the technical descriptions of the plants were in Latin. The collaboration broke down, however, in 1895. Durand was overwhelmed by his official duties at the Brussels garden and was forced to abandon his work on the Costa Rican material. Undaunted, the Costa Rican naturalists continued their work on the book, turning to the eminent North American botanist John Donnell-Smith for help with classification. Donnell-Smith, an expert on the flora of Guatemala, single-handedly worked on the classification of all the families of plants that had not yet been assigned to a specialist. Additional volumes of the *Primitiae Florae Costaricensis* thus continued to be published in the *Anales*.[7]

The *Primitiae Florae Costaricensis* was more than a simple list of plants. Classification had generated new scientific insights about Costa Rica's plant distribution: although naturalists had long recognized that Costa Rica had an unusually great variety of plants given its size, they now began to discern patterns in the distribution of its plants where colonial naturalists had seen only a "great and dark sea." Hermann Christ, the eminent Swiss pteridologist responsible for classifying the collections of ferns, found that Costa Rica contained ferns characteristic of three floristic provinces: North America, South America, and the Caribbean. Based on this evidence, he argued that the Central American isthmus was a land bridge between ferns characteristic of North America and those characteristic of South America. Costa Rica was the point where these groups intersected, its sharp mountain ranges preventing the northern species of ferns from moving farther south and the southern species from moving farther north.[8]

Karl Wercklé, an Alsatian botanist long resident in Costa Rica, developed Christ's insight about ferns into a broader theoretical argument that explained why all of Costa Rica's flora was so unusually diverse. Wercklé described Costa Rica as "the privileged region of Tropical America," adding, "in truth, it is unlikely that any other country contains a flora containing the same number of species in a territory of the same size. It is certain that many of those forms that represent the greatest exuberance of tropical nature, have reached their maximum development here." He explained why in a 1909 essay, *La subregión fitogeográfica costarricense.* Wercklé argued that "the extraordinary variation of atmospheric and climatic conditions" in such a small area explained the unusual diversity of Costa Rica's plants. The influence of the Pacific Ocean and the Caribbean Sea, coupled with the "great number of mountains and hills," created a great variety of microclimates, allowing species adapted to many different conditions to live in Costa Rica.[9]

Official support for the theoretical botany characteristic of the *Primitiae Florae Costaricensis* and *La subregión fitogeográfica costarricense* diminished after 1900. A sharp drop in the price of coffee reduced government revenues, and it began to cut costs. Recognizing that it could not support two centers for botanical research, the government amalgamated the IFG and the National Museum. Even so, annual government appropriations for the IFG fluctuated wildly in the early 1900s. In 1904 Pittier resigned in frustration, leaving Costa Rica to take up a position as a tropical botanist at the Smithsonian Institution. Costa Rica's most prolific botanical collector, Adolphe Tonduz, had left the IFG several years before to take a post with the United Fruit Company. A few botanists in Costa Rica—most notably, Alberto Brenes, Anastasio Alfaro, and Karl Wercklé—continued collecting but found it difficult to get funds to continue classification and publication. Publication of theoretical botany, including the *Primitiae Florae Costaricensis,* effectively ceased.[10]

After the turn of the century, botany in Costa Rica took a more explicitly practical turn. Costa Rica's National Agricultural Society published Wercklé's essay on the phytogeography of Costa Rica in 1909, but this was one of the few works of theoretical botany to appear during these years. The government continued to fund some publications on Costa Rica's natural history, although they emphasized agricultural problems rather than theoretical botany. In 1907 the Costa Rican government invited Pittier, then working at the Smithsonian, to write a small volume on Costa Rica's common and useful plants. This new book, *Ensayo sobre las plantas usuales de Costa Rica* (Essay on the Common Plants of Costa Rica), was aimed at a different audience than the *Primitiae Florae Costaricensis.* Whereas the latter was intended for foreign naturalists, the *Ensayo* was written in Spanish and intended for a general audience with a practical interest in Costa Rican plants.

The *Ensayo,* like many Latin American floras of the time, opens with a historical essay and bibliography that synthesized earlier botanical research in Costa Rica. Historical sketches such as this played important scientific and intellectual functions. They helped to reverse the extractive pattern of natural history that had characterized botany in Latin America until then by synthesizing and translating earlier foreign research and publishing it in one convenient location, readily accessible to local readers. With this information available, Latin Americans interested in the nation's plants no longer had to read foreign journals or root through herbaria overseas. Pittier also used the historical sketches to lobby for a renewal of public support for natural history. He reviewed the significant achievements made by botanists working in Costa Rica (not the least of whom was Pittier himself), noting acidly that earlier governments had not "skimped on my resources, nor cut short my programs."[11]

The *Ensayo* standardized the names of Costa Rica's common plants, placing emphasis on useful plants. By the late nineteenth century, the botanical nomenclature of Costa Rica had become quite confusing, because each group of people who worked extensively with plants—farmers, doctors, natives, scientists—had its own idiosyncratic set of names for them. One plant could have several different names, and occasionally different plants could have the same name. Plant names reflected exchanges and conquests that had begun even before Columbus. The dominant influences on the common plant names of Costa Rica were Spanish and the local indigenous languages, but Pittier also found the influences of Nahuatl and *chiapaneco* (from Mexico), *taíno* (from the Caribbean), and Quechua (from the Andes). He found that Costa Rica's indigenous groups alone had five different names for the cacao tree (*Theobroma cacao* in the Western botanical nomenclature): *tsirukurú, tsirú, kaokrá, ko,* and *kaxu-tsía.* The Spanish name for the plant, *cacao,* is itself derived from the Nahuatl name *cacahuatl.* The vernacular Spanish nomenclature used by cacao growers also distinguished several varieties of cacao: the *Matina,* the *criollo,* the *Matinita,* the *calabacillo,* the *Matinita grande,* and the *forastero.* Several of these names referred to the same variety of cacao, while others referred to plants that were not, scientifically, varieties [Figure 2.6].[12]

To sort out this linguistic and analytical confusion, Pittier compiled a standardized list of Costa Rica's common plants. This list is, in effect, a dictionary that translates the popular names of Costa Rican plants into their scientific names, and vice versa. Each plant was listed by its common name, followed by its scientific name and a general description of the plant and its uses.[13] Pittier argued that most tropical products still lacked a civil status. By giving the plant a Linnaean name and thus a firm identity, he was making it legible to scientists, to the state, and to anyone else who might be interested. Once Pittier had completed the *Ensayo,* however, official interest in botany languished again.[14]

The *Primitiae Florae Costaricensis* and the *Ensayo de las plantas usuales de Costa Rica* had constructed new representations of Costa Rica's nature, which gave it new economic and scientific value. The economic value was most clearly de-

FIGURE 2.1

Botanical collectors in Costa Rica, circa 1900.

scribed in the *Ensayo;* it reflected the government's priorities of defining the national space and rationalizing the descriptions of its "useful" plants. Even such utilitarian projects, however, could generate insights of broader scientific interest. The scientific value of Costa Rica's nature had first been described in the *Primitiae Florae Costaricensis,* which had been researched and published as part of Pittier's broader project, producing Costa Rica's first national map. Pittier's, Christ's, and Wercklé's writings presented Costa Rica as a nation whose nature had great *scientific* value because it contained an unusually wide variety of plant species, many of which were rare or endemic.

The publication of the *Primitiae Florae Costaricensis* and the *Ensayo* did not generate sustained public support for botany in Costa Rica, however. Costa Rica's governments were interested primarily in science that contributed directly to a program of national development. They preferred to finance specific projects rather than provide sustained support to research institutions. While Pittier was producing the first national map, for example, the government provided relatively generous (if uneven) funding to the IFG. Once the map was complete, the government reduced its funding to the IFG, and Pittier ultimately left. After Pittier's departure, scientific research in Costa Rica fell into decline. Throughout the 1910s and 1920s Costa Rican naturalists such as Alberto Brenes and Juvenal Valerio continued to build large collections,

FIGURE 2.2

Cacao tree in the wild.

but they had neither the time nor the resources to classify the plants or publish their findings. No new floras of Costa Rica were published until the mid-1930s.[15]

BOTANY AND DICTATORSHIP IN VENEZUELA, 1913–1933

Botany in twentieth-century Venezuela emerged as part of a series of projects to consolidate the dictatorship of Juan Vicente Gómez, who had assumed the presidency after a bloodless coup in 1908. The Gómez dictatorship ushered in a period of relative peace, or what the historian Manuel Caballero more aptly

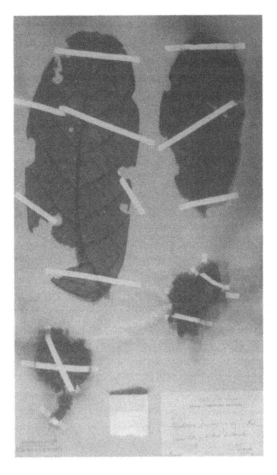

FIGURE 2.3

Dried herbarium specimen of cacao.

describes as an "absence of war." Gómez's cabinet ministers managed most of the dictatorship's practical policy issues, although Gómez jealously guarded his political power. Their projects for modernizing Venezuela reflected the positivist doctrines of science and progress that many of them had learned at the Central University of Venezuela. They believed that a strong central government, with rational, scientific planning, could help Venezuela to break from its anarchic, violent past and move toward a stable, prosperous future. Gómez's ministers founded a series of scientific institutions to address the country's most critical problems—and to consolidate Gómez's power. In 1910, for example, Gómez's Ministry of Public Works organized three Explo-

FIGURE 2.4

Henri Pittier in the herbarium at Caracas, 1940s. Courtesy of the Hunt Institute for Botanical Documentation, Carnegie Mellon University, Pittsburgh, Pennsylvania.

ration Commissions to begin mapping the national territory so that the government could build a network of roads. The Ministry of Public Works was also responsible for producing a general map of Venezuela.[16]

In the view of Gómez's ministers, one of Venezuela's most pressing needs was to rationalize its agriculture. Gómez's minister of education, José Gil Fortoul, suggested that the government should organize an agricultural college for training Venezuelan farmers in the methods of scientific agriculture. The government invited Henri Pittier to Venezuela to help plan the college's curriculum. After surveying the state of botany in Venezuela, Pittier argued that plans to establish an agricultural college were premature. So little was known about Venezuela's botany, he contended, that professors at the college would

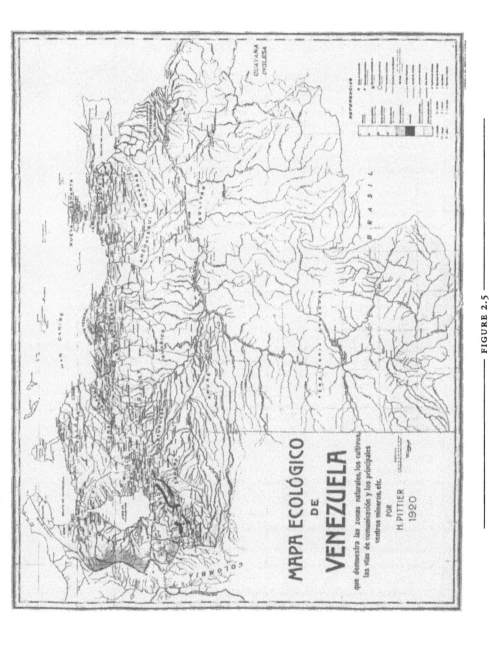

FIGURE 2.5

Visual representation of nature: Pittier's Mapa ecológico de Venezuela (1920).

Cacahuate—Etim.: del nahuatl *cacahuatl*, cacao—Véase **Cacao maní.**

Cacao.   Sterculiaceae.

Theobroma Cacao L. Sp. Pl. 2: 782. 1753.   Pl. III, V, VIII, IX.

El cacaotero es probablemente indígena en Costa Rica, como lo es tambien en las demás partes de América Central. Se encuentra silvestre en los bosques de Nicoya y de la parte Sur de la vertiente del Pacífico y se cultiva desde los tiempos más remotos. En la actualidad, nuestras principales variedades comerciales son el *cacao Matina*, que es sin duda el *criollo* de los antillanos, y que puede considerarse como una raza mejorada de la especie indígena; el *Matinita*, traído, según se afirma, de la Martinica y cuyo nombre legítimo sería *calabacillo;* en fin el *Matinita grande*, que correspondería al *forastero*, si no es sencillamente un híbrido inestable entre las dos anteriores variedades.

El nombre *Matina* se deriva de la circunstancia de haber gozado el producto de las fincas del lugar así denominado de especial fama entre los costarricenses, desde los tiempos coloniales. *Matinita* y *Matinita grande* son expresiones que no requieren explicación y que, siendo muy impropias, deberían abandonarse. En cuanto á la palabra *cacao*, se deriva del nahuatl *cacahuatl*.

El *criollo* ó *Matina* es ciertamente un producto exquisito y es posible que su cultivo sea de mejor provecho para el consumo interior. Pero en lo referente á la exportación, el calabacillo es ciertamente preferible: el agricultor no debe esforzarse en producir una calidad superior para mero aliciente de su vanidad, sino que debe concretar exclusivamente sus esfuerzos en hacer su trabajo lucrativo. Ahora bien, los fabricantes de chocolate prefieren el grano del *calabacillo*,—pequeño, de mala apariencia y de calidad ciertamente inferior,—porque, siendo este más amargo, gastan más azucar, producto baratísimo, para endulzar la pasta. Prodúzcase, pues, cacao calabacillo tanto más cuanto que éste rinde regular cosecha á los cuatro años, mientras el criollo hace esperar hasta doce y dieciseis años, y que el primero es, término medio, cuatro veces más prolífico que el segundo. Agréguese á estas desventajas del criollo que parece poco adaptado á la costa del Atlántico, y que es muy delicado, mientras el calabacillo es planta rústica y robusta que aguanta sin perjuicio la lluvia y el sol.

La producción cacaotera ha recibido en Costa Rica un impulso notable en los últimos años, habiéndose establecido varios grandes cacaotales, con sus respectivos *beneficios*, en la costa del Atlántico. En 1895, se importaba todavía algo de este grano para abastecer el mercado interior: en 1905, se exportaron cerca de 140,000 kilogramos, sin mengua del consumo del mismo país, que no deja de ser considerable.

Cacao de ardilla.   Sterculiaceae.

Herrania sp. nov.

Arbusto de los bosques inferiores de la vertiente del Atlántico, de troncos sencillos, de 3 á 4m. de altura, hojas digitadas de cinco hojuelas y mazorcas pequeñas, sésiles y fijas del tronco; estas frutas cubiertas de pelitos caedizos ó irritantes, se vuelven amarillas en su madurez y encierran numerosas semillas del tamaño de un grano de maíz, envueltas en una pulpa agridulce, como las del cacao común. Los indios bribrí, quienes llaman esta especie *uis-ub*, usan dichas semillas, despues de tostadas, para preparar una bebida algo amarga.

Cacao simarrón—Véase **Cacao de monte.**

Cacao de mico.   Sterculiaceae.

Theobroma simiarum Donnell-Smith in Pitt. Prim. Fl. Costar. 2, 52. 1898.

Theobroma angustifolium Moç. & Sessé ex DC. Prodr. 1, 484. 1824.

El *Theobroma simiarum* es un arbol de mediano tamaño, cuyos frutos alargados, aterciopelados y de color castaño crecen en el propio tronco. El nombre de *cacao de*

FIGURE 2.6

Textual representation of nature: The entry on cacao from Pittier's
Ensayo sobre las plantas usuales de Costa Rica *(1908).*

have little to teach. The government shelved their plans, and Pittier returned to the Smithsonian. In 1917 the government invited Pittier back, this time to direct a new agricultural experiment station on the outskirts of Caracas. After just over a year, Pittier resigned his post because of conflicts with the minister of development, Gumersindo Torres.[17]

Shortly after Pittier resigned as director of the agricultural experiment station, he was appointed director of the new Commercial and Industrial Museum of the Ministry of Foreign Relations. The museum was the brainchild of Lisandro Alvarado, director of the ministry's Department of Commerce and one of Venezuela's leading positivist intellectuals. Alvarado had persuaded Esteban Gil Borges, minister of foreign relations, to organize the museum and appoint Pittier director. Alvarado intended that the museum would collect, classify, and display Venezuela's natural resources so as to promote Venezuela's economic potential to foreign businesses and governments. Pittier welcomed the job as an opportunity to further his research on the botany of Venezuela. The museum was established in an office in the home of the Ministry of Foreign Relations, the Casa Amarilla, on Caracas's Plaza Bolívar. From the beginning, however, Pittier secretly feared that the museum would soon close because of financial or political problems. He told a colleague in the United States that his position as museum director "must . . . be considered merely a transient one."[18]

From his fragile institutional position, however, Pittier began to mount a public campaign in support of botanical research. In the museum's periodical and in general magazines, he observed that all Latin American countries had natural history museums that should, in principle, have been responsible for the classification of natural products. They were, however, little more than "national junk shops." Their collections were frequently so disorganized that "whoever visits them will leave as ignorant as he entered, and it is not from such clutter that the classification of products can be profitably undertaken."[19] Museums in Venezuela were no exception. When Pittier arrived in Venezuela for the first time in 1913, he found only one significant herbarium, which belonged to Adolfo Ernst, the great positivist scientist and plant collector. Ernst's herbarium also contained rare and valuable plants from the herbarium of José Maria Vargas, a physician who had been president of Venezuela for a short time in the 1830s. Ernst's herbarium had fallen into neglect after his death in 1899. When Pittier took it over, he found that the climate and pests had destroyed many of its most important specimens. His goal was to build a new herbarium that would survive even if he died or left Venezuela.[20]

Beyond the decaying herbarium and the threat of institutional instability, at first Pittier also found it difficult to collect new material. The practice of botany in Venezuela was "in a lamentable state of indifference, in spite of the opportunities that any amateur ha[d] of making important discoveries." In Costa Rica, a small but active group of professional and amateur naturalists had continued to collect plants even when money for publications and research had almost entirely dried up. In Venezuela, by contrast, Pittier could find only two amateur collectors: Alfredo Jahn, a politician, and José Saer D'Heguert, a high school science teacher.[21] In spite of the weak institutional support and the shortage of local collaborators, Pittier dedicated himself with enthusiasm and energy to collecting whenever he had the chance. He collected plants around his farm in Maracay, seventy-five miles southwest of Caracas. He also took advantage of opportunities to collect as they arose. In 1922 he collected some seven hundred plants from the states of Zulia and Trujillo while working on the Venezuela-Colombia Boundary Commission.[22]

To classify his growing collections, Pittier turned again to foreign experts. As in Costa Rica, Pittier had neither the time nor the manpower nor the expertise to do the entire job himself. But help was readily available. Botanical institutions in Germany and the United States were vying for the privilege of classifying Pittier's Venezuelan plant collections. When Pittier worked in Costa Rica during the 1880s and 1890s, he had sent most of his plant collections to Germany. While working as a tropical botanist for the USDA, he became closely connected to the botanists at the National Herbarium of the Smithsonian Institution. After he left for Caracas, he sent many of his plant collections to Washington, D.C. This was part of a broader rivalry between German and North American botanical institutions that had begun in the 1890s, at the center of which were Ignaz Urban at the Botanisches Museum in Berlin and Nathaniel Lord Britton at the New York Botanical Garden. Urban had begun a painstaking study of Neotropical flora, published in a series of papers titled the *Symbolæ Antellanæ*. In contrast, Britton's work depended on briefer studies of the plants. Both gardens cultivated contacts among collectors living in the tropics and sometimes hired collectors of their own. In Cuba, for example, the French monk Brother León sent his specimens to New York while the Swedish collector Erik Ekmann sent his to Berlin. Often the two collectors worked side by side and sent their respective collections to Berlin and New York, where the northern botanical gardens raced to classify the plants and get the descriptions into print. "Before Urban could complete his minute dissections, his ponderous descriptions, and his erudite discussions," wrote one of Britton's colleagues, "Britton had his brief diagnoses actually in print and the type specimens, christened with a Brittonian name, safely deposited in the herbarium of the New York Botanical Garden."[23]

Pittier used the competition between U.S. and German herbaria as a way of maintaining control over the classification of Venezuela's plants. This competition also reflected in part the growing U.S. interest in the Caribbean basin.

Botanists from the United States began to arrive in Venezuela in larger numbers, eclipsing their European counterparts. The Allied naval blockade during World War I isolated Latin America from Germany, giving U.S. botanists an advantage in getting Latin American material during the war years. In 1918 the New York Botanical Garden, the National Herbarium in Washington, D.C., and the Gray Herbarium at Harvard University began a cooperative study of the flora of northern South America. As part of this study, Pittier sent thousands of Venezuelan plant specimens to the National Herbarium in Washington.[24]

By 1924 Pittier found that herbaria in the United States (particularly the Smithsonian) were "better prepared than those of England, Germany, or France, for the study and classification of collections from tropical America, since they have sent and are constantly sending scientific expeditions to all the countries in the region, and have many naturalists who specialize in the study of our products." Nonetheless, Pittier accused the Smithsonian botanists of being slow and careless. The Berlin herbarium tried to lure Pittier back by offering to classify his plants quickly and carefully and publish them in a special series. Pittier was tempted by the offer, telling a colleague at the Smithsonian, "[E]ven though I have broken relations almost entirely with Berlin, I still think it would be in everybody's interest to let them do part of the work of naming my plants."[25]

Pittier allowed foreign specialists to classify his plant collections, but he struggled to retain ultimate intellectual control over classification and naming. Most of the time everything went smoothly, but there were occasional disagreements. For example, Pittier classified his plants according to the Vienna Code, a standard nomenclature adopted at the 1905 International Botanical Congress in Vienna.[26] Most taxonomists in the world used the Vienna Code, except for those working at a few herbaria in the United States who used the American Code, which had first been used by Britton in the 1890s. By the 1920s, however, the American Code was becoming outmoded, and even most botanists in the United States followed the Vienna Code. The only exceptions were the botanists at the New York Botanical Garden and a few at the Smithsonian Institution. When botanists at the Smithsonian renamed some of Pittier's plant identifications according to the American Code, he was incensed. "That kind of tyranny in the so-called free America is discriminating, not to say more," he fumed. "The majority of American botanists are against the so-called American code and the fact that you want to force all the contributors to official publications to abdicate their own opinions is simply outrageous."[27] The taxonomists in Washington appear to have yielded to Pittier's demands, since he never complained about this problem again. Pittier also fought to protect his personal research specializations. At one point he feared that J. N.

Rose, a Smithsonian botanist, had begun to work on a genus of plants that was Pittier's specialty. Pittier asked Rose to stop his research. "I do not believe in botanical imperialism," complained Pittier, "and you know quite well that I have been working on the group for several years."[28] Again, the Smithsonian yielded.

Once Pittier had crossed the hurdles of collecting his plants and having them classified, he faced the challenge of getting his results published. He complained that although his research was producing valuable results, they, "disgracefully, had little impact because there [was] nowhere to publish them and so they stay locked in our archive."[29] In spite of his complaints, Pittier published widely. He published the results of his extensive botanical research in the *Commercial and Industrial Bulletin* of the Ministry of Foreign Relations, in *Cultura Venezolana*, the magazine of the Venezuelan intellectual elite, and, perhaps most important, in the magazine of the Caracas Chamber of Commerce, the *Boletín de la Cámara de Comercio de Caracas*. His research articles dealt with issues ranging from forestry to systematic botany to the agricultural ecology of cotton, wheat, cacao, and coffee.[30]

Among Pittier's many publications in these years was the first ecological map of Venezuela [Figure 2.5]. Although he had initially hoped to publish the ecological map in the United States, he remained in Venezuela to look after some business interests. In 1920 the Venezuelan government offered to publish the map in Spanish, and Pittier agreed. To accompany the map, he published a sixty-page paper titled "Plant Formations and the Main Agricultural and Natural Products of Venezuela." This short essay, he wrote, contained "all we know about plant formations in Venezuela and can be used as a base for more extensive work." The discussion of Venezuela's main agricultural exports, such as coffee and sugar, was essentially optimistic. After the disruptions caused by World War I, Pittier foresaw a resumption of Venezuela's agriculturally based prosperity.[31]

In the early 1920s Pittier began to work on a full inventory of Venezuela's plants, modeled after his *Essay on the Common Plants of Costa Rica*. In it, he would synthesize all the dispersed published research on Venezuelan plants as well as his own extensive findings. As always, Pittier worked quickly. By the middle of 1925 the manuscript reached more than nine hundred typed pages. Pittier submitted the manuscript to the Ministry of Development for review, with the support of the Caracas Chamber of Commerce and the Venezuelan Academy of Medicine. At the ministry, it initially received "a first class burial."[32] Pittier had sent another copy of the manuscript directly to President Gómez for approval some months before and had not even received an acknowledgment. Later in 1925 Gómez's secretary finally acknowledged receipt of the manuscript and told Pittier that the government would publish the book after it had been reviewed and approved by the appropriate ministers.

The ministerial review showed Pittier that even representations of Venezuela's nature could be politically contentious. The ministers censored statements that "contained any allusion which could be construed as critical or disrespectful of the Venezuelan people and government." Pittier's draft introduction, for example, criticized Venezuela's forestry legislation for being "essentially unilateral, ignoring important issues like conservation and reseeding." President Gómez would tolerate no criticism of his government, however indirect. The minister of development, Antonio Alamo, asked Pittier to "correct" this passage because it was "certain that during the sage and prescient administrations of General Gómez, there has been much attention paid to these issues." Alamo also said that he realized "the intention of our friend Pittier has never been to attack any national custom or institution but rather to cooperate with his great knowledge and noble efforts in the progress of Venezuela, where, justly, he is regarded as one of the most enlightened, useful, and correct foreigners."[33] Alamo recommended that the book be published once Pittier had made the necessary "corrections." It was published in 1926, duly dedicated to President Gómez. Pittier thanked Gómez for his "boundless concern for forest conservation and agricultural development." Pittier had bowed to Gómez's absolute authority, expressing a gratitude he certainly did not feel.

The *Manual de las plantas usuales de Venezuela* (Guide to the Common Plants of Venezuela) blended theoretical and applied botany. It remains the foundational work of Venezuelan botany. It cataloged approximately 6,800 Venezuelan plants, based mainly on Pittier's collections but also on the collections of European explorers and his Venezuelan predecessors. Like the *Ensayo sobre las plantas usuales de Costa Rica,* Pittier's book on Venezuela began with a historical review of botanical exploration, an ecological sketch of the nation's plant life, and general essays on the country's useful plants. The main body was a detailed list of the country's common plants organized by their common names.

As in Costa Rica, standardizing the vernacular botanical nomenclature was important for both scientific and commercial reasons. Scientifically, the *Manual* would contribute to "the great work of stabilizing the nomenclature, so important from the point of view of the world economy, which is being heroically brought about under the auspices of an international commission, which can only with difficulty arrive at any results before each country on this continent has a proper catalog of its native plants."[34] Commercially, it could provide Venezuela with a well-defined list of its tropical crops. Pittier and his boss, Lisandro Alvarado, were particularly interested in standardizing the names of tropical hardwoods. Mahogany, for example, was known by many different popular names in the Spanish Caribbean. If a foreign timber company were to use one of these other names when inquiring about Venezuela's mahogany supply, they might be told that no wood by that name was available. Such problems could be avoided by connecting the popular nomenclature in each country with the international scientific nomenclature. This confusion impeded the growth of timber exports, Alvarado argued in the preface to the *Manual*, because Venezuela could not provide foreign companies with the essential data concerning the "scientific name of a wood, its specific gravity . . . , the regions where it can be found, and the roads which connect these regions to the ports."[35] Pittier frequently returned to the theme of the scientific and economic utility of plant taxonomy in his public arguments in favor of botany.

Although the *Manual* could not directly criticize the government, it did criticize agricultural practices in Venezuela generally. The picture Pittier painted was significantly different from the optimistic analyses that had accompanied his ecological map of 1920. In the *Manual*, Pittier presented Venezuela as a country whose essential export crops were being poorly managed. He noted that annual coffee production in Venezuela was 230 grams per tree, while in neighboring countries the average was closer to 500 grams. He extolled Venezuela's soils and climate, claiming they could not be the cause of the low yields. He argued instead that Venezuela's low coffee yields were attributable to planters who allowed the shade trees in the plantations to grow too large. Once the shade trees grew to a certain size, they competed with the coffee trees for nutrients in the soil. Similarly, Pittier found that Venezuela's sugar agriculture "ha[d] remained virtually stationary, to such an extent that what Humboldt wrote about the sugarcane of Antímano and Adjuntas [in Venezuela] a century ago, could have been written yesterday."[36]

Pittier's critiques of agricultural practices might have been accurate, but he was writing at a time when the Venezuelan state was rapidly losing interest in export agriculture. During the 1920s, petroleum exports overtook agricultural exports as the major source of the country's income. Lack of official interest in agricultural research was quickly becoming apparent. The Ministry of Foreign Relations authorized Pittier to publish the first issue of a botanical journal for which he had long been lobbying, but Pittier feared it would be the last. As Pittier predicted, the minister of foreign relations refused to authorize a second issue. Pittier argued vehemently that publication was an essential function of the museum and that his research would be useless if it was not available to the public. He also argued that the journal was valuable as a means of promoting science within Venezuela and of increasing the museum's library through exchange. "[The minister] told me to shut up," Pittier later told a friend.[37] No further issues of the *Commercial and Industrial Bulletin* were ever published. Pittier continued to work at the Commercial and Industrial Museum until 1933, when he was fired because he had publicly criticized a political ally of Gómez. Although Pittier was allowed to stay in Venezuela, he was prohibited from having access to his herbarium. The state took little interest either in botany or in export agriculture until after Gómez's death in 1935.[38]

Pittier had long feared for the institutional stability of botany in Venezuela, and his fears turned out to be wholly justified. Because he had anticipated such a possibility, however, he managed to ensure that his work would not suffer the fate of his predecessors, Ernst and Vargas. Both of these nineteenth-century naturalists had built significant herbaria of Venezuelan plants, but neither man published much, and when they died most of their knowledge died with them and their herbaria were abandoned. Since Pittier had sent duplicates of most of his Venezuelan plants to the National Herbarium in Washington, D.C., the loss of the Venezuelan herbarium would not mean that later botanists would have to start all over again. Similarly, the publication of the *Manual de las plantas usuales de Venezuela* provided (and continues to provide) a starting point for all further research into the natural history of Venezuela.

CONCLUSION

The Latin American floras produced between 1885 and 1935 demonstrate the complex place of science and nature in the process of nation building in Latin America. Institutionally, naturalists in Latin America had shown that it was possible to organize national scientific research communities differently than did the more developed nations of Europe and North America. They showed, in fact, that it was possible to pursue a nationalist scientific agenda with the help of foreign scientists. Complete scientific independence was not possible in such a small country, but that did not mean the only alternative was complete dependence on a foreign scientific metropolis.

The floras nationalized nature from a scientific perspective. The work of assembling a national plant inventory involved repatriating, translating, synthesizing, and therefore reappropriating foreign research. This meant that under certain circumstances it was possible for Latin Americans to reverse the patterns of intellectual extraction that had characterized most of the region's history before the late nineteenth century. The historical and bibliographic essays that introduced most national floras were reassertions of national sovereignty over scientific knowledge. In retrospect, this strategy has worked. Most contemporary botanical research in Venezuela takes Pittier's *Manual* as the foundational text for Venezuelan botany. The inventories and ecological maps in these floras commodified and represented each nation's nature in new ways. The floras identified new and rare plants, which had great value to the scientific community. The work on plant geography also began to assign value to certain ecosystems. By the late twentieth century, Costa Rica's singular biological diversity—a feature first recognized and explained in the early floras—had become a defining national characteristic.

The floras also nationalized nature from a commercial perspective. The commercial utility of botanical surveys had, in fact, been a key reason that Latin American naturalists had succeeded in gaining government support in the half century between 1885 and 1935. The floras gave Latin American states, for the first time, a clear and systematic idea of the plant resources contained within their national borders. This utilitarian vision of nature in the national economy was reflected in Pittier's *Ensayo sobre las plantas usuales de Costa Rica* and *Manual de las plantas usuales de Venezuela*, which organized plants by their common names and emphasized useful plants. Primarily, however, the commercial utility of these lists lay in their enumeration of export commodities. Such utilitarian surveys sometimes pointed out shortcomings in national agriculture, as did Pittier's critique of coffee growing in Venezuela. At other times they pointed out incipient conservation problems, as in the *Ensayo sobre las plantas usuales de Costa Rica,* where Pittier warned that rapid deforestation was leading to soil erosion. By emphasizing the commercial utility of inventorying botany, however, naturalists had also made scientific research vulnerable to fluctuations in the international markets for export commodities. Pittier's experiences in Costa Rica and Venezuela make it clear that both governments were primarily interested in useful science. In the end, neither government was committed to sustained funding for additional inventories. In this they were typical of most countries in the Spanish Caribbean. Finding sustained support for agricultural research, however, was easier.[39]

✍

THREE

BUILDING CREOLE SCIENCE

Science and Ideologies of Agricultural Development
in Cuba and Puerto Rico, 1898–1930

✍

> *For any country to fail to keep a watchful eye on the progress of other*
> *countries and take advantage of their natural resources and the*
> *improvements they have made in the products of the soil is to fall behind*
> *in the race of life and publicly acknowledge a lack of enterprise.*

S. A. KNAPP, *AGRICULTURAL RESOURCES*
AND CAPABILITIES OF PORTO RICO (1900)

The first stable agricultural research centers in the Spanish Caribbean were founded in Cuba and Puerto Rico. Between 1898 and 1927 five major centers were organized on the two islands. In Cuba, the national government established an experiment station at Santiago de las Vegas, just outside Havana; Edwin F. Atkins, an American planter who owned a sugar mill near Cienfuegos, founded an experimental garden devoted to cane research; and the Cuba Sugar Club, an association of Cuban and North American planters, organized another sugarcane research station at the Central Baraguá. In Puerto Rico, the USDA's Office of Experiment Stations operated the Porto Rico Agricultural Experiment Station (PRAES) in the western city of Mayagüez, and the insular government organized the Insular Experiment Station at Río Piedras, on the outskirts of San Juan.

All these centers were modeled, in one way or another, after U.S. centers for agricultural research, and all their staffs included U.S. scientists. This transfer of U.S. institutional models to Cuba and Puerto Rico was, at least in part, the product of U.S. economic and political expansion in the Spanish Caribbean. After the Spanish-American War in 1898, the United States had annexed Puerto Rico and, under the provisions of the Platt Amendment, reserved the right to intervene in Cuba. The U.S. government used science and technology as tools to consolidate effective control of the islands and as an ideological justification for this control. For example, U.S. public health campaigns to control yellow fever early in the twentieth century improved living conditions for many Cubans and Puerto Ricans while also reducing the mortality among U.S. troops and colonial officials there. Most U.S. agricultural scientists and government officials who visited the islands in the years immediately following the war shared this imperial ideology of science and progress, arguing that science was the key to agricultural modernization. However, it is impossible to reduce the history of the research stations solely to U.S. economic and political interests. In any case, these interests were far from monolithic: colonial officials, scientists, and businesses were often at odds over the exact path modernization should take.

Cubans and Puerto Ricans participated actively in the construction of the experiment stations. Pursuing their own ideas of national development, they appropriated, adapted, and sometimes rejected North American models. Local demand for agricultural science predated the U.S. occupation by several decades. In the late nineteenth century, for example, agricultural associations in Puerto Rico had convinced the Spanish imperial government to establish agricultural experiment stations at Mayagüez and Río Piedras. The stations quickly foundered in the bitter political struggles between islanders and the Spanish metropolis, but it is surely not a coincidence that the two experiment stations established after U.S. annexation of Puerto Rico were located in the same two cities. Local agricultural and political interests could even influence U.S. imperial decisions. It was the city of Mayagüez that found a permanent site for the PRAES, which was beholden (at least in theory) only to the USDA's Office of Experiment Stations in Washington, D.C. Similarly, Cuba had a tradition of agricultural innovation and research that dated to the pioneering work of Alvaro Reynoso, and by the late nineteenth century many Cubans were anxious to modernize the nation's agriculture. Since many of them had been educated or had lived or traveled in the United States, it is not surprising that they used it as a model for development.

Although U.S. influence was strong in the experiment stations, it was by no means the only—or the most important—influence. Each station's institutional form and research agenda was ultimately shaped by the interplay of local and global economic, political, and ecological forces. The stations, for example, could not simply import scientific knowledge from the United States, as their environment was radically different from that of the mainland. They had to look farther afield and collaborate with stations in other parts of the Caribbean and elsewhere in the tropics. These stations were also shaped by local politics. In Cuba some administrations rewarded loyal party members with jobs at the Estación Experimental Agronómica, to the chagrin of the scientists who worked there. In both Cuba and Puerto Rico, nationalist (and often, therefore, anti-American) politics led to an exodus of U.S. scientists from the public stations. Wherever possible, they were replaced by local scientists. The stations were also influenced by the region's cycles of boom and bust, particularly in terms of sugar prices: when sugar prices were high, funds for both public and private research were ample; when they were low, agricultural research suffered. This fusion of Cuban, Puerto Rican, U.S., and foreign influences made the research stations distinctively creole institutions.[1]

Two major issues dominated agricultural research in Cuba and Puerto Rico. One was the ideological debate over which model of agricultural development should be supported by research. Both islands imported a large percentage of their food, using their best agricultural lands to plant export crops, including tobacco, coffee, and, above all, sugar. Some scientists and government officials wanted to end the quest for export-led development and break the islands' dependence on large plantation agriculture. They held that the experiment stations should devote most of their resources to research on food crops, which would promote domestic food production and thereby reduce dependence on imported food. Others argued that the islands should continue to produce export crops but diversify so as to reduce dependence on sugar. Those involved with the sugar industry, including growers, government officials, and scientists, wanted to use agricultural science to make the sugar industry more efficient and productive. Their goal was to optimize the model of export-led development, not subvert it. They argued that it was better to produce as much sugar as possible and to continue to purchase food abroad with income from sugar exports.

The second, related issue was to figure out how to use the research to change agricultural practices in the countryside, with the goal of solving pressing agrarian problems. To do this, each station had to develop effective ways of communicating their research to their agrarian constituents. Some stations, however, found it difficult to reach—or clearly define—their constituencies. Agricultural extension services were chronically weak through most of the period, making it difficult to disseminate research results. While the relative effectiveness of experiment stations can be evaluated by many criteria, a compelling criterion is how well they met the needs of their various constituents. During the first three decades of the twentieth century, the stations were more successful in meeting the needs of the sugar industry than they were in meeting the needs of small farmers.

CUBA

The Estación Experimental Agronómica at Santiago de las Vegas

The first task of the Cuban republic was to rebuild the island's ruined agriculture. Cuba's once-powerful planter class had been devastated by the war of independence and its aftermath. In part, the damage was material. Many of Cuba's sugar mills were destroyed during the war of independence: less than 20 percent of the mills in operation in 1894 survived. Cane fields had been burned, mills and equipment destroyed. The war also ruined Cuban planters financially. They were faced with crippling debts from the war and declining sugar prices. After the United States assumed control of the island in 1898, many planters were unable to obtain loans or grants from either the United States or commercial banks. The U.S. occupation government argued that loans would destroy the planters' "self-respect" and suggested that they seek financing from banks. Banks, however, were reluctant to lend them money because sugar prices were so low. To liquidate their debts, many Cuban planters sold their property to U.S. investors.[2]

The recovery of Cuba's export agriculture was a top priority for the republic's new government, which assumed power in 1902. The administration of Tomás Estrada Palma sought to rebuild Cuba's ruined economy as best it could. Given the "newer and more intimate" relations between Cuba and the United States, Emilio Terry, Cuba's secretary of agriculture, decided to look to the United States for help. On his behalf, Gonzalo de Quesada, the Cuban ambassador in Washington, asked James Wilson, U.S. secretary of agriculture, to recommend a scientist who could organize and operate an experiment station in Cuba. Wilson suggested Franklin Sumner Earle, an expert on sugarcane then employed at the Louisiana Experiment Station. Wilson, Quesada, and Earle met in Washington, D.C., in February 1904 to discuss the job, which Earle accepted. The station was established in April 1904, on the site of a former orphanage at Santiago de las Vegas, just outside Havana.[3]

Earle modeled the Estación Experimental Agronómica after agricultural experiment stations in the United States. Rather than focus on sugar alone, Earle's plans included all facets of Cuban agriculture. He organized the station into two divisions, one of which would concentrate on practical work, the other on basic research into Cuban plants, soils, and ecology. The practical division consisted of the departments of general agriculture, animal industry, and horticulture. The research division consisted of the departments of chemistry and soil science, botany, and vegetable pathology. Earle stressed the importance of the research division, particularly the departments of botany and vegetable pathology, as they would provide vital information about Cuba's economic crops. The department of botany was to study the floral regions of the country, identify and study medicinal plants and other plants of economic value, explore the possibility of the exploitation of trees that could provide timber for construction, identify ways of controlling and destroying weeds, and, perhaps most important, identify and breed varieties of economically useful plants. The department of vegetable pathology would identify and control organic plant diseases.[4]

Earle built up the station's research capacity by using his personal connections in the world of tropical agricultural research to forge links with institutions in Cuba and abroad. He organized a transnational network of collaborators, similar to the networks Pittier had organized in Costa Rica and Venezuela. In the U.S. journal *Science,* he promoted the station as a tropical laboratory for American botanists, offering its facilities "to any properly accredited botanist who cares to make use of them for any line of botanical investigation." The station rapidly became one of the most important centers for the study of Cuban natural history. The station's herbarium—housing its collection of Cuban and Caribbean plants—was "already larger and more important than any other in the Antilles." The bulk of the specimens came from three collections on loan from the station botanist, the Cuban Academy of Sciences, and the New York Botanical Garden. The herbarium represented a scientific baseline, which could be used as the starting point for more detailed surveys of Cuba's flora and for agricultural research. Earle's old experiment station in Louisiana and the newly founded Federal Agricultural Experiment Station in Puerto Rico sent sugarcane varieties. The New York Botanical Garden sent a series of its publications and offered to cooperate in a survey of Cuba's flora. The station also received help from the Agrarian League of Cuba and the Cuban Academy of Medical Sciences.[5]

The station's North American directors sought to reach all Cubans involved in agriculture. Both Earle and the station's second director, J. T. Crowley, also an American, were determined that the station should serve small farmers as well as large agricultural interests. Both men emphasized the importance of extension work. "If the work we are doing is of sufficient value to Cuba to justify the maintenance of this station," Crowley wrote, "certainly it is of sufficient value to justify teaching it to the people." He suggested that the Cuban government fund lecture tours, agricultural substations, and cooperative experiments. He was happy that the station's research reached "progressive agriculturalists" (a term that appears repeatedly in the accounts of North American scientists), but he was not satisfied with reaching just them. He was also concerned about "the vast body of people tilling the soil that we do not reach."

He argued that agriculture should be taught in the schools and colleges, so that Cuba could eventually count on a body of educated agriculturalists who could promote modern agriculture.[6]

The station also produced a range of Spanish-language publications. The station sent circulars, which discussed agricultural issues of current interest, to Cuban newspapers. It distributed a series of bulletins, simple treatises on aspects of Cuban agriculture that were based on the station's research, directly to farmers. Its annual reports included more detailed scientific documents, of interest to the national and international agricultural and scientific communities. The station researched and published on cane agriculture, but these efforts, published in Spanish, were primarily directed at the few remaining Cuban mill owners and, perhaps, the Cuban *colonos*, cane planters who worked under contract for U.S. mills. In its first year of operation alone, the station published fifteen circulars and one bulletin. The station's persistent financial difficulties, however, limited its capacity to do extension work.[7]

In spite of these early achievements, Earle's project to create an American-style institution in Cuba foundered on the rocks of Cuban politics. By 1905 Estrada Palma's administration began awarding public service positions based on party affiliation. Middle-class Cubans, excluded from much of the rest of the economy, clamored for positions in the public service. Each change of administration brought a high turnover in the station's staff. Another problem was the pay scale. As employees of the Cuban government, the station scientists were paid according to civil service scales, which were often far below the salaries of agricultural scientists in the private sector. Because of the patronage appointments (known as *botellas*), low wages, and demoralizing working conditions, many of the staff quickly resigned. Earle himself resigned in 1906, after only two years as director. During the three years Crowley served as director, there were "eighteen resignations from important positions and twenty-two appointments." Crowley blamed the turnovers on low salaries, which did not reflect length of service or skill level.[8]

Nationalist policies of the Cuban government also discouraged the station's North American staff from remaining. In 1909 the Liberal government of José Miguel Gómez assumed power. Gómez greatly expanded the public administration, undertook a series of public works projects, and began promoting Cuban interests over U.S. interests. Early in 1909 the Gómez government demanded the resignation of all the station's North American staff, including Crowley. The director who succeeded Crowley was a Cuban, the engineer Ramón García Osés. Franklin Earle, the station's former director, expressed outrage at the forced resignations, denouncing them as a "purely political move made to supply more spaces for the horde of hungry office seekers."[9]

This rejection of all things North American extended to the station's research program. Osés canceled all of the research projects begun under Earle and Crowley, projects that one Cuban scientist later lamented "should have been continued for three to six years more to obtain conclusive results." The sudden departure of the station's North American staff caused most of its experimental programs to grind to a standstill. The station's botanist, Juan Tomas Roig y Mesa, later complained that the herbarium, library, and seed collection had been "left to the mercy of insects and fungi." Under the Gómez administration, Cuban politicians had also taken the best animals from the station and used its resources for personal ends. Osés committed suicide in 1913, after Mario Menocal's Conservative Party defeated Gómez's Liberals in national elections. The reasons for Osés's suicide are unclear, but some sources suggest that the new administration had uncovered irregularities in the station's finances.[10]

The Menocal administration was not as hostile to the United States as was that of Gómez. In 1914 Menocal's Conservative government rehired Crowley. In spite of the administrative and political turmoil, the station's small group of scientists undertook a broad range of research, focused along two principal lines: the diseases and pests of crop plants and plant taxonomy and acclimatization. The department of vegetable pathology did research on the diseases of mango flowers, avocados, and tobacco. In response to the growing frequency of insect infestations in Cuba's sugar crop, in 1915 the station organized a department of entomology. When a citrus cancer struck Florida, an entomologist and a pathologist were detailed to prevent the spread of the disease to Cuba. In doing so, they identified another plague that had recently hit orange groves in a remote area. To ensure that infected plants were not imported into the country, Cuba established the Commission of Plant Inspection.

The scientists in the department of horticulture performed experiments on the acclimatization of vegetables, including spinach, peppers, radishes, and carrots, and also worked on decorative flowers and fruit trees. One of the station's main achievements was the publication of a flora of Cuba by Roig. To deal with the growing interchange of plants and seeds abroad and the collection and distribution of plants and seeds within Cuba, the department of botany organized an acclimatization garden, a propagation garden, and an arboretum. The department also sponsored collecting expeditions to various parts of the island. Nonetheless, Cuban politics again fell into disarray, after President Menocal won a second term in office. A brief Liberal insurrection known as the February Revolution broke out early in 1917, although it ultimately failed. Apparently unhappy with the political situation, Crowley resigned again. Crowley was to be the station's last North American director.[11]

Under Menocal's second administration, the station enjoyed relative stability and official support for research. This renewed official interest in research was reflected in the appointment of Eugenio Sánchez Agromonte as secretary of agriculture, commerce, and labor. Sánchez Agromonte, a physician who had been a separatist leader in the uprising of 1895, took a genuine interest in ensuring that the station functioned properly. In October 1917 he named an Italian agronomist named Mario Calvino as Crowley's successor. Sánchez Agromonte charged Calvino with reforming the station. He couched his charge to Calvino in metaphorical, and revealing, terms:

> I would like to see if you can make this tree, now in such bad condition and so little appreciated by those who were expecting its fruits, recover its luxurious growth and produce what the country can reasonably expect. Do not let "goats" eat it, and do not believe that it can be watered by "bottles." I give you a machete with which to prune it. Use it well. You have the opportunity to do something good in Cuba.[12]

"Bottles" refers to the political patronage appointments, or *botellas*, that had plagued the station for much of its existence.

With this clear mandate from the secretary of agriculture, Calvino reorganized the station. In his report, he reviewed the status of Cuban agriculture. He argued that Cuba's "socioeconomic system" was backward, "because it pays less attention to small farmers [*campesinos*] than it should, and distances the new generations from the soil. Cuba's problem," he continued, "lies in the great expanses of soil that still need to be brought under cultivation; in making production less expensive without sacrificing the wages of laborers; and in obtaining from the soil many of the products that are now imported from abroad."[13]

Reflecting this new understanding of Cuba's agricultural problems, Calvino hired new researchers and placed more emphasis on the study of food crops. He also developed ties with the University of Havana and revamped the extension system, making it easier for small farmers to consult the station. In the first year of Calvino's administration, the station distributed more than 26,000 of its publications around the island and offered 889 consultations. Calvino also reported that the station received an average of forty-five letters a day. All of this suggests that the station was becoming more actively involved in Cuban agricultural development.[14]

Calvino's 1918 report responded to Sánchez Agromonte in metaphorical terms similar to the charge he had been given:

> I had to . . . prune gangrenous roots and initiate a systematic struggle against the many parasites, animal and vegetable, which in tropical climates multiply in such a manner that they do away with even the strongest plants. There were

those who did not want the tree to prosper, because its shade bothered them or hurt them. . . . A few shakes were sufficient to ensure that the tree was almost free of them. The wasps which buzzed around the trunk bit me repeatedly[,] . . . but we have continued shaking and working to defend the tree and its fruits, even in spite of the skepticism of some observers who, watching us with almost apathetic eyes, as if we were illusions, told us that we were wasting time, since the tree was in such bad shape that any attempt to help it recover its natural lushness was useless.[15]

Certainly the "tree" prospered under Calvino's custodianship. The turnover in the station's staff began to diminish. By early 1920 the station had sixty-three employees and student assistants, including seventeen scientists and engineers and seventeen technicians.

Sugar research came to play a more prominent role in the station's agenda during the 1920s. Calvino retired from the directorship in 1923, lured away by an offer to organize and direct a private station for sugar planters in Cuba's Oriente province. The directorship passed to the Cuban agronomist Gonzalo Martínez-Fortún. Martínez-Fortún had previously been the head of the station's department of agriculture, the one department whose research work had focused heavily on sugarcane and tobacco. Martínez-Fortún continued Calvino's main lines of research but also placed new emphasis on sugar. The sugar experiments were directed by the station's lone North American employee, Stephen C. Bruner. When Puerto Rico's sugar industry was stricken with the mosaic disease, Bruner developed a series of experiments that showed the disease was also causing severe losses in Cuba, although it did not manifest itself as dramatically. He also helped to introduce hybrid sugarcanes to the island. The botanist Juan Tomás Roig continued his pioneering research on the flora of Cuba. The station's pure and applied research programs continued steadily through the 1920s, even though a hurricane destroyed its main building in 1926. The government quickly financed the construction of a new, better building to replace the old structure.

The history of the Estación Experimental Agronómica illustrates how the course of agricultural research in Cuba was shaped by its complex ties with the United States. Two Cuban historians argue that the station was primarily a center of scientific support for the problems of agricultural businesses and foreign interests in Cuba, since they were the only entities with the economic and technical resources to assimilate scientific research. The Cuban station consistently tried to reach a wide Cuban audience, rather than business and foreign interests alone. Most of the station's early publications under the U.S. directors were in Spanish, reflecting the station's orientation toward a Cuban audience. The station also promoted agricultural extension and primary agricultural education, to try to create a community of Cubans with the resources to assimilate scientific research well.[16]

Another historian argues that although the station established a national agriculture, introduced varieties of cane, fruits, and other plants, and obtained results in the methods of planting, cultivating, and harvesting major crops, this work represented a minuscule part of what could have been accomplished. The vagaries of Cuban politics had disrupted the station's development, especially in the early years. But it is hard to know just what the station could have accomplished even under the best of circumstances. The problems of Cuban farmers, as Calvino himself had noted, were primarily socioeconomic rather than biological. As these socioeconomic problems remained unresolved, science could play only a small role in Cuba's agricultural development.

The Atkins Garden, the Central Soledad, Cienfuegos

Private agricultural concerns, particularly the large U.S.-owned sugar corporations, promoted agricultural research in Cuba. By 1920 most sugar *centrales* had experimental plots of at least one or two acres to study many facets of cane growing, including breeding, fertilizers, and diseases and pests. Since the sugar corporations enjoyed high profits during these years, they were able to employ some of the best agricultural scientists in the tropics, often luring them away from more poorly paid positions at public agricultural experiment stations. The earliest private station in Cuba was established in 1900 by the E. Atkins Company at their *central* at Soledad, near the city of Cienfuegos. The Atkins Company, like many other U.S.-owned corporations in Cuba, imported experts from the United States to make their Cuban operations more efficient. By the 1890s much of Cuba's sugar industry was particularly well suited to benefit from agricultural research, as most other aspects of production had already been optimized.

The garden had its roots in Atkins's quest to rationalize sugar production on his estates. He had already rationalized most of the operations on the *central*, building railroads and importing the latest milling machinery. In 1893 Atkins's Soledad Mill was, in the words of an American journalist, "one of the largest and most efficient mills on the island."[17] Nonetheless, Atkins and other planters in Cuba faced growing pressures to modernize their operations so as to increase production and lower costs. In part, the pressure to modernize came from competition from Europe, which began producing more beet sugar in the late nineteenth century. It also reflected the apparent "degeneration" of the Cristalina variety of sugarcane, which was then the variety most widely planted in Cuba. As Atkins himself described it, "[P]lanters were likely

56

to be confronted by two serious difficulties; either the plants might degenerate through successive stalk cutting, or they might be attacked by disease." Planters like Atkins began to look for sugarcane varieties better adapted to Cuban conditions.[18]

Until the late nineteenth century, the only way to obtain new cane varieties had been to import and acclimatize wild varieties from Asia. Improvements in shipping during the nineteenth century greatly accelerated the global exchange of new cane varieties. The Cristalina cane had first arrived in Cuba in the mid-nineteenth century and became popular among planters for its adaptability to a wide range of growing conditions and its high sugar content. For a long time, planters had supposed that it was impossible to breed hybrid strains of sugarcane, since the practice of planting cane from stalks apparently caused the flowers to become sterile. In 1886, however, scientists working independently in Java and in Barbados bred a hybrid sugarcane. This discovery made it possible, at least in theory, to breed a hybrid cane that would be self-sowing, adapted to local conditions, resistant to plagues and disease, and high in sucrose. In practice, however, breeding such a cane proved to be difficult. The botanical gardens in Java (the Dutch Proef-Station Oost-Java) and Barbados began to produce hundreds of hybrid canes, which were quickly distributed to sugar-growing regions around the world. Cuban planters experimented with many of these hybrids, with little success. They found that imported hybrids with high sucrose content and purity were often unsuited for Cuban growing conditions and that hybrid canes that were durable and vigorous were often low in sucrose content. For these reasons, most sugar planters in Cuba continued planting the Cristalina cane, which remained the best compromise between durability and sugar content.[19]

Atkins was not content to continue planting Cristalina and decided to establish an experimental garden for acclimatizing and breeding economically viable cane hybrids. Atkins, whose family was from Boston, turned to botanical experts at Harvard for advice. In 1900 Atkins invited two Harvard biologists to Soledad: Oakes Ames, director of Harvard's botanical gardens, and George L. Goodale, professor of economic botany. The three men, along with a plant breeder named Robert M. Grey, set out the plans for an experimental cane garden at the Colonia Limones at Soledad. Atkins named the new experimental garden the Harvard Botanic Station for Tropical Research and Sugarcane Investigation. In spite of its name, the garden's official affiliation with Harvard was initially unclear. Grey, who had remained in Cuba to operate the garden, sent monthly reports to the director of Harvard's Botanical Museum. But the university had little direct involvement in the operation of the garden, which was wholly funded and controlled by Atkins.[20]

Grey aimed to breed a hybrid cane that had high sugar content and was more durable than the Cristalina variety. The two varieties most widely planted in Cuba, the Cristalina and Cinta canes, had frail sexual organs that made breeding them difficult. To begin his breeding program, then, Grey imported hybrid canes from around the world. The first hybrids to arrive at the Atkins Garden were several strains of Barbados Hybrid (B.H.) cane, sent by Barbados's commissioner of agriculture early in 1901. By 1903 the garden had fifty-one varieties of cane, including hybrids from Java, Jamaica, and Mexico. By the 1904–1905 season, Grey had produced a new Cuban hybrid cane, which he named the "Harvard" cane. The Harvard hybrid was less susceptible to cold and produced more seed than the traditional Cristalina variety.[21] At the Second National Cuban Exposition at Havana in 1912, the garden exhibited thirty Harvard hybrids. Grey noted proudly that these were the "only canes of Cuban origin displayed among the numerous cane exhibits at the Exposition."[22] Grey bred hardier hybrid canes in the following years, but none were widely planted beyond the Atkins estates.

Acclimatization of exotic plants, both ornamental and economic, also played a large role in the garden's early research agenda. In fall 1901 Oakes Ames sent the garden a collection of ornamental flowering plants from Harvard's botanical garden in Cambridge. Atkins sent the garden a collection of tropical fruits and other crops from Florida. The garden quickly expanded to include these plants. In 1902 Atkins opened a second section of the garden, dedicated to fruit experiments. Just three years after its founding, the botanical garden at Soledad contained "243 genera and 400 species of plants, shrubs, and trees." Important experiments were undertaken on the cultivation of "bananas, cacao, castor bean, coca, coconut, coffee, cotton hybridization and selection, rubber, tea, and various fibre plants." Not all of these experiments were successful. Those on cotton had initial promise, but most of the plants succumbed to insect attacks. Tea did not flourish at Soledad either. During its first two decades, the garden continued to expand rapidly to accommodate the research on cane and plant acclimatization.[23]

The garden's research mission began to change during the early 1920s. During its first two decades, the garden's relationship with Harvard had never been clarified, and it remained wholly dependent on ad hoc appropriations from Atkins. In December 1919, after discussions with Ames, Atkins sought to make its relations with Harvard more official. He offered to donate $100,000 to Harvard to establish "a Fund for Tropical Research in Economic Botany." He also offered to continue funding the experimental garden, so that the income from the endowment could accumulate. Atkins told Ames that he wanted to provide a permanent endowment for the garden because, as Ames described it, he "has been well satisfied with the results accomplished and has, as a business man, realized the practical value of the work undertaken to the development of the sugar industry in Cuba."[24] In 1924 Atkins provided funds for the establishment of the Harvard Biological Laboratory at the Atkins Garden and turned over the administration of the garden to "a committee of Harvard Professors." When Atkins died in 1926, he left a permanent endowment to the laboratory. In the following years, Atkins's widow continued to donate money for the station's scientific work. By the early 1930s the garden had grown from eleven acres to more than two hundred.[25]

Under the influence of the Harvard biologists, the garden's research mission expanded from a narrow focus on economic botany to embrace much broader studies of tropical biology. Atkins, with the encouragement of the Harvard biologists, had funded scholarships for Harvard students "who wish to pursue investigations in any branch of tropical biology." Atkins hoped "that the work of this Harvard Station [would] be of real value to the scientific world."[26] Under the custodianship of the eminent Harvard zoologist Thomas Barbour, the garden began to promote exchanges with researchers in Cuba and elsewhere in the tropics. In addition, the garden became an integral part of the training of Harvard graduate students, who for the first time had access to a biological laboratory in the tropics.

Under the new administration, the garden began collaborating with many individuals and institutions in Cuba. It freely distributed seed throughout the country and exchanged plants and seeds with public and private institutions in Cuba and abroad. Cuban scientists, particularly those from the Estación Experimental Agronómica, "[enjoyed the garden's] hospitality at their convenience."[27]

Although general biology played a more important role in the garden's research, biologists there continued to do research on sugar and other crops of economic value. Scientists also did work on acclimatization of vegetables—it grew the first white potatoes in Cuba—on forage grasses, and on shrubs and fruit trees. Results of general interest were forwarded to the Cuban government, which published them in its *Official Bulletin*. Work on sugar also continued, although the control of diseases and pests became more important than the breeding of new hybrids. In 1925 the garden's directors signed an agreement with the Cuba Sugar Club and the U.S.-based Tropical Plant Research Foundation (TPRF) to undertake a collaborative research project on the causes of sugarcane root disease. This disease was then one of the most significant limiting factors in sugarcane production in Cuba, particularly around Cienfuegos.[28]

The Atkins Garden evolved from an institution that served the interests of a single North American sugar planter to one that served a broad range of Cuban and international interests, at least as understood by the station's researchers. Like many other U.S. institutions in Cuba, the Atkins Garden had a complex relationship with the Cuban people and Cuban institutions. Having been established to promote the interests of the Atkins corporation, its work was initially very closely tied to Cuba's sugar economy. Under the influence of the North American biologists who worked at the station and who consulted with Atkins, however, the garden's role evolved and broadened. They encouraged Atkins to provide the garden with an endowment, which would insulate the garden from the rapid fluctuations that plagued Cuba's sugar economy in the 1920s.

Unlike the Estación Experimental Agronómica, the Atkins Garden's organization, funding, and location kept it insulated from the political turmoil that afflicted public life and institutions in Cuba. In spite of this insulation, or perhaps because of it, scientists at the Atkins Garden began to work on a wide range of projects related to both export and subsistence agriculture in Cuba. The universalist ethos of the sciences promoted ties between the garden and scientific institutions in Cuba and abroad. Notwithstanding these growing ties with Cuba and with the global scientific community, the Atkins Garden remained a fundamentally North American institution. Most of its professional employees were from the United States, and North Americans continued to define its research agenda.

The Cuba Sugar Club Experiment Station of the Tropical Plant Research Foundation, Central Baraguá, Camagüey

In the 1920s sugar agriculture in Cuba was threatened by an unprecedented wave of diseases and pests. A viral disease of cane, known as the mosaic disease, was discovered to be widespread on the island. The sugarcane root disease and an insect known as the moth stalkborer were also reducing sugar yields throughout the island. The Cuba Sugar Club decided to organize an agricultural experiment station to address these problems. The station was established at the Central Baraguá in the eastern province of Camagüey. Unlike the Estación Experimental Agronómica or the Atkins Garden, research at the Central Baraguá station was focused almost exclusively on a single crop.

The Central Baraguá experiment station was organized, staffed, and operated by the TPRF, which had been established in Washington, D.C., in 1924 to "promote research for the advancement of knowledge of the plants and crops of the tropics; to conduct investigations in plant pathology, entomology, plant breeding, botany and forestry, horticulture, and agronomy, and to publish the results thereof; and to establish and maintain such temporary or permanent stations and laboratories as may be necessary for the accomplishment of these objects." The driving force behind the organization of the TPRF was the Committee on Phytopathology in the Tropics of the U.S. National Research Coun-

cil. The TPRF's structure closely matched that proposed by the U.S. sugar researcher Franklin Earle in 1920. Given the growing problems in tropical agriculture after World War I and the shortage of scientific experts in tropical
agriculture, such a central organization made sense to scientists, agricultural
interests, and governments in both the United States and Latin America.[29]

The foundation formalized an existing network of North American experts
in tropical botany. The network was small: the same names crop up in articles,
reports, and organizational charts throughout the Caribbean. For example,
research on sugarcane varieties at the Baraguá station was done by Franklin
Sumner Earle, who had been the founding director of the Cuban Agricultural
Experiment Station and had also worked for private Cuban sugar growers, for
the USDA, and for Puerto Rico's insular government. The board of the foundation was composed of nine trustees, five of whom were "scientific men" and
four of whom were to represent "business interests." The scientific representatives were assigned by the National Research Council, the American Phytopathological Society, and the American Association of Economic Entomologists. The most prominent businessman on the board of trustees was Victor
Cutter, president of the United Fruit Company.[30]

Using funds contributed by "organizations or individuals interested in
tropical plant products," the foundation's primary missions were to collect
information on tropical crops and to organize scientific research in tropical
Latin America. During the foundation's brief six-year life, much of its consulting work and research was done on behalf of U.S. business interests in
Latin America. But the foundation was not simply an instrument of U.S. business interests. It also did consulting work for Latin American organizations
and governments. Often, the line between U.S. and Latin American business
interests was blurred, as in the case of the Baraguá research station.[31]

The experiment station at Baraguá was the foundation's flagship, designed
to demonstrate to countries in tropical Latin America what the foundation
could achieve. It was established in 1925 and published its first bulletin the
same year. The foundation's first annual report to the Cuba Sugar Club proudly
described the station as having "one of the best equipped laboratories in the
West Indies for general experimentation work in the field[s] of plant pathology, entomology, agronomy, chemistry, and soil study."[32] Research focused
on four problems relating to sugarcane: the mosaic disease, the root disease,
the moth stalkborer, and the selection of cane varieties. The principal research
work was undertaken at the station at the Central Baraguá. Three branch stations were maintained for testing varieties of sugarcane, studying insect pests,
and investigating the mosaic disease.[33]

The Baraguá station also collaborated with the Atkins Garden on sugarcane
research. Early in 1925 the TPRF met with the Harvard committee in charge of

the Atkins Garden. They formally agreed to cooperate on sugar research in Cuba. At the top of the agenda was a study of the root disease of sugarcane, which had hit the Cienfuegos region especially hard.[34] After completing this research, the two stations continued to cooperate in other ways. In 1928, for example, Robert Grey, the superintendent of the Atkins Garden, sent eight Harvard hybrid seedlings to the Baraguá station for inclusion in their research collection.[35] There is no evidence that the Central Baraguá scientists undertook similar cooperative projects with the Estación Experimental Agronómica, even though it was doing important research on cane breeding and cane diseases.

Although the station was funded by an organization of Cuban and North American sugar planters, in many respects it favored North American interests over Cuban interests. Labor relations at the station were similar to those at U.S.-owned sugar *centrales*. Cuban technical and professional staff played essential roles in daily operations but were generally excluded from upper management. At the Baraguá station, North American scientists defined the research agenda. The station employed some Cuban scientists and technicians, many of whom had long experience in tropical agriculture and botany, but at best they were junior partners in the research.[36]

Similarly, the station sometimes withheld findings that might have favored the *colonos,* the Cuban planters whom the sugar companies contracted to grow the sugarcane. In one of the foundation's English-language publications on sugarcane varieties in Cuba, its director, William Orton, noted, "Since questions of cane varieties sometimes involve plantation policy and *colonia* contracts, we have not prepared a Spanish edition of this letter for distribution to the *colonos,* but we shall be ready to do this through the Sugar Club if the contributors desire it."[37] The issue was sensitive because the *colonos* often received payment in the form of a fixed weight of refined sugar per ton of cut cane they delivered to the mill. Introducing higher-yielding cane varieties would increase the mills' profits at the *colonos'* expense.[38]

The Central Baraguá research station did important research on sugar in Cuba during its brief existence. Its research agenda evolved little, unlike that of the Atkins Garden or the Estación Experimental Agronómica, which ultimately reflected (not always equally) the interests and concerns of several groups. At any given moment, these groups included some combination of politicians, large and small farmers, Cubans and North Americans, and the scientists themselves. In contrast, the research mission at the Central Baraguá was set by the Cuba Sugar Club alone. The Cuba Sugar Club expected its research station to address specific problems of sugar agriculture, in particular, increasing sugar yields and limiting the impact of diseases and pests.

In the case of this station, it is difficult to sharply delineate Cuban interests and North American interests, although North American interests dominated.

The station did serve one class of Cubans: the planters who were members of the Cuban Sugar Club. But it is not clear how big a role Cuban planters played in the club, which also included powerful U.S. members. The station's research systematically excluded other Cubans, particularly the lower-class *colonos* who grew and harvested much of Cuba's cane crop. Most Cubans employed at the station were limited to secondary roles. Like the Atkins Garden, the experiment station at the Central Baraguá was a place where U.S. scientists could gain valuable research experience in the tropics. For most of these scientists, however, Cuba was simply a temporary stop in their careers. Most returned to work for museums, corporations, or universities in the United States. The station contributed little to the development of a scientific community in Cuba.

PUERTO RICO

The Laboratory of Empire: U.S. Visions of Agricultural Development

While the United States occupied Cuba after the 1898 war, it annexed Puerto Rico. The island remained in political limbo for almost two decades after 1898. It was no longer a Spanish colony, but neither was it formally a U.S. territory. The island was ruled by a presidentially appointed governor. Tariff restrictions on trade with the United States were abolished, and as a result the island's sugar economy grew rapidly. U.S.-owned sugar companies came to dominate this burgeoning industry. In contrast, the Puerto Rican coffee industry entered a period of decline in these same years, a decline that was at least partially caused by the political and economic transformations brought about by annexation. The Jones Act of 1917 took steps to clarify the island's status. Puerto Ricans were granted U.S. citizenship, and Puerto Rico's elected Senate was given more authority over the island's governance. Nonetheless, the governor, as a presidential appointment, could override the Senate's decisions. In the 1920s the sugar industry increased its economic dominance in Puerto Rico while the coffee industry collapsed almost completely.

The government officials who came to Puerto Rico after 1898 saw it as a perfect laboratory for U.S. models of agricultural research and agricultural development. Puerto Rico was one of four tropical possessions the United States had acquired that year, along with Hawaii, the Philippines, and Guam. U.S. officials did not always agree on what form agricultural development on these islands should take. Some argued that they should simply rationalize their existing export economies; others proposed alternate paths. U.S. Secretary of Agriculture James Wilson, for example, suggested that the new tropical colonies could help the United States to achieve agricultural self-sufficiency by producing crops that could not be grown on the temperate U.S. mainland. Whatever model of development they promoted, most colonial officials shared Wilson's view that there was "a pressing need for the establishment of experiment stations" in the new possessions.[39]

Wilson's arguments for establishing experiment stations in the new tropical colonies also had a strong moral component. He was anxious to prevent the spread of plantation monocultures, which he associated with the pre–Civil War society in the southern United States. Wilson wanted the experiment stations instead to promote the development of small farms. The presence of "practical scientists" in the colonies would provide small farmers with "not only an object lesson, but the foundation of a farm literature." Permanent agricultural experiment stations were essential "for giving to the people of those islands information regarding their staple crops, their development, and the insect and bacteriological pests to which they may be liable." Educational efforts such as agricultural extension "established among the peoples of the islands will not be the least potent influences in elevating them to higher intellectual levels." Wilson's interest in promoting small farms and staple crops seems difficult to reconcile with his hope that Puerto Rico and the other islands would become major suppliers of tropical commodities to the United States. Perhaps he envisioned that small farmers could produce enough for both domestic consumption and export.[40]

Not all U.S. experts shared Wilson's vision of development. The first agricultural expert to visit Puerto Rico was Brigadier-General Roy Stone of the U.S. Volunteers, who conducted an agricultural survey of the island in 1898. He praised Puerto Rico's agricultural potential, its good crops, and its diligent laborers. He argued that for Puerto Rico to fulfill its agricultural potential, it needed better transportation, irrigation, and agricultural experiment stations. "No country or region," Stone wrote, "is more in need of a system of official experimentation in agriculture like that of the United States than Puerto Rico." Agricultural experiment stations would help to make Puerto Rico's agricultural potential a reality:

> Under an efficient experiment station system every one of the scores of products of the island could be experimented with and tested, selections and crosses made, diseases studied and cured, fertilizers tried, and methods of preservation and transportation devised, whereby, in time, intelligent cultivation and shipment would take place of haphazard operations.[41]

Unlike Wilson, Stone argued that Puerto Rico ought to focus on developing its export crops rather than its staple crops. Stone predicted that Puerto Rico, with the help of U.S. capital, would become a base for the export of tropical crops to the United States. In Stone's view, Puerto Rico should continue to import most of its food for domestic consumption so that it could devote "its whole area to tropical productions, thereby securing the best use of its matchless soil and climate." He predicted that the island would continue to export its current plant resources and also develop new export crops, including potatoes, tomatoes, and other vegetables, and medicinal plants, fibrous plants, and "many kinds of tropical fruits not now shipped for the want of the necessary quick transportation." Stone's vision more closely matched prevailing U.S. ideas about the development of its tropical colonies.[42]

Yet a third vision of agricultural development in Puerto Rico was articulated by Seaman A. Knapp from the Louisiana Experiment Station. In 1899 the USDA sent Knapp to Puerto Rico to study the agricultural conditions of the island. Like Stone, Knapp found the sugar industry "primitive." Puerto Rican planters, for example, knew little about techniques of fertilization. Knapp was impressed with the potential of Puerto Rican rice, corn, beans, bananas, and vegetables. However, he found the coffee situation precarious. Most coffee growers were deeply in debt, a condition made more difficult after the hurricane of 1899 destroyed their plantations. Without money to rebuild, many coffee planters abandoned their plantations; those that had recuperated were producing at lower levels. Knapp predicted that coffee could easily be grown profitably in Puerto Rico if the yield were tripled or quadrupled, which would lower the cost of production correspondingly. Fertilizers, yields, and productivity were precisely the kinds of problems that an agricultural experiment station could readily address.[43] The new station, as Knapp saw it, would have "a wider range of investigation and application than is usually given to such institutions." Initially, research would emphasize the development of coffee, sugar, and tobacco. In this respect Knapp agreed with Stone.[44]

But where Stone envisioned Puerto Rico as a producer of export crops alone, Knapp saw the rationalization of export agriculture as just one phase in the island's agricultural development. Once the cash crops had provided an adequate economic surplus for the island, Knapp proposed that the experiment station would promote agricultural diversification, focusing on the production of crops and livestock for domestic consumption. The station would also do forestry research with the aim of reestablishing Puerto Rico's forests, which had been almost completely destroyed during the Spanish colonial period. Knapp also proposed a program of cooperation with local farmers, instruction in local schools, and demonstrations.[45]

No matter what their vision of agricultural development, the U.S. advocates of agricultural science had to navigate among a host of competing interests, between the federal and territorial governments and between the governments and the agricultural interests in the territories. The agricultural interests were quite complex and included large and small farmers from the United States and from the territories themselves. For example, Wilson's vision of favoring small farms over corporate plantations frequently met with resistance in the territories. In Hawaii, large-scale sugar planters actively resisted the USDA's attempts to "Americanize" Hawaiian agriculture by promoting small farms.

The federal and territorial governments fought for control of the territorial experiment stations. This mirrored the struggle between the federal and state governments to control the state agricultural experiment stations on the mainland, which had been resolved a decade before. On the mainland, the federal government funded the stations but let the states determine the stations' research agendas. The territorial governments of Hawaii and the Philippines wanted this pattern to be extended to them. Instead, the Office of Experiment Stations (OES) of the USDA was granted control of all the insular stations. The desire to retain federal control over agricultural research in the colonies was motivated in part by paternalism. The historian Richard Overfield argues that "the USDA leadership believed that they knew better than their constituents what constituted a proper experiment station." The social, economic, and political conditions in Puerto Rico, however, forced the USDA to modify this paternalist vision.[46]

The Porto Rico Agricultural Experiment Station, Mayagüez

The USDA's Office of Experiment Stations founded the Porto Rico Agricultural Experiment Station in 1901. The station was first located at Río Piedras, on the outskirts of San Juan. The following year, however, it moved to Mayagüez, in the coffee region at the western end of the island. Promoting alternative paths of agricultural development in Puerto Rico proved to be more difficult than the station's scientists or the USDA had imagined. Over the next three decades, the station's directors often found themselves trying to catch up with Puerto Rico's rapidly changing agricultural economy.

Although the PRAES enjoyed strong political support from the USDA, it got off to a weak start. The experiment station was not eligible for many federal grants because the island's political status with respect to the United States remained unclear. Most important, the PRAES was not eligible for federal funds under the Hatch Act, which granted $15,000 in federal money to each state and territory, to be used for agricultural research. Without funding from the Hatch Act, the station depended on annual appropriations from the U.S. government and Puerto Rico's insular government. Federal funds alone were not enough to finance the station, and its first director, Frank D. Gardner, could only hope "that the insular government [would] continue its liberal policy toward the station." These appropriations fluctuated significantly from one year to the next. At first the station did not have enough money to buy a plot of land. Gardner leased thirty acres and several houses at Río Piedras. The next year, the insular government and the city of Mayagüez appropriated enough money to buy the experiment station a permanent location on the outskirts of the city.[47]

The station's original research goals included "systematically studying all of the problems of agriculture, with the end of acquiring useful and practical information for the farmers of this country." Gardner emphasized the importance of "practical work" over "scientific work." He was well aware that he had to convince Puerto Rican farmers that the station would be useful to them. He publicized the station's utility by testing new crops and new methods of cultivation. During the station's brief time in Río Piedras, Gardner had begun experiments that would give quick results and concrete evidence of its usefulness, focusing on studies of vegetable crops and of noxious insects. He put aside longer-term work on sugarcane and coffee. Gardner argued that for the station to succeed, it needed, not only "the greatest efforts of the station officials, but also the interest, cooperation, and support of all the people in the island who are interested in agriculture."[48]

In spite of Gardner's good intentions, much of the station's early research was of little use to Puerto Ricans. The scientists, most of whom were from the mainland, showed little awareness of the agricultural and botanical research that had been carried out in Puerto Rico in the nineteenth century. Instead they treated the island as a scientific tabula rasa. Their research programs often reflected their personal interests. They began experiments with "nearly all agricultural and horticultural crops grown on the island, and also with others believed to be adapted to the conditions." The station's botanists began to build a large collection of economic tropical plants, "permitting a comparison of varieties, testing their adaptability, and making possible plant-breeding work on an extensive scale."[49] They also tried to acclimatize North American plants to Puerto Rico. "It would not have been so bad if the species from temperate climates had been tried at higher altitudes," wrote the Puerto Rican agronomist Edmundo Colón several decades later, "but in Mayagüez these efforts are merely entertaining. The mere contemplation of an apple tree, seen by us in a hill in Barranquitas, would have been enough to make anyone desist from such attempts at acclimatization, except as a sport."[50]

The station ran an agricultural extension program from 1902 until 1924. It published bulletins and reports in Spanish and answered requests for consultation. It translated, verbatim, some twenty-four USDA bulletins, which, Colón later pointed out, were more suited to the temperate climates of the United States than they were to the tropical climate of Puerto Rico.[51] In 1909, for example, the station sent out some 2,250 letters responding to requests for information and "many thousand bulletins, reports, circulars, seeds, and plants, for the purpose of bringing the investigations of the station before the people and enabling them to obtain the greatest benefit from its efforts." The station developed few programs to reach the larger masses of poor Puerto Rican farmers, relying instead on informal means of disseminating knowledge. "It is impossible for the station to reach all classes of inhabitants," wrote the director, "but in every community there are progressive planters who are taking up improved agriculture and are also imparting instruction to their neighbors." Most of these "progressive planters" appear to have been either Puerto Ricans involved in export agriculture or planters from the United States.[52]

The station did little systematic research on Puerto Rico's staple food crops until the mid-1910s. Puerto Rico's rapidly increasing population forced the station to address the issue of food crops. In the view of the station's director, the challenge was to "produce foodstuffs, or other crops of sufficient value to be exchanged for foodstuffs, for the maintenance of the ever-increasing population." He argued that Puerto Rico's agricultural laborers, "in order to maintain themselves during periods of idleness as well as to place themselves in a position to secure better pay, must become more independent of their daily wage."[53]

There was a brief flurry of interest in food crops during World War I, when it was feared that the island might be isolated from its food supply. After the war the station resumed its attention to cash crops. It took up research in vegetable growing during the early 1920s, but these efforts too were directed at exports for the U.S. market rather than for domestic consumption. The last reported experiment aimed at ordinary Puerto Ricans was a demonstration to show that it was not necessary to wait for certain phases of the moon to plant crops. The experiment was a success, but it is not recorded what effect, if any, it had on traditional planting practices. The experiment station did little work to promote subsistence agriculture among Puerto Rico's poor. It focused instead on the production of cash crops that would provide the laborers with the wages they needed to buy their food.[54]

The station devoted much of its research to reviving Puerto Rico's ailing coffee industry, the one agricultural sector still firmly under the control of Puerto Ricans. The industry had suffered under the U.S. occupation. Before 1898 Spain had been the principal consumer of Puerto Rican coffee. After 1898 Spain placed a prohibitively high tariff on Puerto Rican coffee, meaning that Puerto Rico effectively lost access to the Spanish market. The removal of tariffs on coffee exports to the United States did not make up for the loss of the Spanish market, as U.S. consumers were not accustomed to the varieties of coffee grown in Puerto Rico. The 1899 hurricane aggravated the problem even further. The coffee industry, therefore, seemed ideally suited to benefit from technical assistance. The experiment station acquired a coffee plantation outside Ponce and began a large-scale program of coffee experimentation "along several lines such as introducing those coffees that bring the highest prices in the States markets, and also increasing the yield and improving the quality of the native product." It introduced coffee varieties from the Philippines, Hawaii, Java, and Ceylon to determine if Puerto Rico could grow varieties more palatable to the American consumer. By 1911 some coffee plants on the station were producing eight hundred pounds of coffee per acre, or roughly four times the average yield on the rest of the island.[55]

In spite of these successes, the core problems of Puerto Rico's coffee industry could not be solved through science. Puerto Rican coffee still continued to sell poorly in the U.S. market. Even had it sold well, coffee agriculture in Puerto Rico might not have been profitable. Coffee prices in the early twentieth century were volatile because Brazil, the main supplier of coffee to the United States, had been overproducing coffee. Gradually, the American-owned fruit plantations took over much of the best land previously occupied by Puerto Rican coffee plantations. By 1907, "as a rule, inaccessible lands in the interior [were] being planted to coffee, while the old plantations, especially where they [were] near macadamized roads, [were] being planted to more remunerative crops." In the mid-1910s the station's director conceded that the "most favorable outlook for the coffee grower is along the lines of diversification." The station nonetheless continued with small-scale coffee experiments through the 1920s.[56]

Although the early USDA rhetoric had emphasized the importance of Puerto Rican farmers and staple crops, the station's research quickly began to focus on North American farmers and export crops, principally fruits and coffee. This research agenda was shaped in part by changes in Puerto Rico's agricultural economy. Tropical fruit farming in Puerto Rico expanded rapidly after 1898, largely under the impetus of planters from the United States. At first, Puerto Rico's poor roads and port facilities made it difficult to ship fresh fruit, so early exports were mostly canned fruit. Improvements in transportation under the U.S. administration, however, made Puerto Rico's fruit industry increasingly profitable. Fruit growers frequently looked to the station for advice, and tropical fruits quickly assumed a dominant place in the station's research agenda. By 1903 the station had "nurseries of citrus fruits, mangos, aguacates, and other sorts" and a banana plantation. The station dedicated much of its research efforts to pineapple. Station scientists discovered that chlorosis, a crop disease that affected Puerto Rico's pineapple and citrus fruits, was caused by an excess of carbonate of lime in the soil. Because of this and because soil conditions in Puerto Rico were generally poor for citrus plants, the station undertook a research program on fertilizers. Between 1900 and 1911 the value of Puerto Rico's exports of pineapple and other fruits jumped from $100,000 to $2.1 million. To earn some badly needed operating funds, the station itself even began exporting pineapples.[57]

The station's relationship with Puerto Rico's sugar industry was complicated. Because Puerto Rican sugar was exempt from U.S. tariffs, the industry grew rapidly after 1898. North American sugar corporations established large, modern sugar *centrales*, particularly in the southeastern half of the island. The sugar industry quickly overtook the coffee industry as the island's leading source of agricultural exports. Although the station's director noted that it was "very urgent" that the station begin cane experiments, he argued that limited funding prevented the station from developing a full line of cane research. As with coffee, the station concentrated on the introduction of new varieties and on studies of fertilizers. Puerto Rico's small size meant that the sugar companies quickly ran out of new land to plant, and by 1908 they had begun to look for new ways to increase sugar yields, largely through the introduction of new varieties and the application of fertilizers.[58]

The station's reports, however, regularly criticized the intensive agriculture that characterized the American-run sugar plantations. "As long as the present prices of sugar continue," wrote the station's director in 1908, "the land now devoted to cane will continue to be planted to that crop. The production of the crop on the same land year after year is against the best practices of agriculture and cane growers must study the methods of overcoming the drawbacks in soils continually subjected to a lack of diversification." The lack of new land and the growing threat of soil exhaustion encouraged sugar planters to pay more attention to the scientific problems of sugar growing. Instead of turning to the Porto Rico Agricultural Experiment Station for help, however, Puerto Rico's sugar growers' association founded their own station in 1910. While the federal experiment station continued experiments with introducing new varieties and crop rotation, sugarcane occupied a relatively minor place in its research agenda for most of the 1910s.[59]

Sugar assumed a more prominent role in the station's research in the late 1910s and early 1920s when the mosaic disease was first detected on the island. For years, scientists at the PRAES had urged planters to grow sugar in rotation with other crops, particularly rice or beans. Instead, sugar planters had adopted even more intensive methods of sugar cultivation, spurred on by the high prices that sugar commanded following World War I. Rather than rotate their sugar crops, they applied more fertilizer. The station's chief agronomist argued that fertilizers were a poor substitute for "rational agricultural techniques."[60]

After sugar prices fell in 1921, the director again scolded the planters, noting that "it is only by continued losses . . . that the [sugar] planters can be made to realize the necessity of practicing a rotation, which will result in the production of many foodstuffs for a number of years instead of growing a single remunerative product for the present." Eventually, the station conceded that the sugar growers were not going to take up crop rotation. Now scientists encouraged them to at least rotate cane varieties, which would carry some of the benefits of a broader crop rotation. For the rest of the 1920s, the station's sugar research focused on the introduction of cane varieties, especially the new hybrids from Barbados and Java that became common after about 1924.[61]

The station abandoned its extension activities after 1922 and devoted itself completely to research. The director of the station wrote, "For many years after the establishment of the Porto Rico Experiment Station it was necessary to translate its work to a public not familiar with scientific agriculture. Fortunately this period is passed and the station can now turn more to the investigation of tropical agriculture, leaving to other agencies the popularization of its work." [62] In 1924 it transferred all its extension activities to the experiment station operated by the insular government in Río Piedras.

In short, the PRAES had great difficulty building a constituency in Puerto Rico during its first three decades. Station scientists tried to revive Puerto Rico's coffee economy, but the industry's problems were not ones that scientific research could solve. Rather, the coffee industry was doomed by restrictive tariffs on its principal markets overseas, its inability to break into the U.S. market, and globally depressed coffee prices. The sugar industry should have been a natural constituency for the station, but sugar growers showed little interest in the station's efforts to convince them to rotate their crops. Crop rotation might have been a sound practice ecologically and agriculturally, but the sugar planters did not feel it was sound economically. They expressed their dissatisfaction with the PRAES by founding their own research station in 1910. The one solid constituency that the station built was the fruit growers, although this represented only a small fraction of Puerto Rico's agriculture.

For a variety of reasons, the station never built a relationship with the vast majority of Puerto Rico's small farmers. Issues of language and literacy no doubt presented a large barrier to communication. Organizational problems presented another difficulty: the station was best equipped to deal with agricultural associations, which were interested in applying research to their crops. It was more difficult for the station to disseminate its results to widely scattered small farmers. Perhaps the greatest obstacle to reaching Puerto Rico's small farmers was the station's commodity-centered vision of agricultural development. Station scientists argued that food crops could be purchased using wages from producing export crops. In these three decades, the station had little room for agricultural projects that were not directly connected with agricultural exports.

The Insular Experiment Station, Río Piedras

The second large experiment station in Puerto Rico was organized to address particular agricultural problems rather than to promote a general vision of agricultural development. It was founded at Río Piedras in 1910 by the Porto Rico Sugar Growers Association, an organization dominated by planters from the United States. The sugar planters hoped that the station would find a way to control the white grub, an insect pest that was drastically reducing Puerto Rico's sugar yields. The association hoped that agricultural research could emulate the success of the Hawaiian Sugar Producers' experiment station. Scientists there had successfully eradicated the sugarcane leafhopper, a serious insect pest. Unfortunately, scientists at the Puerto Rican station were not as successful. For three years, three full-time and two part-time scientists tried unsuccessfully to find a way to eradicate or control the white grub. In 1914, frustrated by the lack of results, the association donated the experiment station to Puerto Rico's insular government, specifically the Board of Commissioners of Agriculture.[63]

The Board of Commissioners of Agriculture was a quasi-public organization in charge of creating an administrative and research apparatus for the development of agriculture in Puerto Rico. The insular government established the board in March 1911, after lobbying from Puerto Rico's powerful agricultural associations. The board was composed of seven members, two designated by the insular government and one appointed by each of Puerto Rico's five major agricultural associations: the Association of Farmers of Puerto Rico, the Sugar Producers Association, the Puerto Rico Fruit Exchange, the Tobacco Growers Association, and the National Coffee Growers Association.

The board's main tasks were scientific and technical. It was to "publish from time to time statistics relative to agriculture; to study insects, pests, and diseases harmful to the agricultural interests of Puerto Rico, and to devise ways to exterminate them; to dictate measures for the development and improvement of livestock; to enforce quarantine against plants and insects; and various other powers beneficial to agriculture." From the sugar planters' perspective, then, donating the experiment station to the board was the ideal solution. They could still benefit from the station's research without being obliged to pay its operating expenses. In fact, the only condition that the sugar growers' association placed on the donation was that the station distribute three hundred tons of select cane seed annually. Reflecting its new public role, the sugar growers' station was rebaptized the Insular Experiment Station in September 1914.[64]

The Jones Act of 1917 shifted control of the station decisively from the agricultural associations (which had dominated the Board of Commissioners of Agriculture) to the insular government. The station was transferred to the insular Department of Agriculture and Labor, which had been created under the Jones Act. The head of the department, the commissioner of agriculture and labor, was also a member of Puerto Rico's cabinet. While the U.S.-appointed governor had the power to appoint all members of his cabinet, the Jones Act gave the Puerto Rican–controlled Senate the right to veto gubernatorial appointments to several cabinet positions, including the commissioner of agriculture and labor. The Senate used the veto—or the threat of the veto—to ensure that the governor appointed Puerto Ricans to these positions.

Through the 1910s and early 1920s, however, most of the station's scientific staff was from the United States. Unlike the PRAES, the station was swamped with requests for information about tropical agriculture. Like the PRAES, the station's North American scientists initially knew little about tropical agriculture. As one director wrote, "The agricultural textbooks in our schools and colleges not having been based on Porto Rican experience, there being no agricultural libraries or even well-stocked, up-to-date general libraries throughout the island, and the popular publications of our experiment station in the Spanish language having been few and far between and of limited circulation, the people of the island have no choice but to write one of the two stations for the desired information." Many requests were routine, while others required original research. The requests came from all levels of agriculture, from *colonos* to the president of a sugar corporation.[65]

Because of these requests, the Department of Agriculture and Labor and the Insular Experiment Station began systematic programs of agricultural extension. The Department of Agriculture and Labor, through public lectures and publications, was "extremely valuable in 'putting over' the results of these investigations with less enterprising plantations and colonos."[66] The department also published two important periodicals, the *Journal of Agriculture of Puerto Rico* and the *Revista de Agricultura*. The *Revista* was intended for a general audience, particularly the farmers of Puerto Rico. For this reason, it was written almost entirely in Spanish. It described new crop varieties and agricultural techniques developed by the station. In contrast, the *Journal* was aimed at an international audience of tropical plant specialists, and it was written largely in English. Its early issues dealt extensively with sugar diseases and pests. It also published more abstract research, such as a survey of the insects of Puerto Rico. These two periodicals ensured that the station's research was widely disseminated both to specialized audiences of scientists and to the farmers who could use it.

Even after the agricultural associations had lost much of their control over the experiment station, its scientific work continued to focus on the island's export crops, including tobacco, coffee, and citrus fruits. Nonetheless, sugarcane—particularly the study of sugar diseases and pests—dominated the station's research agenda until the early 1930s. Scientists at the Insular Experiment Station worked in close contact with sugar *centrales* on several crucial sugar experiments. The Central Guánica helped the pathologist J. T. Stevenson in his 1919 study of the cane varieties it had imported from the Dominican Republic. In 1923 the experiment station began a long-term cooperative study of sugarcane varieties with some of the largest sugar *centrales* on the island whose goal was to identify the varieties of cane best suited to the different parts of the island. A new cane disease, first known as the "mottling" disease, appeared in Puerto Rico's cane fields in 1917. It was widely feared that this disease could wipe out Puerto Rico's sugar industry. All branches of the experiment station worked furiously to identify and control the disease: plant pathologists and entomologists hunted for its cause, while plant breeders and botanists worked to breed or introduce new cane varieties that would reduce it. Ultimately, a young scientist at the station, Carlos Chardón, discovered the insect that transmitted the disease. Over the next several years, the station found ways to manage it.[67]

By the late 1920s the research agenda had diversified considerably from its early years, although sugar research continued to dominate. Station chemists did research on fertilizers and, in the words of one researcher, "the sugar mills and *colonos* were made 'fertilizer-conscious' and the mystery surrounding its use was broken."[68] The Division of Horticulture studied fruit and vegetable crops. The Division of Soils did regional soil surveys of the island and soil analyses for planters and farmers. The Division of Entomology finally cracked the solution to the problem of the white grubs, the problem that had led to the founding of the station. They imported the Surinam toad, which fed on the grub, from Barbados. The toads brought the problem effectively under control. The Division of Plant Pathology successfully controlled four cane diseases that had threatened the island's sugar industry in the early 1920s. The plant breeders worked at breeding new plant varieties and acclimatizing imported varieties.

The Insular Experiment Station was plagued by the same financial problems that hampered the work of its sister stations in the tropics. In 1922 the station's director complained, "One of the problems that confronts this station at present is, no doubt, that of securing a permanent staff, a body of scientific investigators who will stay here long enough to see the end of their own experiments and who will, therefore, be of fundamental use to the institution." In 1922 only seven out of the station's sixteen researchers had been there for more than a year. Poor salaries were the main culprit. Only the year before, the insular government had reduced the salaries of public officials as much as 23 percent. In contrast, the well-funded *centrales,* with their own experimental gardens, offered much higher salaries. The departure of Franklin Sumner Earle, the sugar expert who had done so much to bring the mottling disease under control, was a serious blow to the station.[69]

Gradually, however, the station began to achieve some measure of stability. The Department of Agriculture and Labor prospered under the able direction of Carlos Chardón. In 1923, at the age of twenty-five, Chardón was named commissioner of agriculture and labor. From that moment onward he worked ceaselessly to promote agricultural science in Puerto Rico. The following year, the salaries of the director and the division heads were raised, which provided for more institutional continuity. In the 1918–1919 fiscal year, the Department of Agriculture's budget had been $200,000. By the 1924–1925 fiscal year, Chardón had managed to increase the budget to more than $490,000. Yet, in spite of its successes, the station's finances remained fragile. Its budget still depended on ad hoc appropriations made by the Puerto Rican legislature every other year. Chardón worried, "Each time the station is given a lease of life for [two years] only, . . . it is possible, although not probable, that it might be entirely suppressed in any one of these recurring instances."[70] Finally, Chardón managed to have a bill put through the insular legislature that would put both the department and the experiment station on a more solid footing.[71]

The researchers at the station were much more successful at addressing problems related to the sugar industry than they were at addressing problems related to other crops. This success has to do in large part with the allocation of scientists and resources to deal with sugar problems. It also had to do with the much more detailed body of scientific knowledge about sugar. There were probably more scientists working on sugar than on any other tropical crop in these years. Puerto Rican scientists were able to build on that body of knowledge in ways that they could not for other crops.

CONCLUSION

The pace of science-based agricultural modernization in Cuba and Puerto Rico was uneven at best. Before the Great Depression, agricultural research had helped to raise the productivity of the sugar industry to new heights while having little impact on the cultivation of food crops. Ironically, some of the strongest advocates for developing domestic agriculture had been foreign scientists and government officials, such as the USDA secretary James Wilson, the scientist Franklin Sumner Earle, and the Italian agronomist Mario Calvino. The public experiment stations and the Atkins Garden did some research on food crops. Both the Estación Experimental Agronómica and the Insular Experiment Station published magazines, circulars, and bulletins aimed at small farmers. The impact of this research, however, was limited by poor internal transportation networks and widespread rural illiteracy. The agricultural extension services in both countries, which could have reached even illiterate farmers in remote rural areas, were rudimentary. The small farmers could not assimilate the research as easily as could producers of export crops, since they were not well organized. Finally, many of the problems faced by small farmers had no scientific solution.

Not surprisingly, scientific research made the largest difference in crops whose producers were well organized and whose core problems (at least in the short term) were biological. Even with these crops, however, the stations had only mixed success. While the PRAES helped to increase the production and export of citrus crops in Puerto Rico, it was helpless to prevent the decline of the island's coffee industry. Scientists argued that increasing coffee production could rescue Puerto Rico's coffee industry, but its main problems—including chronic shortages of labor and capital, declining prices in volatile foreign markets, and hurricanes—were beyond the scope of a simple scientific fix. Even in the sugar industry, the stations' ability to change sugar cultivation depended entirely on the planters' willingness to adopt the methods proposed. They seldom adopted scientific innovations that might limit their profits. In spite of repeated attempts, for example, scientists at the PRAES could not convince planters to rotate sugar with other crops. Similarly, scientists at the Estación Experimental Agronómica faced great difficulty convincing Cuba's sugar planters to plant hybrid canes, even after having proved the impact of the mosaic disease on the island.

Between 1898 and the Great Depression, the needs of the sugar industry dominated agricultural research in Cuba and Puerto Rico, as they dominated many other facets of life. Most scientists, including many Puerto Rican and Cuban scientists, believed that agricultural exports were the key to developing a strong nation. Sugar producers were well organized, politically powerful, and prosperous enough to fund their own agricultural research. They could also easily assimilate new research, through their experiment stations and associations. Agriculturally, the sugar industry was well placed to benefit from scientific research. Many of the industry's short-term problems were biological. Small improvements in cultivation could give planters an edge in the volatile and competitive global sugar markets. Sugar research contributed to a substantial increase in sugar production on the two islands and fended off a potentially disastrous disease.

FOUR

AGRICULTURAL SCIENCE AND THE ECOLOGICAL RATIONALIZATION OF THE CARIBBEAN SUGAR INDUSTRY, 1780 – 1930

Sugar cane problems are present in every country. In this period of intense world competition, sugar has become the cheapest food, and production of sugar cane at a profit depends on methods that will lower the cost of cane per ton. Cheap production in the Tropics has hitherto been based on the utilization of virgin lands, where cane grows almost without cultivation and without need for replanting for many years, but soon there will be no more forests to clear, and cane growing must pass from a pioneer condition of soil mining to a settled permanent agriculture.

W. A. ORTON, "BOTANICAL PROBLEMS OF TROPICAL AMERICAN AGRICULTURE" (1926)

In 1917 W. V. Tower, director of Puerto Rico's Insular Experiment Station, wrote proudly that "the cane grinding season just closed has given the largest yield in the history of the Island, as well as the most profitable." Nonetheless, Tower saw a dark cloud on the horizon: "In spite of the greatly increased plantings, the average tonnage was below that for the previous crop. This is attributed in part to the disease known as 'mottling' which has appeared on the sugar lands in the western half of the Island and is proving most serious."[1] In the Arecibo valley in central Puerto Rico, cane production had dropped between 10 and 100 percent. The plant pathologist of the Insular Experiment Station, John A. Stevenson, was dispatched to make an inspection of the affected areas. Stevenson noticed that the leaves of the sugar plants were strangely mottled. This phenomenon gave the disease its popular name in Puerto Rico: the *matizado,* or mottling disease.[2]

In the coming years, the *matizado* spread quickly to sugar fields throughout Puerto Rico. One sugar mill in the affected area tried to sustain its revenues by increasing the volume of cane it ground. The mill's owners brought three thousand new acres into production and imported cane from other districts. Even though the mill ground more cane, its net sugar production was far lower than it had been the year before. The disease had an even greater impact on the *colonos*. Mills often refused to accept diseased cane for grinding, since it had low sugar content, and many *colonos* went bankrupt. "A considerable number of small planters," Stevenson noted, "have been completely forced out of cane growing in two years' time." [3] Searching for clues to the origins of the *matizado*, Stevenson reviewed the work of his Puerto Rican predecessors. He found that in the nineteenth century Puerto Rico's cane fields had been afflicted by several epidemics similar to the *matizado*. Several scientists suggested that the *matizado* was a severe manifestation of the root disease that had occurred during the 1870s. The root disease, in turn, was thought to be the result of soil exhaustion from intensive agriculture. Nonetheless, Stevenson concluded that the *matizado* was a distinct problem. He commented pessimistically that "the widespread feeling of alarm over the future of the sugar industry of the Island is completely justified by the course of events to date." [4]

The outbreak of the mosaic disease was not an isolated event. By the early twentieth century, all of Latin America's leading export crops were afflicted by epidemic diseases. These were not "natural" events. Rather, they were the products of complex interactions between Latin America's natural environments and local and global political and economic forces. Three factors are necessary for a crop disease to develop: a susceptible host plant (or community of host plants), a pathogen (such as a fungus, nematode, bacteria, or virus), and an environment favorable to the disease. Humans have intentionally or unintentionally modified each of these factors, thereby shaping the course of many epidemics. They have altered the environments in which plants grow, they have learned how to manipulate the plants themselves, and they have often unintentionally promoted the spread of pathogens. This sudden outbreak of regional and global tropical crop epidemics suggests that humans were manipulating their agricultural ecosystems in new ways, thereby creating new disease regimes. [5]

It is not a coincidence that these epidemics erupted at the same time that the volume of Latin America's agricultural exports reached new heights. In the pursuit of profit, planters had refashioned many of Latin America's agricultural landscapes. The spread of monoculture created genetically homogeneous plant communities that were particularly susceptible to disease. As soon as planters attempted to reserve a piece of land "for the plants of a single desired species," argues the mycologist and historian E. C. Large, "the multiplication of all the pests and parasites of that species was enormously favoured." These pests and parasites "were provided with unlimited food, and many of their natural enemies were destroyed. There was nothing to stop their spread until they reached the limit of the clearing, or came to another crop on which they could not grow. In short, specialized cultivation *invited* epidemics of plant disease."[6]

The epidemics transformed environmental and social relations of production in the areas they struck. In some places they destroyed industries and contributed to the decline of the planter class, such as with cacao in Ecuador and rubber in Brazil. Sometimes they greatly increased the costs of production. The high cost of pesticides forced many small banana producers out of business, allowing large U.S. banana corporations to consolidate control over the industry. The socially and naturally constructed sugar mosaic disease similarly transformed the social and environmental relations of production in Puerto Rico and Cuba.[7]

INNOVATION AND DEGENERATION IN SUGARCANE AGRICULTURE, 1780–1910

The conditions favorable to the eruption of the mosaic disease in Puerto Rico were created by the reorganization of the global sugarcane industry in the nineteenth century. Historians have focused heavily on the nineteenth-century technological innovations that brought dramatic and visible changes to the cane fields around the world but have devoted less attention to the subtler but equally significant transformations in cane agriculture itself. Agricultural innovation in the sugar industry lagged behind technological innovation until the mid-nineteenth century. The sugar industry in the colonial Caribbean had been based on a single variety of sugarcane, which "needed no special name for the first three centuries of its growth in America, since it was the only sugar cane known." Its precise botanical properties were not known at the time, but scientists working in the 1930s found evidence that this cane was a naturally occurring hybrid of *Saccharum officinarum* and the wild cane *S. barberi*. When other varieties finally reached the Americas, this variety was dubbed *caña criolla,* or Creole cane. The Creole cane was a "a short-jointed, medium-slender, greenish cane of poor tonnage, but with sweet juice and soft tissue that made it easy to mill and pleasant to chew." It was soft and therefore easy to grind on the ox-driven *trapiches* (wooden rollers) then used throughout the Caribbean for crushing cane. The softness of the Creole cane, however, meant that the *bagasse* (the woody crushed sheath of the cane, left over after the sugar juice had been extracted) was of little use as a fuel for the boilers used to process the sugar.[8]

Caribbean planters began to feel pressure to innovate in the late eighteenth century. Growing international demand for sugar and increased competition among producers fostered innovation, as did changing environmental conditions in the cane fields. Most of the early innovations focused on how the cane was processed. For example, the nineteenth century saw the introduction of the steam-powered three-roller mill, which allowed for a much higher percentage of juice to be extracted from the cane. Railways sped the voyage of cane from the fields to the mills. Sugar chemists worked to increase the purity of the product. By the late nineteenth century, the large modern sugar *central* came to epitomize the technological transformation of the sugarcane industry. These technical transformations more than doubled the industrial yields —measured in tons of refined sugar per ton of raw cane. In 1913 modern sugar mills in Cuba extracted 13 tons of refined sugar for every 100 tons of raw cane; in 1878 the industrial yield had been only 5.5 tons of sugar for every ton of raw cane.[9]

Another way of improving the industrial yields was to find new varieties with higher sugar content. Planters had concluded that it was impossible to breed sugarcane, because the Creole cane did not produce viable seeds. Efforts focused on finding new wild cane varieties in the Pacific islands. The French explorer Louis-Antoine de Bougainville discovered a new cane variety in Tahiti in 1780. Unlike the Creole cane, it was pure *S. officinarum*—a class of canes that scientists later called "noble." This variety, which came to be known as the Otaheite or Bourbon cane, produced high sugar yields on virgin lands in Mauritius, so it almost completely supplanted the older varieties. By the early nineteenth century, the Otaheite cane "was the standard variety of Mauritius, the West Indies, British Guiana, Mexico, Brazil and other countries, and was widely grown in Java and India." From Réunion and Mauritius, the French sent the Otaheite and other cane varieties to their New World colonies in Cayenne (now French Guiana), Martinique, and Guadeloupe. From the French Antilles, Otaheite cane quickly spread to the rest of the Caribbean. A Cuban named Francisco de Arango y Parreño imported the Otaheite cane to Cuba in 1793. It probably made its way to Puerto Rico from Cuba, but its arrival on the island is undocumented. Otaheite cane may also have been imported directly to Puerto Rico from Jamaica. Captain Bligh of *Bounty* fame had brought the cane from Tahiti to Jamaica in 1791. Since the Otaheite cane was also known in Puerto Rico as *caña inglesa,* it may have been imported to the island from an English colony, and Jamaica seems the most likely candidate.[10]

The Otaheite cane was popular because it offered planters several advantages. According to Humboldt, it yielded 15 to 20 percent more sugar than the Creole cane. It grew well on the virgin cane lands of Cuba and Puerto Rico. It stood about thirteen feet high, roughly twice as tall as Creole cane. It produced a thick, woody *bagasse* that could be dried and burned as fuel for boiling the juice; this helped to relieve the problem of deforestation, which was then occurring throughout Puerto Rico and Cuba. Sugar milling technology was quickly adapted to the new variety. At first the thick, hard bark of the Otaheite cane frequently broke the wooden rollers that planters had traditionally used to crush the Creole cane. Planters adapted to the new variety by covering the rollers with iron sheaths, which made the large-scale processing of Otaheite cane feasible. Planters throughout the Caribbean were enthusiastic about Otaheite cane, and soon it became the variety of choice to help feed the booming sugar markets of Europe and North America.[11]

Other innovations in cane agriculture had only limited impact in the Spanish Caribbean. Planters in the British West Indies had long been interested in agricultural improvements. In the seventeenth century, Barbadian planters had developed a practice called cane-holing, which minimized soil erosion and permitted food crops to be planted among the cane. This practice was not picked up in Cuba or Puerto Rico, whose planters did not face the same space constraints as their counterparts on the smaller Caribbean islands. Caneholing was also highly labor-intensive, which further discouraged planters in the Spanish Caribbean from adopting the system. Beginning in the midnineteenth century, they began to express some interest in applying scientific principles to agriculture. The Cuban Alvaro Reynoso published his famous scientific treatise on the cultivation of sugar, the *Ensayo sobre el cultivo de la caña de azúcar*, in 1862. His suggestions for agricultural improvements in cane agriculture were eagerly taken up by Dutch planters in Java, but ironically Reynoso's system received little attention in the Spanish Caribbean. Planters in the Spanish Caribbean appear to have preferred industrial innovations, since these did not require dramatic transformations in labor arrangements.[12]

Planters complained of declining sugar yields more frequently in the nineteenth century. As early as the 1840s, the sugar yield of the Otaheite canes in the Caribbean began to decline. Data for sugar yields in nineteenth-century Puerto Rico are hard to find, but repeated references to varietal degeneration suggest that cane varieties were, in fact, declining in vigor and in sugar yield. Data from late-nineteenth-century Cuba point more clearly to decline in agricultural productivity, measured in the weight of cane produced per unit area. In 1878 Cuban mills produced between 80,000 and 100,000 arrobas per *caballería*. By 1913 yields had declined substantially, ranging from a low of 26,600 arrobas per *caballería* in Santa Clara to a high of 83,000 in Oriente.[13]

There was disagreement about the exact causes of the decline. Planters blamed it on the plant rather than the soil, arguing that the variety itself was degenerating. According to the planters, the degeneration of a variety was a logical consequence of asexual reproduction. During the 1890s, the director of Puerto Rico's short-lived Mayagüez experiment station blamed the degeneration of cane varieties on the practice of "selecting as seedlings the pieces which are least likely to sell because of their poor condition." He recommended that planters instead save the best pieces of cane for later planting. Planters argued "that cultivated varieties of plants of all kinds that are continuously propagated asexually have, like individual animals, their definite period of life— that they flourish for a certain length of time, each according to its special nature, then degenerate and finally disappear from cultivation or die." [14]

Not all scientists accepted this model of varietal decline. The North American sugar expert Franklin Sumner Earle pointed out that some varieties of plants, such as Bartlett pears and navel oranges, had been cultivated for centuries yet had shown no signs of degeneration. Earle argued instead that so-called varietal degeneration was caused by external factors, especially soil exhaustion. Sugar planters had not used fertilizer at first, because the cane prospered on the natural nutrients in the virgin soils. The Otaheite cane grew best in "a well aerated soil abundantly supplied with vegetable matter," which was characteristic of the newly cleared lands of Puerto Rico, Cuba, and Santo Domingo. But varieties were adapted to a narrow range of cultural conditions, Earle argued, and they deteriorated quickly if there was any change in those conditions. [15]

The exact causes of varietal decline in sugarcane remain unclear. As planters in the nineteenth century recognized, particular cane varieties lose vigor after a time. Recent research points to external factors as the principal cause of varietal decline, although the factors vary widely for each cane variety and each location. As Earle and others had noted earlier, "cultural practices may lead to the inability of the soil to continue supporting high yields." The role of soil exhaustion alone in varietal decline is less clear. Pointing to the case of sugar agriculture in Queensland, Australia, the sugar researcher A. C. Barnes argued that varietal decline is not caused by "the gradual depletion of organic matter in the soil, caused by prolonged crop production in tropical soils." Other environmental factors, such as nematodes, insects, and fungi, contributed directly and indirectly to the gradual decline in productivity of certain varieties. The one cause of varietal decline that appears widespread is ratoon-stunting disease. Whatever the specifics, varietal degeneration prompted sugar planters to continue the search for new cane varieties. [16]

DEVELOPMENT AND DISEASE IN THE
SUGAR INDUSTRY, 1840–1915

Gradual varietal degeneration was not the only problem confronting sugar planters. In the mid-nineteenth century epidemic cane diseases struck sugar plantations around the globe. Two factors contributed to the spread of these diseases. One was the rapid growth of the sugar industry, which had created large populations of genetically homogeneous and therefore highly susceptible cane plants. The botanical specialization of the sugar industry in the nineteenth century had unintentionally fostered the growth of disease. "As with other economic plants," Barnes wrote, "the increasingly high population of sugar cane grown in closer proximity brought about more favourable conditions for attacks by pests and diseases." Monocultures were not new to Latin America, however, so they alone cannot account for the rapid increase in the incidence of crop epidemics. The second factor was the global exchange of sugar pathogens. Until the mid-nineteenth century, most sugar diseases had been local, as pathogens had no easy way to move from one region to another. Improvements in transportation facilitated the global transfer of diseases. When Latin American planters imported new varieties of cane, they often unintentionally imported cane pathogens. Some of these pathogens, which were harmless in their native environments, became virulent when they were transplanted to their new homes. The first global cane epidemic struck in 1840, devastating the cane industry of the Indian Ocean islands of Mauritius and Réunion. These islands had depended exclusively on the Otaheite cane, as did most sugar plantations worldwide. Over the next three decades, the disease spread to Brazil and northward to the Caribbean islands, reaching Hawaii in the early twentieth century.[17]

The widespread "failure" of the Otaheite cane because of disease led to a global scramble to find new varieties of *S. officinarum*. In 1850 the planters of Mauritius imported a new variety from Java, known as the Cheribon cane. Variants of the Cheribon cane were soon planted worldwide. The light variant of the Cheribon cane was particularly popular in Cuba, where it was known as the Crystalina cane. The Crystalina cane grew better than Otaheite in Cuba's exhausted soils and was more drought resistant. On the downside, it yielded less sugar than the Otaheite cane. Faced with the epidemic, however, planters worldwide replaced the old Otaheite canes with varieties of the Cheribon cane. Otaheite cane did not disappear entirely, however. It continued to be cultivated in Mauritius, where planters had discovered a resistant variety of Otaheite named Lousier. If this variety circulated beyond Mauritius, it might explain why sugar planters in Puerto Rico continued to plant Otaheite. Fearing renewed outbreaks of disease, planters continued to search for new varieties. Planters worldwide began to collect and exchange cane varieties.[18]

Unfortunately, the practice of collecting and exchanging seed cane accelerated the global spread of sugar diseases, as planters took few precautions to ensure that the cuttings were free of disease. Several global epidemics can be traced to such exchanges. An outbreak of gum disease in 1860 almost entirely wiped out the Otaheite crop of Pernambuco in northeastern Brazil. The Botanical Gardens at Rio de Janeiro imported cane varieties from around the world in search of an immune variety. In 1869 the disease was accidentally carried from Brazil to Mauritius in a shipment of cane varieties. The disease did not affect Mauritius, because the Cheribon cane then planted there was immune. From Mauritius, however, the gum disease was carried to Australia, whose canes were not resistant. In Australia, the disease caused large losses. One scientist summed it up thus: "The history of the cane-sugar industry inevitably becomes more and more the history of the introduction and distribution of cane varieties, such introductions usually being caused by the outbreak of epidemics that have seriously threatened the local industry."[19]

In the face of these global epidemics, planters and governments began to fund scientific research to find cane varieties that were resistant to disease. In Java, for example, the Dutch government founded and staffed three sugar experiment stations. The Dutch scientists were especially anxious to cure the "sereh" disease, which first appeared in 1882 and threatened to destroy Java's large sugar industry. The sereh disease caused canes, principally the black Cheribon variety of S. officinarum, to grow erratically. The mature cane plant resembled what one biologist described as a "worthless bushy stool." In searching for cane varieties that showed immunity to the disease, scientists eventually noticed that sereh afflicted only canes growing in the lower parts of Java. To get rid of the disease, then, scientists established seedbeds at higher altitudes. Although the scientists had not identified the biological causes of sereh, they had at least found an agricultural solution to the problem. The search for resistant varieties in Java continued, since the high-altitude seedbeds proved to be expensive and inconvenient.[20]

In the late 1880s scientists working in Java and Barbados independently discovered that sugarcane sometimes produced fertile seeds. This was a momentous discovery, as it meant that cane could be bred sexually and that high-yield, disease-resistant hybrid canes could be produced. For a long time, planters and scientists alike had assumed that the sugarcane was sterile. This assumption was based on long experience with Creole cane, which produced no viable seeds. Scientists later discovered that Creole cane did not set seed because it was a hybrid. The noble canes imported in the nineteenth century were all varieties of S. officinarum and did produce viable seeds. There is some evidence that cane workers and plantation owners earlier in the century had recognized that these varieties sometimes set seed but saw it simply as a curiosity. Scientists first tried crossing noble canes (S. officinarum) with wild members of the same genus, including S. barberi and S. spontaneum. The wild canes were immune to sereh, although they could not be used for commercial sugar cultivation. These early crosses between noble canes and wild canes, known as nobilized canes, did not at first produce commercially viable hybrids. Over the next several decades, the Java and Barbados stations produced hundreds of nobilized canes, trying to optimize the balance of hardiness and disease resistance from the wild canes with the sugar yields of the noble canes. They distributed the hybrids around the world. Those produced at Java were known as P.O.J. canes; those produced at Barbados were known as B.H. canes.[21]

The Barbados and Java stations became models of agricultural research throughout the tropics. In the Caribbean, experiment stations were established in British Guiana, at St. Croix in the Danish Virgin Islands, at Guadeloupe in the French West Indies, in Cuba, and in Puerto Rico. Farther afield, stations were established in Louisiana, Hawaii, Argentina, and India. Their success depended heavily on consistent and strong support from planters' associations, businesses, or governments. The Barbados station enjoyed the support of the Royal Botanical Gardens at Kew, and the Dutch stations in Java were funded by generous donations from the Dutch government. The station in Hawaii, with the backing of the Hawaiian Sugar Planters Association, grew to include fifty researchers and a host of technicians and other workers. Official support for agricultural research was more sporadic in Cuba and Puerto Rico.[22]

THE MOSAIC IN PUERTO RICO, 1917–1924

Before the mosaic outbreak in 1917, sugar planters in Cuba and Puerto Rico had been slow to adopt the new hybrid canes. Their reluctance made economic sense. In Puerto Rico, the Otaheite cane continued to be highly profitable in the early twentieth century, as did the Crystalina cane in Cuba, although planters saw some early signs that the noble varieties were slowly degenerating. An insect plague of the sugarcane leaf cutter prompted the Puerto Rico Sugar Growers Association to organize an agricultural experiment station in 1910. And gradually declining sugar yields began to worry some planters. But planters did not consider these problems critical, so they felt little need to switch from the varieties that had served them so well.

The scientific efforts to determine the cause of the *matizado* that struck Puerto Rico in 1917 exemplified the new ecological thinking that characterized early-twentieth-century biology. Scientists focused their attention on all the factors in the agricultural ecosystem. The search involved scientists working in laboratories and in the field. Between 1916 and 1918 mycologists at the Insular Experiment Station conducted life history studies of more than one hundred types of fungi to see if there was any relation to the disease. Other researchers studied field conditions, to see if rainfall, elevation, or other environmental factors could be directly linked to the disease. They found no

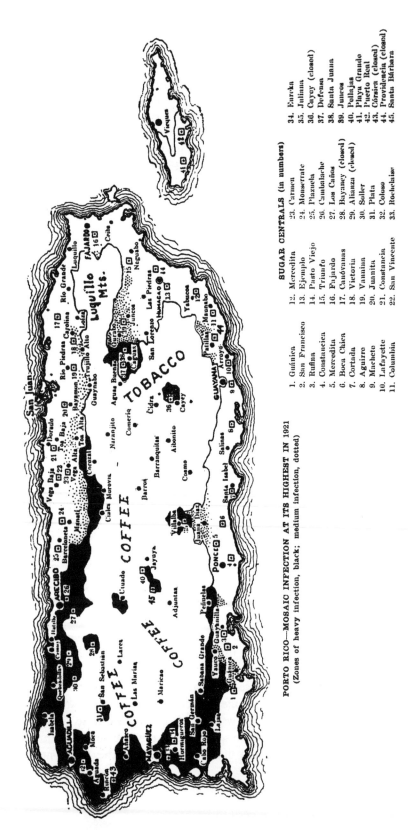

PORTO RICO—MOSAIC INFECTION AT ITS HIGHEST IN 1921

(Zones of heavy infection, black; medium infection, dotted)

1. Guánica
2. San Francisco
3. Rufina
4. Constancia
5. Mercedita
6. Boca Chica
7. Cortada
8. Aguirre
9. Machete
10. Lafayette
11. Columbia

12. Mercedita
13. Ejemplo
14. Pasto Viejo
15. Triunfo
16. Fajardo
17. Canóvanas
18. Victoria
19. Vannina
20. Juanita
21. Constancia
22. San Vincente

SUGAR CENTRALS (in numbers)

23. Carmen
24. Monserrate
25. Plazuela
26. Canabalache
27. Los Caños
28. Bayaney (closed)
29. Alianza (closed)
30. Soller
31. Plata
32. Coloso
33. Rochelaise

34. Eureka
35. Juliana
36. Cayey (closed)
37. Defensa
38. Santa Juana
39. Juncos
40. Pellejas
41. Playa Grande
42. Puerto Real
43. Córsien (closed)
44. Providencia (closed)
45. Santa Bárbara

— FIGURE 4.1 —

The mosaic disease in Puerto Rico at its greatest extent, 1921.

obvious connection. The staff entomologist concluded that insects were not the direct cause of the *matizado*. In the laboratory, chemists looked fruitlessly to see if fertilizers somehow caused—or could cure—the disease.[23]

A note of desperation crept into Stevenson's 1918 report on the mosaic disease. He dismissed varietal degeneration as a cause, since both new and old varieties suffered. Otaheite cane was particularly susceptible to the disease, and it became effectively impossible to grow it on the island. The Rayada, or striped, cane was initially resistant to the disease but succumbed after a short period. The Cavengerie variety held out until early 1918, but it too began to lose its immunity. In May 1918 all Stevenson could say was that researchers were testing the susceptibility of many varieties and that almost none of them had proved to be immune. He noted, however, that not all varieties of cane suffered equally from the disease, and so there was hope that it could be controlled through varietal selection.[24]

Scientists slowly pinpointed the cause of the *matizado*. By the end of 1918, Stevenson had reached two conclusions. First, the disease was hereditary but not exclusively so. Cane grown from diseased stalks was also diseased. The disease could not have spread so rapidly by planting alone, but by what other means it might spread was unknown. Second, the disease was an infection caused by a "disturbance" in the cane juice itself. Stevenson argued that this disturbance was so similar to the tobacco mosaic disease that the *matizado* should also be classified as a mosaic disease.[25] By 1918 the crop losses were serious enough that the USDA sent Earle, its top cane expert, to Puerto Rico. Earle had considerable experience in tropical agriculture. He had been the first director of Cuba's Estación Experimental Agronómica from 1904 to 1906. Since then he had worked in the tropics on behalf of sugar companies or the USDA. In Puerto Rico, Earle worked with Julius Matz, a Russian-born plant pathologist who had replaced Stevenson as director of the station. Earle made the first big breakthrough in identifying the mottling disease, observing that it was identical to the "yellow stripe" disease that had first been identified in Java in 1892.[26]

Later research has sketched a rough map of the disease's journey from Java to Puerto Rico, although many of the specifics remain unclear. Dutch scientists in Java first recognized the mosaic disease (then called "yellow stripe" because of the characteristic marking it left on the cane leaves) in 1892, shortly after they had started research on sereh. At the time they considered it a minor problem. Ironically, the success of cane breeding in Java contributed to the rapid spread of mosaic around the globe. It appears that mosaic first arrived in the New World as part of a shipment of P.O.J. hybrids sent from Java to Argentina, whether directly or via Egypt is unclear. From Argentina, the disease spread northward to the Caribbean basin. Although widespread, the mosaic disease had relatively little impact until it appeared in epidemic form in Puerto Rico in 1917. The outbreak in Puerto Rico drew global attention: sugar growers were alarmed by the severity of the losses, and scientists were fascinated by the virus, which belonged to a category of organisms that had only recently been discovered. In the 1920s and 1930s mosaic was found to be present in cane fields worldwide, except for Mauritius. It is not clear why the impact of mosaic was so visible and dramatic in Puerto Rico. One possible explanation is that a new, more virulent strain of the mosaic virus emerged there. Scientists later found several strains of the virus, each of which has widely varying effects on different cane varieties. A second possible explanation, related to the first, is that most sugar-growing areas planted varieties of the Cheribon cane or hybrid canes, while Puerto Rican planters continued to prefer the older Otaheite cane. All of these cane varieties were susceptible to the mosaic virus, but the Otaheite canes were much more susceptible than the Cheribon.[27]

It is also likely that the geopolitical situation contributed to the course of the mosaic disease. The outbreak of World War I had virtually destroyed the European sugar beet industry, which had been competing heavily with the sugarcane industry. Sugar prices skyrocketed during the war and the years immediately following, and cane planters rushed to meet the demand. As one scientist later noted, "Too little attention was paid to land preparation, drainage, cultivation, and fertilization, and commonly the good cane was sent to the mill and only the poorest and most diseased was saved for seed purposes." For this reason, later observers have questioned whether all of the losses could be attributed to the mosaic disease alone or whether poor agricultural practices also contributed to the decline. Rather, the speed of the decline suggests that a disease was at work. Poor agricultural practices contributed by weakening the cane plant, thereby making it especially susceptible to disease. Mosaic's impact was felt severely on the smaller, Puerto Rican–owned plantations on the north and west sides of the island, while it had a limited effect on the U.S.-owned plantations in the south and east.[28]

By 1920 Earle and Matz had established that the mottling disease of the cane was, as Stevenson had suspected, an infectious viral disease similar to the tobacco mosaic disease. They were able to infect healthy cane by inoculating it with the juice of infected cane. Matz wrote that "for the sugar planter, it suffices to know that he is dealing with an infectious disease, which is carried by the sick cane and which is transmitted to the healthy cane by an external agent."[29] The next problem was to identify the elusive "external agent." Some progress was being made in identifying the disease vector. The first clue was discovered by E. W. Brandes, a plant pathologist at the USDA in Washington, D.C., who had briefly worked at the Insular Experiment Station in 1915–1916. At the USDA greenhouses in Maryland, Brandes discovered that under laboratory conditions a small insect known as the corn aphid (*Aphis maidis*) could transmit the disease from sick plants to healthy plants. But there was a difference between showing that transmission was possible in a greenhouse in suburban Washington and proving that it could happen in the field in Puerto Rico. Brandes wrote in 1920, "Just what insects are responsible for dissemination in the cane regions remains to be proved."[30]

Scientists working in Puerto Rico initially devoted little attention to the *Aphis maidis* because it did not attack cane plants under normal conditions. E. G. Smyth, a researcher at the USDA, concluded in 1920 that "the corn aphis . . . can not in any way be considered responsible for the transmission of mosaic disease in Puerto Rico."[31] Stephen Bruner, at Cuba's Estación Experimental Agronómica, concurred. He had been among those who had shown that the *A. maidis* transmitted the disease in the laboratory but argued that "even if the evidence shows that the green corn aphid can transmit the mosaic disease of sugar cane, it does not solve the problem of dissemination, because the insect does not attack cane under ordinary field conditions."[32]

Given the confusion over the role of insects in spreading the mosaic disease, two young Puerto Rican scientists, Carlos E. Chardón and Rafael A. Veve, began field tests in Puerto Rico early in 1921. Planters and scientists alike suspected that an insect known as the sugarcane leafhopper was responsible.[33] This notion made sense, as the insect was common in cane fields and had caused a disease in Hawaii. But Chardón's and Veve's experiments cast doubt on this hypothesis. Chardón began with a simple but elegant experiment. He planted two groups of healthy cane, one protected from insects by a screen, the other left out in the open. Within four months, more than 80 percent of the cane left out in the open was infected, while the protected cane remained completely healthy. Cane in screened enclosures containing the leafhopper did not become infected, and the disease was spreading to parts of the island where the leafhopper was not present. Although Chardón's experiment ruled out the leafhopper as the vector, it strongly suggested that another insect might be responsible.[34]

Chardón turned his attention back to the corn aphid, even though scientists had already rejected it as a possible means of transmission because it did not feed on sugarcane under normal field conditions. In 1921, however, an entomologist named George Woolcott discovered the aphid feeding on the young leaves of sugarcane. Chardón noticed that while the aphid did not feed on sugarcane under normal circumstances, it prospered on weeds that were common in the cane fields. After the fields were weeded, the insects jumped to the sugarcane and remained there for several hours. In these few hours the aphids transferred the virus to the cane. About three weeks after weeding, the cane showed signs of disease. This concurred with Brandes's observation in the laboratory that the incubation period of the disease was three weeks. Veve and other agronomists at the Fajardo sugar mill, which had one of the best sugar research divisions on the island, began a rigorous experimental program and confirmed Chardón's hypothesis.[35]

The etiology of sugar mosaic gives environmental historians an excellent example of the role of humans in shaping the course of a plant disease. It had spread from its home in the Pacific to the New World by hitchhiking on hybrid canes. In Puerto Rico, scientists had quickly recognized that the *A. maidis* could transmit the disease but were also adamant that it could not do so under natural conditions. But humans had unintentionally altered the "natural" conditions through weeding, depriving the *Aphis* of its normal source of food. In the highly artificial ecosystem of the cane field, then, the *Aphis* began briefly feeding on the sugarcane plant, remaining just long enough to transmit the disease. To spread, the sugar mosaic depended on the conjunction of the virus, the *Aphis,* and the regular weeding of the cane fields. Without human intervention, the mosaic disease might have remained a minor disease affecting isolated stands of cane on a few small Pacific islands.

THE VARIETAL REVOLUTION
IN PUERTO RICO, 1922–1928

After the sugar mosaic was identified, the next step was to try to bring it under control. Farmers appear never to have seriously considered the possibility of not weeding their fields, and there was no easy way to control the corn aphids. Scientists, therefore, focused on the cane plant itself. The most expensive, most labor intensive, and thus least popular way of controlling the disease was by pulling out, or "roguing," infected cane, planting healthy cane in its place, and then closely monitoring the cane fields for new outbreaks. Roguing demanded constant vigilance against new outbreaks. In 1918 Stevenson had suggested roguing as an interim measure; it would at least slow the spread of the disease. Planters preferred to plant immune or resistant canes. Immune canes did not succumb to the mosaic disease at all. Resistant canes got infected with the virus but grew to full size and produced as much sugar as healthy cane.

One of the first popular immune canes in Puerto Rico was the Uba, imported from Argentina. The mosaic disease had caused serious losses in the noble canes. Uba cane, however, was a variety of *Saccharum sinense,* a different species, and thus was not affected by the mosaic disease. Widely planted between 1919 and 1922, the Uba cane also gave high sugar yields even in poor soils. For example, between 1920 and 1921 the mosaic disease had cut sugar

FIGURE 4.2

The contrast between diseased Otaheite cane and healthy P.O.J. 2728 hybrid cane in Colombia.

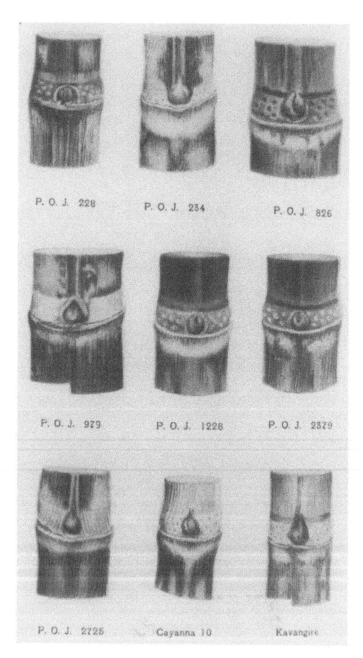

P. O. J. 228

P. O. J. 234

P. O. J. 826

P. O. J. 979

P. O. J. 1228

P. O. J. 2379

P. O. J. 2725

Cayanna 10

Kavangire

FIGURE 4.3

Varieties and hybrids of sugarcane.

yields in the Central Eureka near Mayagüez from 14.5 tons to 8.0 tons per acre. Planting of the Uba cane began in 1922, and in 1923 yields had climbed back to 14.1 tons per acre. In following years yields at the Central Eureka greatly exceeded the premosaic yield, increasing to an average of 20 tons per acre. In other nearby *centrales*, yields of Uba cane fluctuated between 26 and 29 tons per acre. Like the other wild cane varieties, however, the Uba cane was less than ideal commercially because it matured slowly and was difficult to harvest and mill. It was also highly susceptible to another pest that was plaguing the island at the time, the moth borer. Finally, planters began to discover that the Uba cane was not completely immune to the mosaic disease.[36]

Planters turned to resistant canes, most of which were hybrids. Work on the identification and breeding of resistant canes began in earnest after 1922. This research was supervised by Arthur Rosenfeld and Melville T. Cook, two internationally renowned sugar experts. Cook had previously worked at the Estación Experimental Agronómica in Cuba, and Rosenfeld directed the sugar research program at an experiment station in Tucumán, Argentina.[37] At Tucumán, Rosenfeld had worked extensively with P.O.J. canes, hybrids bred at the experiment station in Java that were notable for their vigor and tolerance to disease. Recent innovations in cane breeding in Java had produced even more robust hybrids. Since the 1890s, breeders at the Proef-Station Oost-Java had concentrated on crossing noble canes, varieties of *S. officinarum*. During the mid-1910s, they also began producing more vigorous nobilized canes, hybrids of *S. officinarum* with wild cane species. These P.O.J. hybrid canes, particularly the P.O.J. 105, had been planted in Puerto Rico for several years with considerable success. Like the Uba cane, however, the P.O.J. 105 was slow to mature and had very low sugar content. Newer canes such as the P.O.J. 36 and P.O.J. 213, both hybrids of the black Cheribon variety of *S. officinarum* and the wild species *S. barberi*, were much more vigorous and highly resistant to the mosaic disease. Even when infected with the mosaic disease, these two hybrids continued to grow unaffected. Other P.O.J. hybrids, particularly the P.O.J. 2725 and P.O.J. 2878, both hybrids of *S. officinarum* and *S. spontaneum*, were almost completely immune to the disease. Rosenfeld cautioned against planting them in areas where mosaic was present, though, because he feared that they could spread the disease to more susceptible canes.[38]

Other cane hybrids also showed promise. The Barbados hybrid B.H. 10(12) was popular throughout the West Indies. This cane was a cross of two varieties of *S. officinarum* and thus susceptible to the mosaic disease. But even the infected cane continued to produce high sugar yields, which led Puerto Rican planters to begin planting it in spite of the risks.[39] Another high-yield hybrid cane popular among planters was the Santa Cruz (S.C.) 12/4 cane from the Santa Cruz experiment station in the U.S. Virgin Islands. Although the S.C.

cane was susceptible to mosaic, it was highly resistant to two other major diseases of sugarcane that were plaguing Puerto Rico: gummosis and root disease. The B.H. and S.C. canes depended on advanced agriculture and the use of fertilizer. Earle wrote that both canes "ratoon very well on good lands, but will probably fail more quickly than Crystalina where soils are worn and exhausted. They are decidedly not poor-land canes."[40]

The free global exchange of hybrid cane appears odd, now that corporations and governments have adopted a proprietary attitude toward commercially valuable genes, seeds, and organisms. Yet in the nineteenth and early twentieth centuries, free exchanges of cane varieties were the norm. They took place both formally and informally. Informally, planters in the New World frequently obtained new canes by traveling to Asia or from other planters. Formally, agricultural experiment stations and botanical gardens exchanged plant varieties; breeders from Java exchanged hybrids with those in Barbados, and experiment stations in Cuba and Puerto Rico received hybrids as gifts from stations around the world. Efforts to limit informal exchanges began in the early twentieth century. National governments, at the behest of scientists, began to regulate the importation of plants. The rationale for this regulation, however, was ecological rather than proprietary. Governments, scientists, and even many planters wanted all imported seed and plants to go through quarantine, to control the spread of epidemics such as the mosaic disease. In light of Puerto Rico's experience, such caution was entirely reasonable. The formal exchanges continued, although they too were subject to quarantine.

Two explanations for the continuing free exchange of hybrid canes are plausible, one economic and the other scientific. First, the success or failure of specific hybrids depended heavily on local ecological conditions. Therefore, a hybrid that did not grow well in Java might acclimatize well in Barbados or Cuba, and vice versa. Only a handful of the hundreds of hybrids produced enjoyed any economic success. Thus it was rational economically for planters and research stations to exchange hybrids, in the hope of finding one well suited to local conditions. Second, most scientists at the research centers shared an "internationalist" ethos. They saw the free exchange of plants as part of a broader exchange of ideas and information. These explanations are retrospective, however. To the sugar planters and scientists involved, the exchange required no explanation or justification. They did not see hybrid canes as intellectual property.

The mosaic disease was gradually brought under control in Puerto Rico in the mid-1920s through aggressive roguing and careful selection of immune and resistant canes. Earle, in his 1921 report to the commissioner of agriculture and labor, wrote, "[T]his serious outbreak may now be considered as checked and under control. Instead of the rapid increase of the area of infection which has marked each previous year, we have had this year an actual decrease in the extent of the disease. This favorable result is due to the present widespread knowledge of the nature of the disease and to the vigorous adoption by so many planters of intelligent matters for combating it."[41] Chardón shared Earle's assessment of the farmers, noting that the planters "seem to be using more discrimination in choosing the seeds in regard to the varietal qualities as to resistance to disease and sucrose content of the cane."[42]

Although the mosaic disease was no longer a threat from an agricultural perspective, a complete scientific solution proved elusive. Chardón wrote in his annual report of 1922 that "the study of the scientifically important feature of this disease, the internal characteristics of the infected cane tissues, has been followed as time would permit."[43] With the shortage of station staff and a host of other agricultural problems, time did not permit much. The mosaic disease remained endemic in large parts of the world. Its effects could be managed through the planting of resistant varieties such as the P.O.J. hybrids or susceptible but tolerant varieties such as B.H. 10(12), but it proved difficult to eliminate the mosaic virus itself. New strains of the virus were constantly emerging.

Scientists in Puerto Rico celebrated their role in rescuing Puerto Rico's sugar industry. They had identified the vector of the mosaic virus and had been instrumental in introducing the new hybrid canes from Java and Barbados. Scientists at both the Mayagüez and Río Piedras stations began programs to breed locally adapted cane hybrids, most of them crosses with the P.O.J. 2878 hybrid. They were also well aware of how much diseases benefited the consolidation of agricultural science in the Caribbean. "The outbreak of mosaic," Earle wrote, "being one of the greatest calamities that ever befell the sugar industry, has proven to be one of its greatest blessings, since it led to such an extensive study of sugar cane, and especially of methods of cane breeding."[44] Rosenfeld described how the boll weevil had stimulated scientific research in Louisiana and led to the diversification and improvement of the economy there, and he credited the sugarcane mosaic disease in Puerto Rico for improving its capacity for agricultural research.[45]

Table 4.1 shows the changes in sugar yields in Puerto Rico between 1915, just before the mosaic disease was first noticed, and 1930, after the new hybrid canes had come to dominate Puerto Rican agriculture. There is a brief dip in production after 1918 and a recovery in the 1920 harvest as planters began to use the Uba cane. The most significant jump appears in 1924, when hybrid canes were planted widely. At the Central Mercedita in Ponce, for example, Otaheite yields averaged 3.15 tons per acre between 1917 and 1921. The hybrid B.H. 10(12) averaged 5.2 tons per acre between 1920 and 1924. The managers of the central were apparently convinced of the effectiveness of the B.H. cane: while in 1920 they planted just a little over 3 acres of the hybrid, by 1926 the

TABLE 4.1
Sugar Yields in Puerto Rico, 1915–1930

Year	Total Sugar Production (tons)	Total Sugar Acreage	Average Sugar Yield per Acre (P.R.)	Sugar Yield per Acre (Aguirre)	Sugar Yield per Acre (Central Mercedita)
1915	346,490	211,110	1.64		
1916	483,589	203,491	2.37		
1917	505,081	205,106	2.46	3.47	3.62
1918	453,793	256,431	1.76	3.22	2.97
1919	406,002	238,901	1.70	3.39	2.73
1920	485,070	240,151	2.01	3.49	3.62
1921	489,817	241,372	2.02	3.47	3.85
1922	408,335	244,180	1.67	3.22	3.39
1923	379,171	239,676	1.58	2.79	3.11
1924	447,597	236,600	1.89	2.44	3.35
1925	660,411	240,010	2.75	4.10	5.83
1926	603,240	242,745	2.48	4.23	4.80
1927	629,133	*240,000*	2.62		
1928	748,677	*240,000*	*3.11*		
1929	586,760	237,758	2.46		
1930	866,109	*240,000*	*3.61*		
1935	773,021	299,384	2.58		

Sources: Carlos E. Chardón, "The Varietal Revolution in Porto Rico," *Journal of the Department of Agriculture of Puerto Rico* 11 (July 1927): 9, 10, 16, 31–34, 35; Arthur D. Gayer, Paul T. Homan, and Earl K. James, *The Sugar Economy of Puerto Rico* (New York: Columbia University Press, 1938), tables 3, 7, 30.

Note: Italicized numbers are my own estimates. Sugar yields are expressed in tons of refined sugar per acre.

hybrid covered fully 2,600 of the *central's* 3,400 acres. Between 1923 and 1924 the Fajardo Sugar Company shifted from growing a mix of canes to an almost exclusive reliance on the Demerara hybrid D433. *Centrales* owned by the Aguirre interests had traditionally planted the Crystalina cane, which was less susceptible to the mosaic disease. Nonetheless, they too began major introductions of the B.H. and S.C. canes in the 1925 season.[46]

In the *Journal of Agriculture of Porto Rico,* Chardón reviewed the changes in the Puerto Rican industry in the decade after 1915. While the Puerto Rican industry had produced 315,000 tons of sugar in 1915, before mosaic struck, by 1925 it was producing more than 600,000 tons annually. "American and

Cuban interests are justified in their inquisitive look for the real cause of this remarkable sugar increase," Chardón wrote, "not for fear of its effect in the world's sugar production, since our entire output is too small to materially affect the price situation, but for the objective lesson that the larger Antille could learn from her smaller but more industrious sister, Puerto Rico."[47] He then reviewed the main factors affecting sugar production in Puerto Rico: acreage of land planted, precipitation, disease, and varietal selection.

There had been only small changes in the amount of land in cane production, and although rainfall had traditionally greatly affected sugar yields, by the mid-1920s yields were increasing in spite of reduced rainfall. Chardón argued that this increase in production was almost entirely attributable to the introduction of new hybrid canes to the island by scientists working at the agricultural experiment stations. He echoed Earle and Stevenson when he explained how the mosaic disease helped to generate public support for science:

[Mosaic disease] has been for us an education, for now every *colono* on the Island has awakened to the fact that after all, *only science applied to crop production* can in the end solve his problems. He knows mosaic and fears it; he knows about cane varieties and knows that the ones he has now have originated through the application of botanical science; he uses more fertilizer, he now considers the government expert as his true and unselfish friend, not the "crazy bum running after bugs." What a different man he is now from ten years ago![48]

The mosaic disease and the varietal revolution brought the *biological* problems of sugar production dramatically to the fore. Puerto Rican sugar planters had been concerned, of course, about diseases, pests, and other biological problems for some time. However, they never—within living memory—had to confront a biological problem that threatened to destroy the island's entire sugar industry. Scientists averted the impending crisis by identifying the vector of the mosaic disease and introducing hybrid canes. As Chardón noted, these discoveries helped scientists in Puerto Rico to gain support from the island's sugar growers, from the insular government, and even from overseas. As a result of the varietal revolution, the Insular Experiment Station became a model of agricultural science throughout the Spanish Caribbean. But while science assumed a more important role in sugar production, few planters or *colonos* would have agreed with Chardón that their most pressing agricultural problems could be solved by science alone. As the course of the varietal revolution in Cuba would show, even seemingly straightforward scientific solutions could create new problems in other facets of production.

THE MOSAIC DISEASE AND THE VARIETAL
REVOLUTION IN CUBA, 1919–1930

While the mosaic disease caused sudden and catastrophic losses in Puerto Rico's sugar industry, it was felt more gradually in Cuba, probably because of subtle yet significant ecological differences in sugar agriculture on the islands. Cuban planters had been slow to introduce innovations in cultivation during the early twentieth century. Some planters, such as Edwin Atkins, had experimented with hybrid canes, but Crystalina remained the most widely planted variety. In part, this was a result of the relative abundance of land. After 1898 the sugar industry expanded rapidly in the virgin soils of eastern Cuba. Such options were not available to planters on smaller islands, such as Hawaii, Barbados, or Puerto Rico. The pace of innovation was also slower because Cuba's cane fields were not, apparently, immediately threatened by any of the major cane diseases that had sparked rapid innovation in the cane industries of Java, Mauritius, and Barbados. Although sugar yields in Cuba had been declining since the late 1880s, this was thought to be a consequence of the intensive land use that characterized the Cuban sugar industry. However, given the experience of other sugar-growing areas, it seems likely that diseases also played a role in the decline.[49]

The mosaic disease was first noticed in Cuba in 1915 by a sugar researcher visiting from the Hawaii sugar experiment station. At first Cuban planters were not alarmed because it did not seem to be affecting sugar yields. After the mosaic disease began causing crop failures in Puerto Rico in 1917, some Cuban planters began to express concern. The Cuban government brought in E. W. Brandes, the USDA researcher who had identified *Aphis maidis* as the vector of the mosaic disease for Puerto Rico. Brandes found that cane fields across Cuba were infected with the mosaic disease but that the infection did not seem to be causing serious losses. In any case, Cuban sugar producers at the time were enjoying an economic bonanza because of World War I. With no competition from European sugar beets, Cuban producers were earning a premium price on sugar. By 1917 the price had risen to 7.5 cents a pound, up from a prewar average of 4.2 cents. This bonanza continued after the war: when price controls were lifted the price of sugar began a dizzying upward spiral known as the "dance of the millions," reaching a high of 23.57 cents a pound by mid-1920. With prices so high, profits greatly offset any losses from declining yields.[50]

When the price of sugar plummeted back to 4.2 cents a pound in December 1920, however, the pressure on producers to innovate and make the sugar industry more efficient greatly increased. Sugar growers hoped to offset the fall in prices with an increase in output. In the early 1920s American-owned mills introduced new technology and scientific management techniques. As part of this larger effort to rationalize the sugar industry, planters and scientists in Cuba began to pay more systematic attention to the mosaic disease. E. F. Atkins asked two biologists at the Atkins Garden, Edward East and William Weston, to study the effects of the mosaic disease in his cane fields. East and Weston concluded that it was the same disease that was present in Puerto Rico, even though they could not infect experimental cane with inoculations from diseased cane. They pointed to the work of Brandes, Chardón, and Veve in Puerto Rico as proof that the virus was infectious and was carried by A. maidis. Like their counterparts in Puerto Rico, East and Weston argued that the mosaic disease in Cuba was not caused by the degeneration of cane: "Since there is convincing evidence that a living parasite belonging to the filterable viruses is the effective cause of mosaic, obviously unfavorable environmental conditions cannot produce mosaic." They concluded, "[I]n general it appears that conditions rather favorable to plant growth are also favorable to the development of the disease."[51]

While the two scientists found the virus widespread in Cuba, they doubted that it had been the cause of declining yields. Cuban planters depended principally on the Crystalina cane, which they believed was resistant to mosaic, while their Puerto Rican counterparts preferred Otaheite. East and Weston pointed out that while new diseases tended to spread from a single point of origin, in Cuba the mosaic disease was present everywhere. New diseases were also often lethal to their hosts, but in Cuba the Crystalina canes appeared to be resistant to mosaic. These two observations suggested that the disease had been present in Cuba for a long time. In any case, they saw "no evidence that the mosaic disease at Soledad is cutting down either the tonnage of cane per acre, the yield of juice, the sugar content, or the purity."[52] Based on their observations in Cuba, East and Weston concluded that the mosaic disease had probably not caused the crop failures. Instead, they attributed the losses to environmental factors such as the exhaustion of marginal lands or poor irrigation.

Stephen Bruner, the cane expert at the Estación Experimental Agronómica, drew different conclusions. He found that although the Crystalina cane showed resistance to the mosaic disease, it still suffered. Stalks of diseased cane were shorter and thinner than those of healthy cane, and their root stock was weakened. And although mosaic did not kill the Crystalina cane, it made the cane much more susceptible to death from secondary causes, such as drought. Bruner supported his initial impressions with experimental evidence. He and his fellow researchers planted two fields of cane in fall 1923, one with healthy cane and the other with infected cane. Over the next year the two fields were given identical care. When the fields were harvested in March 1925, the yield of healthy cane was two and a half times greater than that of infected cane. The fields were ratooned four times, and in the 1928 ratoon, the yield of the healthy cane was almost quadruple that of the infected cane. The economic life of infected cane was thus much shorter, requiring more frequent and costly replantings.[53] Bruner's team also did careful experiments on the chemical composition of the cane and found that diseased cane and healthy cane yielded almost exactly the same percentages of sugar. But since diseased cane was smaller and stunted, the total amount of sugar it contained was correspondingly reduced.[54]

One of the early strategies used to control mosaic in Cuba was quarantine. In fall 1919 the Cuban secretary of agriculture prohibited the transportation of seed cane from infected zones of the island. He also prohibited the importation of sugarcane from abroad, unless destined for experimental use and sent directly to the secretary of agriculture. By 1926 Cuba's quarantine measures were beginning to take effect. James A. Faris, pathologist at the Cuba Sugar Club's experiment station, argued that "individuals should refrain from importing sugar cane. No foreign canes should be introduced, even in the smallest quantities, except by duly authorized persons and under the strictest safeguards of inspection and detention in isolated propagation stations." Although Faris was confident that Cuba could remain free of most diseases, he was worried that diseases such as gummosis might be introduced to Cuba from Puerto Rico, "from where we have had numerous varietal introductions within the past few years."[55]

Although it was slowly becoming clear that the mosaic disease was in fact causing severe losses in the Crystalina cane, Cuban planters were reluctant to give it up. They argued that environmental conditions, rather than diseases, were the primary cause of the declining yields of Crystalina. In any case, they saw few economically viable alternatives. Even scientists suggested that "there is no occasion yet to give up Crystalina except where other varieties are demonstrated to give better results under special conditions." Bruner was similarly unenthusiastic about the use of immune canes to combat the disease. He argued that immune canes should be used only as a temporary resort, since it "is difficult to find a substitute for Crystalina cane, which under the diverse conditions of the country, gives such satisfactory results."[56] Carlos Chardón, then Puerto Rico's commissioner of agriculture, visited Cuba in January 1925. He "found no interest in varieties. . . . [I]n fact, the Crystalina seemed to be the universal and only variety known." The only places that had collections of varieties were the experiment stations. The cane in the recently cultivated virgin soils of eastern Cuba was prospering much more than in the long-cultivated areas around Havana and Matanzas in western Cuba. In the tired areas, Chardón found the cane suffering heavily from mosaic. "[L]ittle effort was being done to control the mosaic[,] and most farmers believed that it was due to abnormal conditions."[57]

Some scientists in Cuba held out hope for improvements, though. "We believe that a new varietal revolution is about to take place in the West Indies," wrote Rafael Menéndez Ramos, a Puerto Rican disciple of Chardón who had moved to Cuba to be director of research for the Cuban Dominican Sugar Company. "[T]he 'Pearl of the Antilles,'" he continued, "will soon follow the trail which ha[s] been blazed by the smaller of its sister islands." He appealed to progress: "History is again repeating itself and we believe that Cuba is now ready to look forward to the selection and planting of the best varieties in the right kinds of soils as the next logical, progressive step towards the general improvement of the agricultural phase of its Great Industry."[58] Menéndez Ramos began breeding several dozen promising varieties of cane imported from Puerto Rico. He extolled the virtue of the Santa Cruz hybrid cane S.C. 12/4, whose "vigorous growth and deep green color . . . has been a grand ally to us in helping to convince our *colonos* and field men that there might be something, after all, in this question of new canes."[59]

In spite of the scientific acclaim for the new hybrids, resistance to them came from all levels of the Cuban sugar industry. Some hybrids that were immune to mosaic could not be planted "due to the difficulties in harvesting, since the Jamaican and Haytian labor simply refuses to cut these slender canes." The P.O.J. 2725 cane, almost ideal in the technical sense, was not popular with cutters because of small spines or hairs on the leaves that slashed their skin when they touched the cane. For the same reason, the leaves could not be used as cattle feed. Other hybrids, particularly P.O.J. hybrids, were being tested around the island with mixed results. Some varieties flowered too early, causing them to lose their sucrose. Others did not grow well in some of Cuba's soils. Yet others had weak root systems and blew over quite easily.[60]

The introduction of new canes also presented political problems in the delicate negotiations between *colonos* and the sugar mills. The Crystalina cane remained popular in spite of declining yields because the economic relations of production had been negotiated around this particular variety. Over the years, sugar mills had worked out a system of payment based on the sugar yields of Crystalina. The *colonos*, who grew the cane under contract for the mill, were paid a fixed amount of refined sugar per hundredweight of raw cane. If the *colonos* planted canes that yielded less sucrose, then the mills would lose money. Conversely, if the *colonos* planted canes that yielded more sucrose, then they would lose money. The introduction of new varieties, then, called for a renegotiation of the contracts between the mill and the *colonos*. One scientist in Cuba reported that "the necessity for dependable comparative data upon which to base the new contracts is so great that each season more mills are making comparative plantings under their local conditions to serve as a guide." The renegotiation of these contracts caused a considerable acrimony between mills and *colonos* both in Cuba and in Puerto Rico.[61]

It was only in 1925 that some Cuban planters began to substitute the Crystalina cane with hybrid canes. The switch to hybrid canes was made possible in part by the continuing rationalization of the industry in the 1920s. Mills began to employ sugar chemists, who would measure the sucrose content of the cane delivered by each *colono*. The mill would pay the *colono* on the basis of this assay. This new arrangement freed *colonos* and mills from contracts that would effectively bind them to a single variety of cane. Slowly, *colonos* throughout Cuba began to adopt the S.C. 12/4 hybrid as the standard. By 1931 it was the second most popular commercial cane in Cuba, after Crystalina. Even though Java hybrids, particularly the P.O.J. 2878, became planted widely, Crystalina cane still accounted for more than 13 percent of Cuban sugar production as late as 1949.[62]

CONCLUSION

The surface continuity in the growth of the sugar industry masks some significant environmental and social transformations. The growth of the sugar industry was not a question of simply scaling up older methods of production or of increasing the amount of land under cultivation. The nineteenth-century technological revolution in sugar refining—the shift from *ingenio* to *central*—has been well documented. Historians have, however, tended to draw a sharp distinction between the intensely modern process of sugar harvesting and refining and the supposedly more traditional, static process of sugar agriculture. Under closer scrutiny, however, the distinction between these two processes is not so sharp. The agricultural component of the sugar industry also became intensely modern, dependent first on the global exchange of noble canes and later on the production of sophisticated hybrids. The disease regime was also quintessentially (although accidentally) modern, depending as it did on the radical simplification of natural ecosystems and the global exchange of pathogens, both of which depended on modern developments in economy and transportation. As planters sought to continually increase agricultural production, they embarked on an endless environmental treadmill. The search for new, more productive varieties of sugar entailed the introduction of new diseases, which in turn prompted the search for new varieties, and so on. These differences might have been difficult for a casual observer walking through a cane field to notice. The hybrid canes harvested by the *colonos* in the 1930s looked almost identical to the noble canes they had harvested in 1900, or even in 1840. But everyone concerned with sugar production was aware that the environmental relations of production *had* changed substantially—that sugar agriculture had undergone an environmental revolution.

The varietal revolution produced some social and economic changes. It is more notable for the catastrophic social and economic changes it averted. For examples of what might have happened, we can look at the cases of cacao diseases in Ecuador and rubber diseases in Brazil, both of which developed at about the same time as the sugar mosaic disease. In Ecuador, two epidemic diseases—monilia and witches' broom—wiped out cacao production almost completely. Scientists were hired to address these diseases, but they could find no economically viable solution, and the industry collapsed in the 1920s. Ecuador's cacao planters, hitherto a major force in the country, lost much of their political and economic power. Unemployed laborers from the cacao plantations flooded Ecuador's cities, aggravating urban poverty and unrest. Likewise, a fungus known as the South American leaf blight prevented Brazil from establishing rubber plantations. Many organizations, including the Brazilian government and Ford Motor Company, funded research into the disease. Again, scientists could find no economically viable cure, and Brazil's rubber industry rapidly lost ground to rubber producers in Asia.[63]

In 1917 sugar planters in Puerto Rico feared that the mosaic disease might destroy the island's sugar industry. Had scientists not been able to manage the disease, Puerto Rico's sugar industry could have collapsed, destroying the island's main source of revenue and plunging it further into poverty. If the mills had continued to refuse to grind diseased cane, as they did in 1917, they would have forced most Puerto Rican *colonos* into bankruptcy. The U.S.-owned sugar corporations would have either gone bankrupt or abandoned the Puerto Rican plantations and established new ones elsewhere in the Caribbean, just as the U.S. banana corporations were doing to escape disease in Central America. With no other export commodities that could produce as much revenue as sugar, Puerto Rico's hypothetical crisis of development in the 1920s would have been even more profound than the real crisis of development that struck the island ten years later. It is hard to know what would have happened, but it would likely have led to a significant renegotiation of the economic and political relationships between Puerto Rico and the United States.

The varietal revolution also brought about some subtle yet significant transformations in the social relations of sugar production. The introduction of hybrid canes had forced planters and *colonos* to renegotiate the terms of the contracts that had defined the social structure of early-twentieth-century sugar agriculture in Cuba and Puerto Rico. The efforts to manage the rapid environmental transformation of the sugar industry also led to the formation of a new class of scientific and technical experts. The new *colono* contracts made it necessary for mills to hire sugar chemists to measure the sucrose content of the new hybrid canes. More dramatically, the varietal revolution had decisively proved that agricultural scientists had a central role in modern agricultural production. The dramatic and ultimately successful scientific struggle to control the mosaic disease had given scientists a new legitimacy in Latin America. During the late 1920s, governments and agricultural associations throughout Latin America came to see Puerto Rico's sugar industry as the paradigmatic model of science-based agricultural development. The attempts to reproduce the Puerto Rican model of science-based agricultural development elsewhere in Latin America are discussed in chapter 5.

∽

FIVE

PROMOTING THE "PRACTICAL"

Technocratic Ideologies of Science and Progress in an Age of Fragile Prosperity, 1924–1930

∽

T he sugar mosaic epidemic in Puerto Rico was arguably the first major agricultural crisis in Latin America to be solved through original scientific research. For the first time in the region's history, scientists had demonstrated that they could offer practical solutions to agricultural problems. Until that time agricultural experiment stations in Latin America had not been able to match the successes of tropical agricultural research elsewhere in the world. They had failed to prevent epidemic crop diseases from destroying Brazil's rubber industry in the early 1900s and Ecuador's cacao industry in the early 1920s. Repeated failures such as these caused some people to question whether agricultural research was practical. When scientists at the experiment station of the Puerto Rico Sugar Planters Association could not find a way to control infestations of the sugarcane leafhopper, the association had turned the station over to Puerto Rico's insular government. During the 1910s and 1920s, political and financial support for agricultural research in Latin America remained erratic.

The success of scientists in Puerto Rico in controlling the mosaic disease in the mid-1920s broke this pattern of failure and became a model for agricultural science in Latin America. As a result of this success, agricultural scientists in Puerto Rico gained a measure of political power unprecedented in the Spanish Caribbean. Puerto Rico's governor appointed Carlos Chardón, the young plant pathologist who had helped to identify the insect vector of the mosaic disease, commissioner of agriculture. In this capacity, Chardón worked to consolidate Puerto Rico's agricultural research infrastructure and to export the Puerto Rican model to the rest of tropical Latin America. Other countries in the region hoped to emulate Puerto Rico's success and approached Chardón for guidance. Between 1926 and 1930 Chardón did agricultural consulting for governments and agricultural associations in Colombia, Cuba, Ecuador, Panama, Peru, and Venezuela and for the Pan American Union.[1]

Chardón wanted to do more than simply spread new scientific theories and techniques. He wanted to institutionalize a technocratic ideology of science-based agricultural development. The core principle of Chardón's ideology was that Latin American economic development depended on agricultural science. During the 1920s, economic development in most of the Spanish Caribbean continued to depend on agricultural exports. And the major problems in export crop production, Chardón argued, were biological problems such as epidemic diseases, declining yields, and soil exhaustion. "The solution of these problems," he wrote, "falls strictly within the limits of science as applied to agriculture." Since scientists were the people best equipped to understand these problems, they ought to play a more important role in shaping agricultural policy. Furthermore, since scientists were disinterested professionals outside partisan politics, they were also best equipped to propose rational solutions to Latin America's agricultural problems.[2]

Chardón's technocratic ideology had its roots in the specific circumstances of Puerto Rico in the 1920s. The island's sugar industry was organized in such a way that scientific research could provide immediate and dramatic increases in production. By the 1920s most aspects of sugar production had been optimized and planters had begun to turn their attention systematically to the sugar plants themselves. Most of the problems confronting sugar production in Puerto Rico during the 1920s—as epitomized by the mosaic disease—appeared to be biological problems. Scientists, therefore, had a clear role to play in sustaining the sugar industry. Puerto Rico's unique political situation also shaped Chardón's sense of his mission. As a member of the first generation of Puerto Ricans to grow up entirely under U.S. rule, he sought to fuse the best of Puerto Rican and North American traditions. Chardón's mission was to adapt North American scientific knowledge to the Latin American agricultural, social, economic, and political context. He saw Puerto Rico as a bridge—or a contact zone—between the United States and Latin America.

Although there was widespread interest in the successes of Puerto Rico's agricultural scientists, it proved difficult for Chardón to institutionalize this model in Puerto Rico or to export it to other parts of tropical Latin America. Chardón's two main projects in the late 1920s were to build a Pan-American graduate school of tropical agriculture in Puerto Rico and to build a national agricultural research network in Colombia. For the Graduate School of Tropical Agriculture, Chardón forged a powerful constituency that included Puerto Rico's leading politicians, the U.S. National Research Council (NRC), and Cornell University. All these groups shared Chardón's vision of the role science could play in agricultural development and of Puerto Rico's role in U.S.–Latin

American relations. Even with this ideological consensus, however, raising the necessary funds for the school proved difficult.

It proved even more difficult for Chardón to reproduce his model in Colombia, where the political and agricultural conditions were quite different from those in Puerto Rico. For his projects in Colombia, Chardón had to build a consensus among government officials (both local and national), crop growers, and the scientists themselves. These groups could all agree that Chardón's model of agricultural development was practical, but they differed over what "practical" meant. Chardón, along with other agricultural scientists in Colombia, argued that agricultural science was inherently useful and practical. Many planters disagreed; they wanted quick solutions to their most pressing agricultural problems rather than long-term research programs. For that reason, they were also reluctant to give scientists control over the agendas for agricultural teaching and research. In contrast, government officials and the national agricultural association were more interested in the technocratic facets of Chardón's model. Agricultural science offered, at least in principle, a way to address Colombia's agricultural problems that transcended the partisan agrarian conflict that plagued the country in the late 1920s.

PUERTO RICAN PAN-AMERICANISM: THE GRADUATE SCHOOL OF TROPICAL AGRICULTURE OF THE UNIVERSITY OF PUERTO RICO, 1927–1929

The success of the Insular Experiment Station in managing the mosaic disease offered a new way for Puerto Rico to affirm its identity. The island's political status with respect to the United States had remained unclear from the time it was occupied in 1898 until the Jones Act of 1917. The Jones Act granted U.S. citizenship to Puerto Ricans and gave them a measure of self-government. Although some in Puerto Rico continued to seek outright independence from the United States, by the 1920s most of Puerto Rico's politicians dropped the quest for independence and instead worked toward autonomy within the North American sphere. Puerto Rican intellectuals began to explore and articulate the nature of Puerto Rican identity. Most of these explorations focused on how the United States had either promoted or prevented the formation of a properly Puerto Rican identity. The most famous critical essay was Antonio Pedreira's *Insularismo*, published in 1934. Like Latin American critics of the day, Pedreira criticized the "material" Anglo-Saxon culture of the United States while celebrating the "spiritual" Spanish culture of Puerto Rico. Chardón— and many other Puerto Ricans of his generation—did not see these two traditions as mutually exclusive. Chardón argued instead that the island's culture combined the best of Latin America's traditions and practices with the best of U.S. traditions and practices. Puerto Rico could therefore be a model for U.S.–Latin American relations. Chardón was often critical of U.S. foreign policy with regard to Latin America. He argued that Puerto Rico could mediate a constructive relationship between the United States and Latin America. He articulated this view in his plans for a graduate school of tropical agriculture, to be established in San Juan.

Chardón's efforts to build an independent graduate school of tropical agriculture also reflected a measure of his dissatisfaction with agricultural research and teaching on the island. Puerto Rico already had an agricultural college— the Colegio de Mayagüez, which was part of the University of Puerto Rico. Like the university, the Colegio fell under the jurisdiction of the insular department of education, whose commissioner was not subject to confirmation by the Puerto Rican Senate. Herbert Hice Whetzel, Chardón's former adviser from Cornell, took stock of the situation in 1924: "[T]he commissioner [of education] does not seem particularly interested in developing the college.... Until there is a readjustment in the present attitude of the educational department it is not likely that the college of agriculture . . . can be materially improved or developed." As early as 1924, Chardón was exploring ways to get around the department of education by establishing a separate agricultural research institution in cooperation with Cornell University. Cornell's dean of agriculture, Alfred Mann, expressed interest in the project.[3]

Late in 1926, after a visit to Colombia, Chardón began working on a detailed proposal to establish a graduate school of tropical agriculture based at the University of Puerto Rico. His work in Puerto Rico and Colombia had convinced him that demand for specialists in tropical agriculture would continue to grow. He predicted that "within the coming ten years, every Latin American country will have one or several well-conducted centers for agricultural research, either governmental or private, or both." Given the current state of agricultural research and teaching in Latin America, meeting the demand for researchers would prove to be difficult. Puerto Rico's Insular Experiment Station, which had trained many agricultural researchers, could not continue to meet this demand either. In fact, its very success was undermining its capacity to do agricultural research. The establishment of centers for agricultural research elsewhere in the Americas, Chardón wrote, "has caused a serious drain on the staff of the Insular Experiment Station, and three former directors and a half dozen well-qualified technical men are now scattered in widely separated areas of tropical and subtropical America, like Cuba, Louisiana, Peru, Colombia, Santo Domingo, and Venezuela."[4]

Chardón believed it was up to the United States to help Puerto Ricans train

Latin American agricultural researchers. The United States graduated many trained agricultural scientists, but "the number of them available for tropical work, including a knowledge of Spanish, tropical experience, and the right point of view are indeed very few." There were compelling economic and political reasons for the United States to support the school. First, the United States was the principal consumer of Latin America's agricultural exports. During the 1920s, the United States consumed more coffee, rubber, tobacco, cacao, and bananas than ever before. Second, "cooperation and service" was more politically constructive than military conquest as a way of engaging with Latin America. "The marines," Chardón noted drily, "in spite of their glorious episodes in the World War, have not been quite as successful in the development of friendly relations with Haiti, Santo Domingo, and Nicaragua." Chardón argued that the policy of service, as embodied by a graduate school of tropical agriculture, would be immensely successful in part because such service recognized "no racial or linguistic boundaries."[5]

Chardón looked to the University of Puerto Rico's School of Tropical Medicine as a model for the school of agriculture. The School of Tropical Medicine was a cooperative effort among the University of Puerto Rico, the insular government, and Columbia University. Health, like agriculture, was a very pressing problem in Puerto Rico. Malaria, yellow fever, and other tropical diseases were rampant when the Americans took over the island. For years, the Institute of Tropical Medicine and Hygiene had been in charge of managing the island's health. The institute consisted of several Puerto Rican and several U.S. doctors. After World War I it sought to build a collaborative relationship with a medical school in the United States. Columbia University agreed to provide faculty members and medical expertise for the Graduate School of Tropical Medicine; in return it would have a laboratory for the study of tropical medicine. Disagreements emerged, however, about who was to control the institution. The Puerto Rican physicians in the Institute of Tropical Medicine wanted it to be under Puerto Rican control. As a condition of participation, however, Columbia demanded that it hold the balance of power on the school's board of directors. The insular government finally agreed to Columbia's conditions and signed the formal agreement in 1924. The building was completed by May 1925, a speed of construction unusual for the region. The building embodied the union of old and new, of Latin and Anglo-Saxon ideas: the exterior was modeled after the medieval palace of Monterrey in Spain, but its interior contained all the latest equipment in specialized laboratories for the study of tropical disease. The library, while small, received some seventy-five journals related to tropical medicine and held a nucleus of about five hundred volumes. It opened in 1926 and began operation with great fanfare and success.[6]

For his project, Chardón began by enlisting the support of Puerto Rico's leading politicians and the NRC. The NRC's Committee on Biology and Agriculture had been considering the possibility of establishing a graduate school of tropical agriculture since the early 1920s. The only major decision it had reached by 1927 was that the school should be established "within the boundaries of the Stars and Stripes." This left few options: Florida's climate was subtropical rather than tropical, and the Panama Canal Zone was not well suited for agriculture. The only other tropical possessions under the Stars and Stripes were Hawaii and Puerto Rico. Chardón saw an opportunity for Puerto Rico, and he got support for the school from the president of the Puerto Rican Senate, the speaker of Puerto Rico's legislature (who had been instrumental in supporting the Graduate School of Tropical Medicine), and Puerto Rico's resident commissioner in Washington. In mid-1927, while the four men were in Washington on other business, they put Chardón's proposal before the chair of the NRC's Committee on Biology and Agriculture.[7]

The NRC sent two scientists to Puerto Rico to study the island's suitability as a location for the new school. The NRC scientists shared the Puerto Ricans' vision of the island as a cultural bridge between the United States and Latin America and were impressed by the rapid success of the Graduate School of Tropical Medicine. Not only did this make Puerto Rico a healthy place in which to study, "a graduate school of agriculture, operated similarly, [would] form an excellent nucleus for a Pan-American University." The NRC report pointed to Puerto Rico's unique cultural and political situation within Latin America:

> [I]t is generally agreed that the people of Latin America and the people of the United States fail in large measure to understand each other and therefore to cooperate in their efforts for advancement. This is easily understood when one realizes that they are of very different temperament and have different languages, cultures, and religions. Porto Rico, on the other hand[,] is bilingual and has gone far toward blending both types of culture. They understand and can work with both the people of the States and the people of tropical America. A Graduate School of Tropical Agriculture in Porto Rico will make another step toward a Pan-American University in a place of mutual sympathy. Such a University, in turn, will do much to further an understanding between the peoples of the Western hemisphere.[8]

This vision of Puerto Rico as conduit between the United States and tropical America was also repeatedly advanced by Chardón and other Puerto Ricans in the insular government.

The Graduate School of Tropical Agriculture (GSTA) was to be a cooperative effort with Cornell University, Chardón's alma mater. A Cornell faculty delegation visited Puerto Rico early in 1928. Livingston Farrand, Cornell's president, and Alfred Mann agreed in principle that Cornell would provide faculty and also raise the necessary funds to operate the graduate school. With support from all levels of government in Puerto Rico and the United States, the project was approved with unusual speed. Shortly thereafter, the Puerto Rican legislature proposed and passed a formal resolution to establish the Graduate School of Tropical Agriculture. In April 1928 Governor Towner signed the resolution. Back in the United States, Farrand and Mann set about raising money to fund the college.[9]

By 1928 Chardón had skillfully built a coalition of agricultural, educational, and political elites in Puerto Rico and the United States. These groups broadly shared the technocratic ideas Chardón had articulated in fall 1927, which emphasized the central role of scientific experts in sustaining economic development. All three groups also shared the political vision of Puerto Rico as a laboratory for adapting North American practices to a Latin American context. "Time has only served to strengthen my belief," Chardón told Dean Mann of Cornell, "that nothing more constructive could be accomplished by Cornell and Porto Rico, than to successfully conduct this project which is going to be so far-reaching in helping to promote better understanding between the United States and Latin America." Governments and agricultural associations elsewhere in Latin America apparently agreed. Peru's National Agricultural Society, for example, had expressed interest in the Graduate School of Tropical Agriculture even before the plans had been officially approved. During 1926 and 1927, Chardón had also been working as an agricultural consultant in Colombia. His work in Colombia played a central role in refining his vision of science-based agricultural development. It showed him that exporting the Puerto Rican model of agricultural development to other agricultural regimes could be difficult. His first attempt to reproduce the Puerto Rican model abroad was at the Escuela Superior de Agricultura in Medellín, Colombia.[10]

PRACTICAL EDUCATION? REFORMING THE ESCUELA SUPERIOR DE AGRICULTURA IN MEDELLÍN, 1926–1928

In the 1920s Colombia was in the midst of its second coffee boom. Between 1913 and 1921 coffee exports had doubled from one million bags to two million. This boom had begun after railroads to the fertile regions of Antioquia and Valle del Cauca were completed in 1914 and 1915. The railroads and the newly opened Panama Canal greatly reduced the cost of shipping coffee from Colombia's central valleys and Pacific coast to the markets of Europe and

North America. The center of coffee agriculture shifted from the states of Santander and Cundinamarca in northeastern Colombia down to Antioquia in central Colombia and later to the departments of Caldas and Valle del Cauca in the west.[11]

This growth had taken place during a period of relative political calm in Colombia. For much of the nineteenth century, Colombia's national government had been weak. The Conservative Party emerged victorious from the turn-of-the-century War of a Thousand Days and dominated Colombian politics for the next three decades. During the three Conservative administrations of the 1920s, Colombia's presidents began to systematically strengthen and expand the national government. President Marco Fidel Suárez (1918–1922) financed large-scale public works such as highways and railways by borrowing on international markets, in particular the United States. This orientation to the United States reflected Suárez's "Polar Star" policy, which sought to build closer ties between the two countries by promoting U.S. investment in Colombia. Suárez's successors, Pedro Nel Ospina (1922–1926) and Miguel Abadía Méndez (1926–1930), continued to expand government expenditures for public works—thereby expanding public indebtedness. Nel Ospina spent some 55 million pesos on public works projects, while Abadía Méndez almost tripled Nel Ospina's expenditures to 158 million pesos.[12]

The governments of Colombia's departments also began raising loans to finance public works and modernization projects. Colombia's planters called on the regional governments to direct some of these funds to programs of agricultural development. They also began to organize themselves during the 1920s and in this decade founded many regional and departmental agricultural associations. The economist Jesús Antonio Bejarano estimates that by 1924 there were thirty-eight regional agricultural associations in Colombia. One of their main objectives was to promote technical improvements. For example, the agricultural associations in the departments of Antioquia, Caldas, and Cundinamarca organized agricultural colleges and experiment stations.[13]

Antioquia was arguably Colombia's most powerful and dynamic department during the 1920s. Its capital city, Medellín, was the largest city in Colombia after Bogotá; rivalry between the two was often fierce. Antioquia's importance, however, extended beyond its size alone. While the department produced a significant percentage of Colombia's coffee exports, by the 1920s manufacturing and industry—particularly textiles—also played an important role in the departmental economy. Antioquia's elites, most of them Conservatives, had long pursued organized programs of development. In the nineteenth century the department's economy had been driven by gold mining. In the 1880s Antioqueño politicians convinced the national government to fund a national school of mines on the outskirts of Medellín. The school's motto, *Trabajo y rectitud* (Work and Rectitude), neatly described the Antioqueño approach to development. Of all Colombia's departments, it was Antioquia that showed the most interest in applying science and technology to development.[14]

In 1926 Antioquia's Agricultural Society invited Chardón to reorganize the state's agricultural college. The society's leaders felt a pressing need for agricultural experts, and they were unhappy with the college's recent graduates, whose orientation they felt was excessively "theoretical." This elite concern about "practicality" dated back to the early days of Colombia's independence, when the rulers of the new country had tried, unsuccessfully, to introduce technical education as a means of national development. Chardón's report echoed the Agricultural Society's concerns about the practical. It criticized the school's existing curriculum, which emphasized theory over practice. The school's physical plant likewise emphasized the theoretical over the practical. While the school's classrooms and laboratories were in downtown Medellín, the experimental fields were outside the city. Students seldom visited the fields, most of which were in any case sterile and therefore not useful as experimental plots. Chardón found that the college's budget was inadequate for serious research or teaching. There was not enough money to pay scientists brought from abroad to teach at the school, and "without these scientists, the school cannot and should not exist." The library "barely deserves the name." Other than a mediocre chemistry laboratory, the school had no research or teaching laboratories at all—not even for botany, plant pathology, or entomology.[15]

Chardón's proposed reforms blended the agricultural society's vision of the practical with his own. "We must be careful," he wrote, "that the teaching of [the useful professions] is based on naked practice, based on, that is to say, facts rather than books." The school was to have high admission standards. Prospective students needed to have at least four years of secondary school and ideally a high school degree, the *bachillerato*. Their course of study would be modeled after the U.S. bachelor's degree, and the students would graduate with the degree of agricultural engineer, or Ingeniero Agrónomo. Chardón recommended that the college be relocated to a site near Medellín that had more varied topography and richer lands, which would make better experimental fields. The curriculum would blend classroom work and fieldwork. The fieldwork reflected Chardón's understanding of the main agricultural problems confronting Antioquia, most of which were biological. Chardón's final report indicated that Antioquia's major agricultural ecosystems were riddled with diseases and pests. Many of its coffee trees were infected with an insect plague similar to the leaf miner, which had struck other coffee regions in tropical Latin America. He recommended that the government of Antioquia hire a Puerto Rican plant pathologist to study the region's coffee diseases, after which he could advise the school on lines of research. Similarly, Chardón found that the soils of Antioquia's sugarcane fields were exhausted and that the prevalent varieties of sugarcane were "degenerating." He laid out fifteen agricultural projects, whose solutions were economically important to Antioquia, that could be used as the basis for teaching. They included studies of coffee growing and coffee diseases; on cane varieties and cane diseases; on foraging grasses; and on tobacco, cotton, and cacao.[16]

Chardón's report also echoed a long-standing debate in Colombia about how to encourage young Colombians to pursue technical careers. For example, one Colombian agricultural writer feared that Colombia's ignorance of modern agriculture would remain until "rich and enlightened men dedicate themselves, as they do in England, to cultivation, since in that nation the noblemen consider it proper not to live in the cities, bur rather on their domains, which are developed under their supervision." Chardón's report argued, similarly, that Colombia's elites had long disdained manual labor, which discouraged their children from seeking training in technical professions. Within the technical professions, agriculture had a particularly low status. Chardón argued that it was important to change elite attitudes about science and technology. He saw the college as a means to inculcate the famous Antioquian virtue of hard work and to stem the flood of young educated people to the cities: "We need to dignify hard work, the cultivation of land and our coexistence with it, to obtain its prodigious and generous fruit. The agricultural element is a conservative nucleus, healthy, faithful, and patriotic in the extreme; governments can rest upon it securely. To feed, sustain, and develop agriculture is to create loyal and solid citizens." The reluctance to pursue technical careers was not, however, simply a moral issue. Colombia's economy had historically offered few opportunities for the small group of people who chose technical careers. As Colombia's economy expanded rapidly in the mid-1920s, new opportunities for technical professionals emerged.[17]

The Agricultural Society approved Chardón's plan for reforming the school. Chardón returned to Puerto Rico and sent three young Puerto Rican scientists to implement the restructuring plan and teach the core courses. But Chardón's plan got bogged down in struggles between the Agricultural Society and the departmental government. Although the departmental government had initially approved Chardón's plan, it was slow to appropriate money for the project. Chardón had requested an annual operating budget of $70,000 for the station, with another $150,000 for buildings and equipment, but the government appropriated less than half—$31,000 for buildings and equipment and $60,000 for the operating budget. At the end of the next fiscal year, the government slashed the school's operating budget to $40,000. The college's Colombian director explained the cuts simply as "financial problems." Rafael

Toro, a Puerto Rican faculty member, was more explicit: "The previous [state government] and the present one have always been enemies. The policies of one have been to demean and discredit what the other one has accomplished. . . . [T]he school has received little or no support from the government. Yes, the government did appropriate money—to shut up the Agricultural Society—but they don't allow it to be spent." This problem reflected broader political tensions between Colombia's agricultural associations and the departmental governments. The agricultural associations had considerable political and economic power, but they did not control Colombian politics. Other interests, such as manufacturers and the urban middle classes, were more influential. "So here we sit," Toro wrote to Chardón, "without knowing what to do. With a promise to you to bring about your plans and with delays here which prevent us from bringing them about." Frustrated by the delays in the appropriations and with their accommodations, Toro and the other two Puerto Rican scientists asked Chardón if they could return to their jobs at Puerto Rico's department of agriculture. Chardón responded with a rare fit of temper: "Colombia . . . wants to change, to modernize, . . . and you, my friends, who have been chosen to effect this change have been scared off by a few inconveniences and the horror of seeing houses made out of cow dung! I can't understand how these trivialities can make you lose your enthusiasm."[18]

Chardón also gave his colleagues some suggestions about how to build a public constituency for agricultural science in Antioquia, involving a series of demonstration experiments that would illustrate the rapid economic benefits that agricultural research could provide. First, Chardón suggested that they plant some of the new hybrid sugarcanes, which had raised sugar yields spectacularly in Puerto Rico. The scientists should accompany the planting with lectures to the Agricultural Society. "Make them expect big things of you, and *those things will happen.*" They should also plant new varieties of tobacco, making sure to show the results to Antioquia's Society of Tobacco Growers. Finally, Chardón suggested that they do some work on coffee fertilizers. These three strategies would bring significant material results in a short time and convince Antioquia's main agricultural organizations to support the school's scientific program. Chardón closed his letter with praise and a threat. The praise: "Remember that you are not technicians of salons and hotels, but real *pioneers* who will open the path for Puerto Ricans who are here eagerly awaiting your successes." The threat: "I cannot offer you back any job in Puerto Rico. *Don't count on anything here in Puerto Rico,* because I want to burn your boats just as did Hernán Cortes, to make you struggle and triumph. After the triumph, you can count on me, *but not before.*" It was essential to Chardón's broader vision of agricultural development in Latin America that his Colombian project succeed.[19]

Threats to Chardón's project also emerged from an unexpected quarter. Antioquia's Agricultural Society itself began to question whether Chardón's plan was sufficiently practical. One of the key areas of debate was the extension service. In Chardón's view, the job of extension agents was to disseminate the results of the scientific research carried out at the college. It would take the school several years to train a corps of extension agents because the experiments were just beginning and because the students were just starting the new curriculum. The Agricultural Society argued that basic extension work, which did not depend on original scientific research, could provide the most immediately useful improvements to Antioquia's agriculture. It insisted that Chardón organize an agricultural extension service immediately. Chardón temporized, arguing that there were not enough trained personnel in Antioquia to do extension work and that "the idea of [an extension service] is premature, [but] it is still a good one." [20]

The school's board of directors also began to question Chardón's reforms. One of the directors, a planter named Joaquin Santamaria, wanted the college to begin training estate managers (*mayordomos*) and peasants in basic agricultural techniques. In 1928 the new president of the school's board of directors, Gregorio Agudelo, organized a center for training peasants at the college. Agudelo argued that the peasants, "who because of their poverty, age, and other conditions will not be able to study in the school, will learn something useful alongside the technicians, will improve their crop systems, will transmit to their families, friends, and neighbors their knowledge, while they wait for the extension teaching to come. This way we will be able to make technicians and estate managers without hurting higher education." Training educated peasants and *mayordomos*, Agudelo argued, would be more useful in modernizing Colombian agriculture than research scientists.[21]

Ironically, the high admission standards that Chardón had set undermined his efforts to find students. Chardón had based his plan for Antioquia on his experiences in Puerto Rico, where the system of secondary education was big enough and good enough to provide a small but adequate pool of qualified applicants for Puerto Rico's College of Agriculture. The pool of qualified applicants in Antioquia was not nearly as large: at the time only 5 percent of Colombians attended high school, and a much smaller percentage of those graduated. Few graduating secondary students in Antioquia met the exacting entrance requirements that Chardón had proposed. Rafael Toro told Chardón, "In the towns around here it is hard to find personnel qualified to be admitted according to your plan, so they put everyone who shows up in the school for estate managers and thus there are no students for the school." [22] This debate over the future of the school reflected the widely different interpretations of the "practical." Santamaria and Agudelo agreed with Chardón that the school should focus on practical matters but argued that training technicians who could disseminate quickly known agricultural techniques was more practical than training research scientists whose work offered few short-term economic benefits.

Chardón and the college's Puerto Rican faculty began a publicity campaign to promote the idea that his plan was, in fact, practical. The Puerto Rican faculty, fearing that the school for *mayordomos* was undermining the college's high teaching and research standards, began lobbying publicly for Chardón's vision of the school in 1928. Toro published articles in the Medellín newspapers arguing that the plan "is very well adjusted to the needs of the agriculture of the department. It combines in one institution the three branches of agricultural activity developed by governments. If it has one big defect, it is that of being too PRACTICAL. Given the agricultural conditions of Antioquia, it is the only way to obtain success in teaching." These lobbying efforts, coupled with a change in the departmental government, helped to keep part of Chardón's plan going. "At first the government put obstacles in our way," Toro wrote to Chardón, "but little by little we gained the confidence of the people, first the large planters, later the curates, and these people have given their favorable opinions, such that the government had changed its mind."[23]

Antioquia's new governor, Camilo Restrepo, supported Chardón's project enthusiastically and began to bring the college's budget closer to the levels that Chardón had suggested. With assured appropriations and public support, the Puerto Rican scientists finally began programs of experimental research, some of which quickly bore fruit. Early experiments on hybrid sugarcane varieties showed dramatically increased yields. Other programs proceeded apace, and the school began to attract a small but adequate student body. After long struggles to get appropriations for land and buildings, by late 1929 the school finally had a farm for experimental plots, buildings were slowly being constructed, and the Puerto Rican scientists were able to teach and conduct research. In January 1930 Antioquia's secretary of agriculture and development reported that the school of agriculture was employing "six foreign professors, wholly dedicated to teaching, research, and experimentation." In the short term, at least, Chardón's vision had taken hold.[24]

The debate in Antioquia was a microcosm of the larger national discussion over agricultural teaching and research, succinctly outlined in a 1928 issue of the Ministry of Industry's *Boletín de Agricultura*. The journal argued that agricultural education should be a national priority. It recognized training agricultural researchers as "laudable and necessary" but argued that this training was "expensive and perhaps somewhat deficient" with respect to the agricultural needs of the country. Training agricultural researchers was not, however, as important as "equipping thousands of farmers with enough easily assimilated progressive technical knowledge so that they can carry out their labors successfully." Therefore, the most profitable agricultural teaching is "without a doubt that given to the practical farmer, already trained and capable of assimilating theory to apply it to the concrete reality of the field." To that end, professors should make their lessons "easy to explain and easy to apply." [25]

Chardón's experience in Antioquia shows how difficult it was to reproduce his Puerto Rican model of agricultural development in Colombia. The social, economic, political, and agricultural conditions of Puerto Rico's relatively centralized sugar industry differed greatly from those in Colombia's more decentralized coffee and tobacco industries. Puerto Rico's sugar planters had generally come to share Chardón's vision, after they saw how research could solve their most pressing agricultural problems. But the agricultural problems faced by Antioquia's coffee and tobacco planters could not be reduced to biological problems that could be solved by scientific research alone. Given Antioquia's agricultural problems, not to mention its tiny number of high school graduates, it was reasonable for the planters to prefer a school for training peasants and estate managers rather than research scientists. The relations between planters and political institutions also differed sharply in Puerto Rico and Antioquia. While in Puerto Rico, Chardón sometimes had to deal with political indifference to agricultural research, but he seldom had to confront active political opposition as he had in Antioquia. Chardón saw these difficulties as temporary obstacles, however, and remained convinced that demand for trained agricultural scientists would continue to grow.

RATIONALIZING THE COUNTRYSIDE: THE PUERTO RICAN AGRICULTURAL MISSION TO THE VALLE DEL CAUCA, 1928–1929

Chardón's work in Puerto Rico and Colombia attracted the attention of agricultural reformers in the Colombian department of the Valle del Cauca, on the Pacific Coast. This mountainous department had been recently settled and had quickly begun to prosper. Agriculture in the Valle del Cauca had benefited greatly from technical innovations in transportation. A new railroad connected the departmental capital, Cali, with its Pacific port of Buenaventura. The newly opened Panama Canal made it possible to ship the department's agricultural products to overseas markets quickly and cheaply. The departmental government expressed interest in other technical improvements that could make its export agriculture more profitable. To promote economic development in the Valle del Cauca, the departmental government established a department of industry in 1926, under the direction of an agricultural engineer, Carlos Durán Castro. Given Durán Castro's background, his development programs placed a high value on agricultural research. He looked to the United States as a model and in 1927 visited Louisiana's centers for agricultural research. On his return trip to Colombia, he visited Chardón in Puerto Rico. The two men outlined a plan for the economic development of the Valle del Cauca that proposed the creation of an experimental farm that would become a center for research and innovation on the Valle del Cauca's main crops.[26]

In summer 1928 the departmental government invited Chardón to direct an agricultural survey and to organize the experiment station. Chardón saw the new Colombian project as "evidence of the agricultural awakening of South America" and hoped that it might "be conducive to larger projects in the future." Unlike the planters in Antioquia, the government of the Valle del Cauca shared Chardón's belief in the central role of scientific research in agricultural development. Chardón was charged with studying the region's livestock, economic plants, and plant diseases. Once the mission had identified the main agricultural needs of the Cauca valley, it was to begin work on developing a scientific infrastructure to meet those needs. Specifically, the government asked Chardón to make suggestions for agricultural legislation, to assemble collections of the regional flora and fauna, and, most important, to submit a plan for the organization of an agricultural experiment station.[27]

Under Chardón's direction, the Puerto Rican Agricultural Mission to the Valle del Cauca surveyed agricultural conditions in the department between May and July 1929. Their final report, published in 1930, reflected Chardón's growing awareness of the bureaucratic and administrative obstacles to agricultural growth. The report portrayed the Valle del Cauca as a region that had not reached its full potential for agricultural growth. Basic scientific research could address many of the main obstacles. For example, sugar planters were still using the old Otaheite variety of sugarcane, which had low sugar yields and was vulnerable to the mosaic disease then spreading throughout tropical Latin America. Sugar yields could be doubled or tripled, promised Chardón, if the Cauca planters adopted the new hybrid canes. The cacao and cotton industries, stricken with diseases and pests, did not have a promising future in the short term, but scientific research might offer some solutions over the longer term. The report found that the coffee growers of the Valle del Cauca were not even aware of innovations in coffee agriculture practiced elsewhere in Colombia. It suggested that coffee production could be increased if the Colombian Federation of Coffee Growers sent teams of agronomists to the Valle del Cauca, as it had done with great success in the departments of Antioquia and Caldas just to the north. Not all of the Valle del Cauca's agricultural problems were technical, however. For example, Chardón criticized the Byzantine taxes on the tobacco industry, which discouraged tobacco cultivation. The high costs of tobacco production could be greatly lowered if taxes were levied at only one stage of production. Although the report recognized that not all agricultural problems had scientific solutions, scientific research continued to hold pride of place in its recommendations. It stressed the importance of organizing an agricultural experiment station. The departmental government acted swiftly. By summer 1929, shortly after the mission had left, the government founded an agricultural experiment station on a six-hundred-acre farm at Palmira, near Cali. Durán Castro, who had invited the Chardón mission to Colombia, was appointed director of the experiment station.[28]

The science-oriented agricultural mission to the Valle del Cauca better reflected Chardón's technocratic vision. There, the departmental government already shared the broad outlines of his vision and was prepared to commit resources to make it a reality. "My second trip to South America has further convinced me," Chardón wrote to Herbert Whetzel, his former adviser at Cornell, "of the great necessity of training experts in tropical agriculture, who might be in a position to render some service to these southern Latin countries. Nothing in this way has been done in Colombia, Venezuela, Ecuador, Peru, and the whole of Central America, although some countries, like this, for example, and no doubt the rest will follow in the near future, are showing considerable interest in developing scientific agriculture." Still, there was a long way to go. Although science had traditionally received little support in Colombia, "the people here are waking up and are thirsty for adopting new methods and ideas of how to do things. This has been specially true in agriculture and I have been surprised to see the interest which my visit here has aroused among both governmental and private spheres." Later in 1929 Chardón got the chance to develop his plans for Colombia's agricultural development before a national audience.[29]

TECHNOCRACY TRIUMPHANT: NATIONAL PROGRAMS OF SCIENCE AND AGRICULTURAL DEVELOPMENT IN COLOMBIA, 1929–1930

After the Mission to the Valle del Cauca had completed its work in July 1929, Chardón traveled to Bogotá. His work in Antioquia and the Valle del Cauca had drawn national attention, both from the Colombian government and from the powerful Colombian Society of Agriculturalists (SAC), which were sympathetic to Chardón's vision. While in Bogotá, Chardón sketched out a national plan for science-based agricultural development that would give agricultural scientists absolute control over the research agenda, independence from partisan politics, and an important role in a new national department of agriculture. Chardón's program appealed to both groups for practical and ideological reasons. By 1929 Colombia was in the midst of a political and fiscal crisis. The ruling Conservative Party was deeply divided; international coffee markets were stagnant and coffee prices were falling; foreign loans had dropped from $75 million to $9 million between 1928 and 1929; and laborers on the coffee plantations organized strikes and protests to gain access to land. The government and the SAC were looking for technical solutions to these fundamentally political problems; Chardón's promotion of agricultural science thus meshed well with their needs.

The SAC, founded in 1904, became a quasi-official organization in 1909, when Ramón González Valencia, a founding member who was a coffee grower from the department of Santander, was elected president of Colombia. During its year in office, González Valencia's government recognized the SAC as an official consulting body on agricultural matters. Although the SAC had close links with the ruling Conservative Party, many of its members were liberals. The society explicitly tried to avoid getting caught up in Colombia's often-divisive partisan politics. Instead, the SAC promoted a technocratic program of agricultural development that emphasized infrastructural and technical improvements rather than ideological conflict. At the same time, however, the society agitated for an "agricultural policy that would favor national agricultural interests." It lobbied the national government for a national ministry of agriculture, which was duly created in 1914. As the SAC had requested, the Ministry of Agriculture began to promote agricultural education, research, and extension programs, including a national school of agriculture in Bogotá. The SAC also gained government support for technical projects such as a livestock census and for a campaign to eradicate tropical anemia (a disease that afflicted many agricultural workers in the lowlands), carried out jointly with the Rockefeller Foundation. It published a journal, the *Revista Nacional de Agricultura,* which dealt extensively with technical issues.[30]

In spite of its attempts to insulate itself from partisan conflicts, the SAC lost much of its political and economic clout during the late 1910s and early 1920s. In 1918 opponents in Colombia's congress tried to shut down the Ministry of Agriculture and the National School of Agriculture, on the grounds that neither body was doing anything useful. The SAC mounted a national publicity campaign that successfully fended off the attack. But Colombia's agriculturalists suffered during the global depression of the early 1920s. They also suffered from the national fiscal and banking reforms passed on the advice of the Kemmerer Missions. The national governments of the mid-1920s devoted most of their attention to urban and industrial issues. In 1924 the government disbanded the Ministry of Agriculture and the following year closed the National School of Agriculture. Reflecting the national government's new priorities, the agricultural portfolio was subsumed into the new Ministry of Industry and Commerce. The agricultural depression had also brought the SAC itself to the edge of bankruptcy.[31]

By the late 1920s, however, Colombia's agricultural economy had recovered. To defend their interests, Colombia's planters began to revitalize and reorganize their associations. In 1927 Colombia's coffee growers organized the Colombian Federation of Coffee Growers (Fedecafé) to promote agricultural modernization in the national coffee industry. Financed by a small tax on coffee exports, Fedecafé devoted itself to all aspects of coffee production, from agricultural research to marketing. Fedecafé operated an experiment station and sent agricultural experts to the main coffee zones to advise growers. It also sent experts to centers for coffee research abroad to study modern methods of coffee agriculture. The SAC, likewise, began once again to call for public support for agricultural science. These calls became more urgent during the late 1920s as laborers migrated from the country to the cities and as clashes between Colombia's tenant farmers and landlords intensified. Agricultural science offered the large planters, in principle at least, the possibility of increasing agricultural production without having to expand the labor force.[32]

By 1929 the national government also showed renewed interest in supporting agricultural research. While Chardón was in Bogotá, he met with Colombia's minister of industry. They discussed a bill to reorganize Colombia's agricultural research and teaching programs. An integral part of this, in Chardón's view, was nationalizing the school of agriculture in Medellín, as a way of separating it from the financial and political turmoil that had bogged down his plan for the school. Chardón proposed that the Colombian government provide half the school's budget and that the minister of industry should also be consulted about the appointment of the rector, "who should be, wherever possible, an agronomist of known competence." The school's rector would be directly accountable to the minister for the budget and research programs, on the understanding that the government would withdraw its funding if the school's academic program was not adequate. The reforms to the school (which Chardón began calling the Medellín Agricultural Experiment Station to emphasize the importance of its research function) reflected the broader reforms envisaged in the bill. The bill had the support of the governor of Antioquia, the minister of industry, and several senators. The president of the senate planned to introduce the bill to the Colombian congress shortly.[33]

While Chardón was in Bogotá, he was invited to address the SAC's annual meeting. The SAC was a sympathetic audience. It had recovered from its brush with bankruptcy in 1924 and the closure of the Ministry of Agriculture that same year. Since then, it had continued to act as a national lobby for agriculture, with an emphasis on technocratic issues such as agricultural teaching and research. In the keynote address to the National Agricultural Congress Chardón sketched out his plan enacting his technocratic vision of agricultural development in Colombia. This speech was actually intended for a larger audience. Its central theme was the importance of depoliticizing agricultural research and giving scientists complete control of the research agenda. In this respect, Chardón's aims were similar to the efforts of state agricultural research scientists in the United States to gain control over their research agendas. U.S. agricultural scientists resented the demands placed on them by local farmers, such as routine soil analysis. They began to achieve this fiscal and intellectual autonomy in the 1890s, when the U.S. government passed the Adams and Hatch Acts, which provided federal funding for state agricultural research. Similarly, Chardón argued that scientists, not politicians or planters, should have the final say in decisions about agricultural research and funding. Research should be undertaken by people with good scientific training and with well-equipped laboratories and reliable financial support. If they could remain distanced from "certain influences," their work would be successful.[34]

Two key organizational elements in Colombia's agricultural modernization were agricultural experiment stations and an extension service. Chardón reaffirmed his conviction that experiment stations were "the nerve-center and brain of agricultural work. From them . . . emerge recommendations and changes which can completely revolutionize a crop and even a country." He stressed that the practical benefits of research might not be immediately obvious. The success of experiment stations was the fruit of long and careful programs of breeding and experimentation. Agricultural research should be funded by governments and agricultural associations since "only they have the resources and the time necessary." Staffing these stations was still a problem, which Chardón traced to the continuing preference for white-collar jobs among Colombia's youth. Governments could help to overcome this problem by offering scholarships to send Colombian students abroad for training. Research results would be disseminated by an agricultural extension service. Demonstration farms and traveling agronomists would teach farmers, who Chardón described as "often conservative and distrustful of scientists." Extension work, for example, could have immediate benefits in the Valle del Cauca, where coffee planting and harvesting techniques were still rudimentary. The farmers there were unaware of the significant innovations in coffee agriculture in the department of Antioquia. In contrast, coffee growers as far away as Puerto Rico had adopted the innovations from Antioquia with enthusiasm.[35]

To coordinate these plans for agricultural development, Chardón proposed that the Colombian government reestablish a separate ministry of agriculture. At the time Colombia's agricultural policies were overseen by a board of agriculture, under the direction of the minister of industry. But Chardón argued that the minister of industry was simply too busy to undertake everything required of him. He suggested that the members of the conference form a committee to write a draft bill for the creation of a national ministry of agriculture. Chardón's proposal was no doubt welcomed by the SAC, which had been deeply unhappy with the closure of the Ministry of Agriculture several years before. It was also welcomed by the Colombian government. A Ministry of Industry article on the diseases of cultivated plants stressed the importance of agricultural research. Among other things, the article called for the formation of agricultural experiment stations and concluded that it was necessary to "introduce scientific teaching and scientific experimentation into our national agriculture." The ministry's interest in science remained explicitly pragmatic: plant pathologists could help combat the diseases that were plaguing many of Colombia's crops. Scientific research would still be expected to deliver practical results quickly.[36]

Several months after Chardón addressed the National Agricultural Congress, the Colombian government invited him to help plan a new ministry of agriculture along the lines he had described. Chardón recommended that the new ministry be organized and operated by the Tropical Plant Research Foundation, the agricultural consulting organization based in Washington, D.C. The TPRF could hire staff with the requisite expertise, and it would ensure that agricultural research remain apolitical. The foundation's board of directors consisted of five scientists representing organizations that did research in the tropics and four businessmen representing businesses with interests in the tropics. The best-known board member was Victor Cutter, president of the United Fruit Company. The foundation had been most active in Cuba but had also advised a number of Latin American governments on organizing agricultural surveys, departments of agriculture, and experiment stations. The TPRF began working on its plan for organizing agricultural research in Colombia in fall 1929.[37]

The memorandum of agreement between the TPRF and the government of Colombia sought to embody Chardón's vision of science-led agricultural development. The agreement emphasized that the foundation's work was to be "primarily research or investigation, and that educational work to extend the result among the farming class will be conducted by another agency of the Government, as will be the regulatory work." The foundation would be responsible for establishing and administering three experiment stations, which would conduct research on "problems of importance to the development of agriculture in Colombia." The foundation was also to make collections of plants, fungi, and soils and deposit the original sets of these collections with Colombian institutions. It would distribute seeds and plants, and it requested authorization to enter into cooperative arrangements with the experiment stations in the Valle del Cauca and Medellín and with the station run by the National Federation of Coffee Growers. Notwithstanding such cooperative arrangements, its principal constituency in Colombia was to be the national government. This way the scientists could set the agendas for agricultural research and education without getting involved in regional politics or tensions. The foundation was to "furnish from time to time for publication in the Spanish language in the official series of the government, special reports dealing with the scientific and practical results of its work." Each year the foundation would draw up a plan of work in consultation with the minister of agriculture. Another central goal of the foundation was to "build up a trained technical personnel of Colombian citizenship as rapidly as possible," although it would "be necessary to appoint foreign specialists to many of the leading positions, particularly at the beginning of the period."[38]

Chardón told Colombia's minister of industry that in the event that a formal agreement was reached, the TPRF had authorized him to take charge of the organization of the experiment stations in Colombia. The minister of industry had also been sounding out Chardón on some other projects, including the reorganization of the agricultural extension work of Fedecafé and agricultural surveys of the departments of Caldas and Antioquia. Chardón replied that he preferred to wait until he found out whether the government would sign the contract with the foundation. If the contract was signed, Chardón hoped to bring all of these projects together under one roof.[39]

Chardón's imminent move to Colombia seemed even more likely after February 1930, when the moderate liberal Dr. Enrique Olaya Herrera was elected president of Colombia. Olaya Herrera won a plurality of the votes after the Conservative Party split into two factions. His election marked the end of the three-decade conservative hegemony in Colombia. Although a liberal, he had long experience working with conservatives and was widely seen as someone who could reconcile the interests of the two parties.

Olaya Herrera knew Chardón and supported his vision of agricultural development. The two had met several times in Washington in 1928, when Chardón was lobbying for disaster relief after a hurricane had struck Puerto Rico. Olaya Herrera had also helped to organize several agricultural programs in the Pan American Union. "With [Olaya Herrera's] election," wrote one Colombian friend of Chardón's, "everything will be definitely assured. My greatest hope is that we will once again see our great Chardón in these lands of struggle and benediction, ideally at the head of the national agricultural services. The end of the sea of illusions is nigh."[40]

Olaya Herrera's Liberal government began to enact moderate reforms in labor, education, and the government. For help with these reforms, he looked to the United States. For most of the 1920s, Olaya Herrera had been Colombia's ambassador to the United States and was eager to deepen ties between the two countries. Between his election in February 1930 and his inauguration in August, Olaya Herrera spent several months in the United States meeting with bankers, economists, and other technical experts. His principal goal was to get U.S. capital flowing back into Colombia. He invited the U.S. economist Walter Kemmerer to organize a second mission to Colombia, to complete the task of reforming Colombia's money and banking systems.[41]

During the months between his election and his inauguration, Olaya Herrera also met with officers from the Tropical Plant Research Foundation, to discuss and finalize the contract between the foundation and the government. In April President-elect Olaya Herrera told Chardón that he wanted to enact the TPRF's proposal and appoint Chardón director. During April and May, the two men met several times with the directors of the Tropical Plant Research Foundation in New York and Washington. By May Chardón reported that the Colombian government and the TPRF were close to a final agreement. Only congressional approval was needed. In the meantime, the TPRF had also done a considerable amount of groundwork in the United States, having secured "cooperation from seventeen universities, colleges, and museums." Chardón believed that "the project, if accepted by [the Colombian congress,] will mark the beginning of an ample program of national production."[42] The Colombian government proposed to give Chardón the chance to establish an agricultural research network that enjoyed complete intellectual and financial autonomy.

CONCLUSION

By early 1930 it appeared that Chardón's technocratic vision of science-led agricultural modernization was gaining popularity in Latin America, as shown by his work in Puerto Rico and Colombia. Regional, national, and international organizations began to sponsor agricultural research. Chardón's program of curricular reform at the Escuela Superior de Agricultura in Medellín eventually won the support of a sympathetic governor, as did his project of agricultural modernization in the Valle del Cauca. Both departments came to accept his idea that scientific research ought to drive agricultural modernization. At the national level, the Colombian government had embarked on plans to institutionalize Chardón's vision in the resurrected Ministry of Agriculture. The planned Graduate School of Tropical Agriculture in Puerto Rico promised to train the experts who would implement science-based agricultural modernization throughout the Americas.

Some problems with this vision lurked just below the surface, however.

Planters were reluctant to cede control of the agendas for agricultural research and teaching to scientists. Although they wanted to rationalize and modernize agriculture, they wanted to retain control over how this would happen. Even where scientists gained a measure of control over the agendas for agricultural teaching and research, they were dependent on the political goodwill and economic well-being of their sponsors. In short, since agricultural research and teaching institutions were government supported, they could never enjoy the complete autonomy the scientists sought.

These tensions were complicated by the economic crises that began to emerge after about 1928—first the collapse of commodity prices and then the onset of the Great Depression. These crises shaped the fate of agricultural research both financially and ideologically. At the financial level, the emergent economic problems made it difficult to raise sufficient funds for agricultural research. On the ideological level, the emergent economic crises began to undermine assumptions about growth that had governed most Latin American economies since independence. For decades, Latin American economies had followed a liberal model of export-led growth, in which domestic economic growth was fueled by exports of primary commodities. During the 1920s, in particular, agricultural science had contributed to this model of development by helping planters to sustain and increase crop yields. By 1930, however, it became evident that the economic crisis was not simply another market fluctuation. Foreign markets for tropical commodities were saturated and the days of free trade were numbered. As Latin America's economic and political leaders looked for new paths for economic growth, agricultural scientists began to search for a role in the new economic order. While technocratic solutions remained popular during the 1930s, the role of agricultural experts would change to reflect the new economic order.

〆

CONCLUSION

The Great Depression, the Plant Sciences, and Changing Paradigms of Agricultural Development, 1928–1940

〆

The logical question is, "what next?" Shall we continue to be indifferent to the protection of our natural resources and our food supplies, the same as we have been in the past? Shall Latin America, with all her baggage of old traditions, culture, and idealistic psychology, continue indifferent to these grave problems, or shall she radically change, and awaken to the necessity of a policy of self-protection and adopt a definite line of research and education in the study of her vital crop problems?

CARLOS CHARDÓN, "THE NEW PAN-AMERICANISM" (1930)

Global markets for tropical commodities had been volatile throughout the 1920s. Prices skyrocketed after World War I, only to be followed by a sharp drop in 1920 and 1921. Most markets recovered during the rest of the decade. This growth was fueled largely by growing demand from the United States, which also became an important source for capital. Loans from U.S. banks during the 1920s financed much of the development in productive infrastructure. Latin American producers continued to increase the volume of exports by increasing the amount of land and labor they used. But during the 1920s, plant scientists helped to increase the productivity of a few key crops, particularly bananas and sugar. The introduction of hybrid canes to Puerto Rico in 1923–1924, for example, had helped to increase its sugar production by almost 20 percent. In spite of the continued volatility in international markets, by the late 1920s most countries in tropical Latin America depended on agricultural exports more heavily than ever.

But global markets were no longer able to absorb the increased production. In several key crops, including coffee and sugar, supply was already exceeding demand even before the depression, pushing global prices for these commodities downward. Between 1923 and 1928, for example, the global price of a pound of sugar dropped from slightly more than 6 cents to 2 cents. Global demand for tropical commodities plummeted further after the stock market crash in October 1929, forcing prices even lower. By 1932 the price for a pound of sugar plummeted to a new low of 0.57 cents. Producers of export crops in Latin America could no longer assume that demand for their products would continue to grow or that the world economy would remain open. The Great Depression, therefore, ended the age of export-led development in Latin America.[1]

The Great Depression and its aftermath transformed ideologies of national development throughout Latin America. The singular focus on export crops that had characterized the export boom was replaced by a much broader focus that included domestic agriculture. The narrow technocratic focus on the biological problems of export crops was, similarly, replaced by broader efforts to rationalize all facets of production. Through the 1930s, then, the plant sciences continued to contribute to national consolidation. But during the early years of the Great Depression, it had seemed possible that the plant sciences might not survive the economic and political turmoil.

THE PLANT SCIENCES IN THE ECONOMIC CRISIS, 1929–1932

In Colombia, the worsening effects of the depression and popular dissatisfaction with Olaya Herrera's government through 1930 and 1931 led to increased political infighting and occasional violence in the countryside. Olaya Herrera tried many strategies to maintain Colombia's fiscal stability through the crisis. One was to cancel federal funding for many departmental projects. In the department of Antioquia, the Escuela Superior de Agricultura de Medellín had scaled back its research and teaching, even though it had just finished a new building and hired six foreign professors. The departmental government of the Valle del Cauca reluctantly reduced funding for the departmental agricultural experiment station. Chardón wrote in protest to Ciro Molina Garces, the department's minister of industry. He argued that it was precisely in moments of agricultural crisis when governments should increase funding for agricultural research, to help agriculture become more efficient. Molina Garces reassured Chardón that in spite of the financial crisis, Carlos Durán Castro, the head of the experiment station, "moves ahead . . . and in the experimental gardens everything has been a success. The look of the farm has been changing people's moods dramatically, and even the firmest unbelievers are now beginning to hold out some hope. It will take more time, but we will continue to move forward."[2]

At the national level, the government put plans to create a new ministry of agriculture on hold. Olaya Herrera's government tried to deal with rapidly expanding agrarian protests and a host of other crises. Furthermore, the Tropical Plant Research Foundation, which was supposed to oversee the Ministry of Agriculture's research program, ran into difficulty. The foundation's dynamic leader, William Orton, died in January 1930. Nonetheless, the foundation's negotiations with the Colombian government continued through the spring and summer. Later that year, however, the foundation's financial position became unstable, as it depended heavily on funding from the U.S. government and American corporations such as the United Fruit Company whose profits were heavily tied to global markets for tropical commodities. Early in 1931 the foundation was forced into bankruptcy, and the agreement Chardón had brokered with the Colombian government fell apart.[3]

Not all institutions for agricultural research and teaching in Colombia suffered as badly during the depression. In 1928 the Colombian Federation of Coffee Growers began to reform and modernize Colombia's coffee industry. The federation, privately managed but publicly financed by a tax on all Colombian coffee exports, organized an experiment station to do basic research on coffee problems. The federation also established seven demonstration farms in the country's most important coffee-growing areas and organized small corps of extension agents. Other innovations included the publication of the *Manual del cafetero colombiano*, a guidebook for coffee agriculture written by the society's head, Mariano Ospina Pérez. Fedecafé maintained funding for agricultural research and extension services through the Great Depression. Its technical programs, coupled with innovations in marketing and agricultural credit, helped Colombia's coffee growers weather the worst of the depression.[4]

In neighboring Venezuela, the Great Depression had a less serious impact on agricultural research, largely because under the dictatorship of Juan Vicente Gómez an agricultural research establishment was virtually nonexistent. By the late 1920s petroleum exports, rather than Venezuela's traditional exports of coffee and cacao, fueled the country's economic growth. The government operated three small stations that did some desultory research and consulting work. A few isolated voices in Venezuela, especially the economist Alberto Adriani, called for the government to organize agricultural experiment stations. In response, the government organized the Ministry of Health, Agriculture, and Livestock to "put the country's agriculture on a scientific basis." Little was accomplished, however. The government also granted several scholarships to agricultural students for study in Puerto Rico. The one active center for plant research in Venezuela was the Commercial and Industrial Museum of the Ministry of Foreign Relations, where the botanist Henri Pittier continued his studies of Venezuela's plants. In 1933, however, he was dismissed from his post after writing a report on the National Observatory that criticized one of Gómez's ministers. All botanical research at the museum ceased when he left. The Venezuelan Society for Natural Sciences tried to have the museum's herbarium transferred to its care so that Pittier could continue his research, but the government refused.[5]

In Costa Rica, the plant sciences had suffered from funding shortages since the early part of the century, so, as in Venezuela, the depression did not change the situation significantly. The decline in coffee prices caused the government to withdraw support from the one major scientific undertaking of the 1920s and 1930s—Paul Standley and Juvenal Valerio's *Flora of Costa Rica*. Valerio, head of Costa Rica's National Museum, had hoped to publish a Spanish-language edition of the flora in Costa Rica. When a new government came to power in 1934, publication was canceled. A government minister suggested to Valerio that he publish the flora with a commercial press. Valerio rejected this option, saying that he "did not want to commercialize scientific research." Eventually, he abandoned plans for the Spanish-language edition altogether, and the flora was published by the Field Museum of Natural History, in English. Apart from that, the National Museum produced little research of value.[6]

In Puerto Rico, falling sugar prices on the global market caused the sugar industry to suffer, but Puerto Rican sugar was not subject to U.S. tariffs. Puerto Rican sugar exports and sugar profits thus increased during the early 1930s. Other agricultural sectors did not fare so well. Hurricanes in 1928 and 1932 destroyed many of Puerto Rico's remaining coffee plantations and also seriously damaged fruit groves. In the same years, food prices increased rapidly while incomes dropped. The USDA experiment station at Mayagüez, which received federal funding, was little affected by these upheavals. Likewise, the insular legislature continued to fund the Insular Experiment Station, although appropriations had to be approved every other year. In contrast, Chardón's project to organize the Graduate School of Tropical Agriculture in Puerto Rico was put on hold indefinitely. Cornell University had undertaken to raise the funds necessary to operate the school, but given the economic situation, Cornell's president, Farrand, was unable to raise the $1 million endowment that he felt was necessary.[7]

Cuba felt the collapse of sugar prices much more strongly than did Puerto Rico. The Great Depression drove sugar prices down and caused global demand for sugar to shrink. Even more damaging was Cuba's diminishing share of the sugar market in the United States, the main consumer of Cuban sugar. Cuba's share of the U.S. sugar market fell from a high of 56 percent in the mid-1920s to 37 percent in 1931. The economic turmoil of the late 1920s and early

1930s was compounded by political turmoil. President Gerardo Machado, elected in 1925, immediately began an attempt to amend the constitution so that he could serve a second term. This generated widespread criticism and protests from many sectors of Cuban society.[8]

The political and economic turmoil was soon felt at the Estación Experimental Agronómica. When Machado appointed several people to the station on the basis of their politics rather than their ability, the station's director, Gonzalo Martínez-Fortún, protested. Machado responded by placing the station under the control of a military supervisor. Martínez-Fortún resigned. Many of the station's other scientists—including Juan Tomas Roig, Julian Acuña, and Stephen Bruner—did not resign but were clearly anti-*machadistas*. In spite of this, the government continued to fund the station. In part, this may have reflected Machado's genuine interest in diversifying Cuba's economy. More important, however, the station served as a vehicle for the rampant political corruption that characterized Machado's regime. The station was yet another place where he could place political appointees. The station's staff was thus divided into pro- and anti-*machadista* camps. The station was consumed by political intrigue, and its scientific activity fell significantly until Machado was deposed in 1933.[9]

Harvard's Atkins Garden at Cienfuegos felt the impact of the depression less than any other station in the region. It remained largely insulated from the crises that plagued Cuba during the early 1930s. When the Atkins Company prospered during the 1920s, Atkins had provided a substantial endowment for the garden. The endowment increased in the 1930s. In 1933 Atkins's widow built a dormitory for Harvard graduate students who were doing research there. In addition to academic research, the station began doing significant work in tropical forestry.[10]

The depression ended most sugar research in Cuba. The Atkins Garden had stopped research into cane breeding in 1929, as they saw no point in duplicating the efforts of the Cuba Sugar Club's experiment station at Baraguá. But, shortly thereafter, even the Cuba Sugar Club abandoned sugar research. Declining sugar prices and the collapse of the Tropical Plant Research Foundation led the Cuba Sugar Club to close the Baraguá experiment station in 1932. At first, the club hoped that this closure would be temporary. They sent the station's botanical collections, research library, and scientific apparatus to Harvard's Atkins Garden in Cienfuegos. Although this material was technically on loan to the Atkins Garden, the club agreed to donate it outright if the Baraguá station did not reestablish operations within three years. Scientists at the Atkins Garden were not particularly interested in taking up sugar research anew. As late as 1936, four years after the Baraguá station had closed, scientists at the Atkins Garden had not bothered to move the collection of canes from

Baraguá to Cienfuegos. From the mid-1930s onward, economic botany at the Atkins Garden focused on domestic food crops rather than export crops.[11]

The economic and political repercussions of the Great Depression were felt by agricultural research institutions throughout the Spanish Caribbean. The depression had brought several institutions to ruin. Those that were closely tied to the rural economy were especially vulnerable, while most nationally or independently financed institutions weathered the crisis more readily. The political uncertainty of the period, particularly in Venezuela, Colombia, and Cuba, also limited the effectiveness of national research institutions. More broadly, the Great Depression undermined the economic paradigm that most tropical research stations had been designed to serve. The liberal paradigm of export-led agricultural development had dominated economic policy in Latin America for the previous half century, but by the early 1930s it had become unsustainable.

The countries of the Spanish Caribbean experienced the Great Depression in different ways, but it became apparent everywhere that the export boom was over. The plant sciences, which had been closely tied to the export model of development, risked becoming irrelevant. In Costa Rica and Venezuela, botanical research became moribund as the national governments seemed to lose any remaining interest in the agricultural sciences they might have had. In other countries, the plant sciences were also in turmoil, and scientists—along with many others—began to search for new models of development.

NEW PARADIGMS OF AGRICULTURAL DEVELOPMENT, 1932–1940

During the 1930s, states began to play a more interventionist, managerial role in the region's economies. They began to pursue "inward-looking" models of economic development, which placed new emphasis on building strong domestic economies and finding local solutions for local problems. Governments throughout the region placed a new emphasis on producing food crops for domestic consumption, to feed the rapidly growing urban areas and reduce dependence on food imports.[12]

The new paradigm for agricultural research was succinctly described in a speech given by U.S. Secretary of Agriculture Arthur Hyde. Speaking to the Inter-American Conference on Agriculture in September 1930, Hyde observed that over the previous decades science had played a crucial role in increasing production. Now, however, "the economic problems of the farm are . . . as important and perplexing as the biological problems." Agricultural science should not be "restricted to the field of production alone—to the mere business of producing two blades of grass where one grew before." Rather, it "should also venture into the field of economics. We have now more reason to help the farmer achieve a successful economic result than we have to help him increase further his crop yields."[13]

The technocratic ideology that had guided agricultural research during the 1920s did not disappear; it evolved to reflect the changing paradigms of agricultural development. During the 1930s, few agricultural scientists continued to try to reduce all of Latin America's agricultural problems to scientific problems, as they had done previously. Instead, they saw science as part of a broader program of rationalizing all facets of agriculture. Reflecting these changes, agricultural extension programs became more important in the 1930s. Basic crop research might no longer be central to agricultural development, but it still had an important role. As before, however, plant scientists continued to pursue regular and stable funding and to insulate their institutions from partisan politics.

There was a clear consensus among Latin America's leaders that the agricultural sciences had an essential role to play in this economic and ideological transformation. Governments expected that agricultural and botanical research institutions would help to rationalize all facets of agricultural production. One priority for most governments in the Spanish Caribbean was to build a locally trained community of agricultural experts. Before the depression, they had hired either foreign scientists or local scientists who had trained abroad. Most of the centers for agricultural research that had been established between 1880 and 1930 placed little emphasis on teaching. Because they were affiliated with government departments or agricultural associations, they focused more narrowly on questions of research and production. Before 1930, therefore, it was difficult for people in the Spanish Caribbean to study the plant sciences locally. After 1930, however, teaching assumed new importance as the control of many agricultural experiment stations was shifted from government departments to universities.

Chardón's career in Puerto Rico illustrates this shifting ideology. Late in 1930 he left Puerto Rico's Department of Agriculture and Labor after he was appointed chancellor of the University of Puerto Rico. He immediately began lobbying the island's legislature to transfer the Insular Experiment Station and the Extension Service from the Department of Agriculture and Labor to the university, where he hoped they could be distanced from political infighting. Earlier in 1930, the U.S. Congress had voted to extend the federal Hatch, Adams, Purnell, and Smith-Lever funds for agricultural research and education to Puerto Rico. This move, to take effect in July 1932, aimed to put the Insular Experiment Station on the same footing as state experiment stations on the mainland. It would no longer have to depend on ad hoc appropriations from the insular legislature. But at first the legislature refused to ratify the federal acts. Chardón speculated that this was because the transfer "tended to separate both [the Insular Experiment Station and the Extension Service] from political influence. Naturally, the legislature decided it was best to keep them in the Department of Agriculture where they might be within easy grasp of political interference." In March 1933, however, the legislature relented and voted to accept the funds. In November the Insular Experiment Station became "the Agricultural Experiment Station of the College of Agriculture of the University of Puerto Rico."[14]

Government officials in both Puerto Rico and the United States saw agricultural science as an integral part of the New Deal plans for Puerto Rico's reconstruction. Again, Chardón was at the center of these projects. In 1934 he was appointed to the Puerto Rico Policy Commission, charged with writing a report on economic conditions on the island. Confronted with shrinking foreign markets for sugar and with growing poverty and social unrest on the island, Chardón and his colleagues produced the Plan Chardón, which outlined a series of reforms aimed at reducing the island's dependency on sugar and diversifying its agriculture and industry. Many of its recommendations, such as the rehabilitation of the island's coffee, tobacco, and citrus fruit industries, would require technical expertise in order to be implemented. Other projects requiring technical knowledge were the development of new products from the island's existing crops, such as a fuel based on alcohol derived from sugar.[15]

The federal government approved the broad outlines of the Plan Chardón, but implementing it proved difficult. Chardón was appointed to head the Puerto Rican operations of the Puerto Rican Reconstruction Agency (PRRA), the New Deal organization charged with implementing the recommendations of his report. The PRRA took steps to rehabilitate the island's coffee and fruit agriculture, including the organization of a model coffee farm. It also promoted conservation programs to prevent deforestation and soil erosion. But many of its plans for agricultural rationalization foundered on the shoals of political infighting between the PRRA's Puerto Rican and North American members, between the PRRA and the sugar companies, and within Puerto Rico's legislature. Late in 1935 Chardón was fired from the PRRA and went into self-imposed exile.[16]

The USDA's experiment station at Mayagüez also began revising its research agendas and policies during the early 1930s. The key impetus to change was Rexford Tugwell, an undersecretary of the USDA who had supported Chardón's programs for agricultural reform. Tugwell argued that the benefits of the New Deal should also be extended to Puerto Rico. "As a result of [Tugwell's] suggestions," wrote the station's director, "the agricultural situation has been reviewed not only with the economic reconstruction of Puerto Rico in view, but also with the purpose of exploring the means by which a tropical station such as this may best serve the Department of Agriculture, and agriculture in the continental United States as a whole."[17]

A priority of the Plan Chardón was to revive the island's coffee industry. This had also been a major part of the station's research agenda during the 1900s and 1910s, although coffee research there had slackened during the 1920s. In the 1930s the station renewed its research into coffee. Puerto Rico's export market never recovered, but production for the domestic market remained constant through the 1920s and 1930s. The station also began to act as a consulting center for other countries in tropical Latin America. For example, in 1939 the director of the Mayagüez station was detailed as an agricultural adviser to the government of Haiti. The main agenda of this consulting work was to "point out mutual advantage in developing crops complimentary to, rather than competitive with, the agriculture of the continental United States."[18]

In Cuba, the government made little headway in promoting agricultural reform during the 1930s, even though its sugar industry was in dire straits. Shortly after Carlos Mendieta assumed the presidency in 1934, he convened the Commission on Cuban Affairs to assess the results of Cuba's recent political and economic turmoil and to formulate plans for the future. The commission concluded that "the most important task before Cuba is to develop nonsugar crops to take the place once held by sugar, develop further sustenance farming to support the country population during the dead season, and create an agricultural middle class."[19] Science was to play an important role in these changes. Among other things, the report recommended "the promotion of agricultural research and education," with the goal of agricultural diversification, and a soil survey, "initiated with the assistance of foreign surveyors, for the purpose of providing a scientific basis for diversified agriculture, forestry, and dairying; and for the development of independently owned small farms."[20] Under this plan agriculture would remain the basis of Cuba's economy, but the new goal was to develop other export crops and to develop small-scale farming to meet Cuba's internal needs.

Political conflicts prevented most of these reforms from being enacted. Widespread corruption and bitter partisan struggles continued under Mendieta's presidency. Gonzalo Martínez-Fortún, who had resigned as director of the Estación Experimental Agronómica in protest over Machado's interference, was reappointed in 1934. In April 1934 the government fired thirty of the station's employees and replaced them with political appointees. In protest, Martínez-Fortún and several of the station's leading scientists resigned. The government relented and rehired the original employees. In 1935, however, many of these same employees were fired again, after having participated in a general strike against President Batista. The constant political struggles and turnover in staff made it difficult for the station to accomplish much meaningful research in the 1930s.[21]

Not even Harvard's Atkins Garden could remain wholly isolated from Cuban politics. When strikes against President Machado broke out in August 1933, eight hundred employees of Atkins's Soledad sugar company—including employees of the garden—"gathered around the office . . . armed with firearms or large sticks." The garden's supervisor wrote, "They were in no mood to be refused their demands and as the Company could not rely on the army Mr. Leonard [the mill's manager] thought it advisable to agree to their terms." The strikers were unsure about how to deal with the garden. At first, they threatened to damage it, presumably to harm the sugar company's interests. By the end of September, strike organizers permitted the garden's staff to return to work (albeit at the higher wage rate they demanded) but continued to prohibit laborers at the sugar mill from returning to work.[22] After 1934 the government of Carlos Mendieta enacted laws that altered the shape of the garden's labor force. Cubans and foreigners in each wage category had to be paid equally, and the "50 percent" law required that at least half the workers in every place of employment be Cuban and that all vacancies be filled by Cubans.[23]

Gradually, both Cubans and North Americans began to see the garden as a private institution working in the public interest. As the Cuban highway system was improved during the 1930s, the garden began to receive more visitors—including government officials—from within Cuba. It also continued to exchange plants with Cuban scientists and institutions. For example, the 1939 report notes that "as part of its service to Cuban horticulture and botany, 442 living plants, 113 packages of cuttings, and 456 packages of seeds were distributed during the year, while 67 packages of cuttings and 556 packages of seeds were received." During the 1930s, the garden distributed tree seedlings and other plants "to be planted out on abandoned pasturelands or cane fields." The Cuban Commission commended the garden for its work in forestry. It was particularly impressed with the garden's experiments with mahogany trees, some of which had grown thirty feet in four years. These small accomplishments, however, did little to relieve Cuba's agricultural crisis. In the absence of substantial government support, there was little that could be accomplished.[24]

In Colombia, the governments of Enrique Olaya Herrera and Alfonso López Pumarejo also sought technocratic solutions to the country's serious economic problems. Both governments were confronted with growing peasant unrest and violence in the countryside, particularly over issues of land tenure. During the 1930s, the national government came to play an increasingly important role in addressing Colombia's rural problems. In addition to pursuing legal and political solutions, the government began to promote technical innovations in agriculture as a way of improving economic well-being.

Agricultural scientists were appointed to important positions in both administrations. Olaya Herrera's government appointed Carlos Durán Castro, former head of the Palmira experiment station in the Valle del Cauca, to head the national Department of Agriculture and Livestock, then still a division of the Ministry of Industry. Notwithstanding the economic turmoil in 1931, Olaya Herrera's government also passed Law 132, whose purpose was to commit the Colombian government to developing a national program for agricultural research. In December the government created the National Agricultural Council to help define national goals for agricultural research, teaching, and extension. The council's central goal was to increase Colombia's agricultural production over a broad range of crops rather than focus on export crops alone.[25]

In Colombia, as in Puerto Rico, government programs of agricultural modernization began to emphasize the welfare of the population as a whole rather than simply the welfare of the small elite who produced export crops. In the early 1930s Colombia began a program of reducing food imports and trying to meet its own agricultural needs. Durán Castro argued that it had succeeded in doing so over the short term because of tariff protections, good weather, and a large supply of cheap labor. Still, he found Colombia's agriculture deficient and called for traditional agriculture to be replaced with "the rational exploitation of the soil and other natural products, for the common welfare and the personal prosperity of working men." The basis of this transformation was the "adoption of modern technology and agricultural economics." Among the organizations that could help to bring about this transformation were "experimental stations and demonstration farms, practical schools of agriculture, and extension services." Durán Castro promised that the farmers who knew how to take advantage of the "progress of humanity with respect to agriculture and modernize their enterprises would gain significant advantages and would take the country to a level of development in which not even the vagaries of import policies could harm the national economy."[26]

López Pumarejo promoted even farther-reaching technocratic reforms. He enacted a program of reform and public works known as the *revolución en marcha*, similar to the New Deal in the United States. As part of these reforms, two of Chardón's institutional projects were nationalized. One was the Valle del Cauca's experiment station at Palmira. The experiment station's sugar research program, one of the main emphases of Chardón's efforts, had been particularly successful in introducing new hybrids to the Valle del Cauca and stemming the spread of the mosaic disease in the region. After the station was

nationalized, its research mission expanded to include research projects ranging from corn to cacao to livestock.[27]

López Pumarejo's government also nationalized the Escuela Superior de
Agricultura de Medellín, whose reorganization had presented so many challenges to Chardón. Educational reform was one of the government's top
priorities. During the four years of his administration, López Pumarejo quadrupled the budget for education. He devoted special attention to the reorganization of the National University. He hoped that the reformed university
would have a practical emphasis, training Colombians who would help the
country modernize. As part of these reforms, the Escuela Superior de Agricultura de Medellín became the National University's Faculty of Agriculture.[28]

Agricultural research and teaching in Venezuela followed a similar path
after the long-awaited death of the dictator Juan Vicente Gómez in December
1935. The government of his successor, General Eleazar López Contreras, began a series of initiatives to modernize the country in a number of different
realms. López Contreras's "February Program" announced a series of sweep-
ing government reforms just two months after Gómez's death. The speed with
which the February Program was announced suggests that it had been in the
works for some time. The February Program decreed the founding of a number of agricultural institutions, including the Ministry of Agriculture and Livestock (Ministerio de Agricultura y Cría), faculties of agronomy and veterinary
science at the Central University, and a series of experiment stations. Henri
Pittier was named head of the ministry's newly formed Botanical Service.[29]

Over the longer term, then, the paradigms of development that emerged
during the 1930s defined a new role for the plant sciences in the Spanish Caribbean. The narrowly technocratic paradigm of the export boom was replaced
by a much broader technocratic paradigm. During the export boom, scientists
had tried to redefine agricultural problems as biological problems, which in
turn had a technical solution. This vision, as embodied by Chardón's work in
the 1920s, had gained some support in Puerto Rico and elsewhere in the Spanish Caribbean. The new technocratic vision of the 1930s saw the plant sciences
as one part of a much broader strategy of rationalizing agricultural society and
agricultural production. The transfer of government centers of agricultural research from ministries of agriculture to universities in Colombia, Venezuela,
and Puerto Rico symbolizes this changing paradigm.

SCIENCE, NATURE, AND THE STATE

The central achievement of the plant sciences before the depression was, for
better or worse, a physical and cognitive reorganization of tropical nature,

both agricultural landscapes and wild landscapes. The physical reorganization of nature on the basis of modern scientific principles—the naturalization of commodities—was most evident in the sugar industry in Cuba and Puerto Rico. The introduction of hybrid cane varieties and the control of diseases greatly increased the productivity of the sugarcane industry in the short term. Disease research emphasized the complicated and delicate relations among the organisms, soil, and climate of agricultural ecosystems. Pittier's ecological studies of the coffee industry in Venezuela and Puerto Rico in the mid-1920s emphasized the role of humans as agents in the ecosystem, whose impact was far greater and more subtle than coffee planters had suspected. Colombia's attention to the botanical aspects of coffee production contributed to the resilience of its coffee industry during the depression. The science of ecology gave planters the tools to manipulate their agricultural systems in entirely new ways. In the sugar industry, scientific agriculture was so successful that it contributed to the crisis of overproduction of the late 1920s and the global decline in sugar prices.

The intellectual and commercial commodification of wild nature transformed the way scientists, agricultural elites, and policy makers understood nature. The national floras provided new cognitive maps of the republics and their plant resources. For farmers, businessmen, and governments, the floras were guidebooks to economic potential. The publication of Pittier's *Manual de las plantas usuales de Venezuela* in 1926 sparked some commercial interest in Venezuelan timber. The Venezuelan economist Alberto Adriani, first as a critic and later as minister of agriculture, used the *Manual* when proposing agricultural and conservation measures. Floras also had important implications for scientists. For example, they opened new possibilities for the study of plant distribution. Much collection and research remained to be done. Although the floras published in Latin America before World War II were the first truly national floras, the forests and savannas of the tropics still contained tens of thousands of species unknown to science. The early floras were a starting point and a framework for further research.

The commodification of wild nature also revealed the extent of the destruction caused by the liberal model of development. National floras were intellectual and practical benchmarks with which to measure the rapidly changing natural world in the Spanish Caribbean and so provided the scientific foundation for conservation movements in later decades. For example, the *Primitiae Florae Costaricensis*, the *Ensayo sobre las plantas usuales de Costa Rica*, and the *Flora of Costa Rica* gave Costa Rican nature a conservation value. As early as the 1930s, botanists collecting in the same areas as their predecessors noticed that Costa Rica's rich and varied flora was disappearing. Pittier first commented on environmental destruction in his 1908 essay on the common plants of Costa Rica. He sharply criticized the "lack of interest shown concerning forest conservation by successive legislatures of the country." He feared that the destruction of the forests would lead to "lack of potable water, deterioration of the climate, soil erosion, and the sterilization and annihilation of the productive forces of the land." While Pittier cast his criticism of environmental destruction in utilitarian terms, later botanists couched theirs in more ecological terms.[30]

By the 1930s it was almost commonplace for botanical collectors to comment on the loss of plants. The North American botanists working in Costa Rica saw this mainly as an inconvenience, an impediment to collecting. Paul Standley commented briefly on the deforestation and destruction of plants in the *tierra templada,* particularly in the Meseta Central around the capital city of San José. Similarly, a young American naturalist named Alexander Skutch commented that the countryside around San José was "quite 'peeled,' like all the *meseta central,* and not at all promising for either plants or birds." This environmental destruction alarmed Costa Rican naturalists more than it did their North American counterparts. Rare species of plants and animals were disappearing at a rate that alarmed Manuel Valerio, director of Costa Rica's National Museum. To prevent further losses, Valerio called for official measures to protect rare species: "In the scientific world Costa Rica is famous as a country rich in flora and fauna. There is an enormous quantity of specimens exported, and there is a lot of money in the commerce of birds, plants, and insects. Our forests and mountains are being depopulated of orchids, woods, and birds."[31] In the following decades, naturalists were among the first advocates for governments to adopt policies of conservation. The changing state of nature began to shape the nature of the state in new ways. Rather than frame opportunities, as it had done for most of the export boom, it now determined limits.

NOTES

INTRODUCTION

1. For a comprehensive listing of agricultural research centers in tropical Latin America during the late 1930s, see "Plant Science Institutions, Stations, Museums, Gardens, Societies, and Commissions in Central and South America," in *Plants and Plant Science in Latin America,* edited by Frans Verdoorn (Waltham, Mass.: Chronica Botanica, 1945), 337–349.

2. Two succinct discussions of the liberal era in Latin America are Steven C. Topik and Allen Wells, "Introduction: Latin America's Response to the Export Boom," in *The Second Conquest of Latin America: Coffee, Henequen, and Oil during the Export Boom, 1850–1930,* edited by Steven C. Topik and Allen Wells (Austin: University of Texas Press, 1998), 1–36; and Frank R. Safford, Politics, Ideology, and Society," in *Spanish America after Independence, c. 1820–c. 1870,* edited by Leslie Bethell (Cambridge: Cambridge University Press, 1987), esp. 85–86. On railroads and liberalism, see A. Kim Clark, *The Redemptive Work: Railway and Nation in Ecuador, 1895–1930* (Wilmington, Del.: Scholarly Resources, 1998). On the practical implications of liberal ideologies for coffee planters, see William Roseberry, introduction to *Coffee, Society, and Power in Latin America,* edited by William Roseberry, Lowell Gudmundson, and Mario Samper Kutschbach (Baltimore: Johns Hopkins University Press, 1995), esp. 27–29.

3. John Soluri stresses the importance of understanding the biological dimension of agriculture in "Landscape and Livelihood: An Agroecological History of Export Banana Growing in Honduras, 1870–1975" (Ph.D. dissertation, University of Michigan, 1998), and in "Plants, People, and Pathogens: The Eco-social Dynamics of Export Banana Production in Honduras, 1875–1950," *Hispanic American Historical Review* 80, no. 3 (2000): 463–501. On agriculture as an environmental process, see also Lawrence Grossman, *The Political Ecology of Bananas: Peasants, Contract Farming, and Agrarian Change in the Eastern Caribbean* (Chapel Hill: University of North Carolina Press, 1998).

4. I have adapted this notion of the "republic of rational agriculture" from Steven Palmer: "Central American Encounters with Rockefeller Public Health, 1914–1921," in *Close Encounters of Empire: Writing the Cultural History of U.S.–Latin American Rela-*

tions, edited by Gilbert M. Joseph, Catherine C. LeGrand, and Ricardo D. Salvatore (Durham: Duke University Press, 1998), 311–332.

5. For a detailed discussion of the model of export-led growth, see Victor Bulmer-Thomas, *The Economic History of Latin America since Independence* (Cambridge: Cambridge University Press, 1994), 15–17, 50–57.

6. Elinor G. K. Melville, *A Plague of Sheep: Environmental Consequences of the Conquest of Mexico* (Cambridge: Cambridge University Press, 1984); Warren Dean, *With Broadax and Firebrand: The Destruction of the Brazilian Atlantic Forest* (Berkeley: University of California Press, 1995); Warren Dean, "The Green Wave of Coffee: Beginnings of Agricultural Research in Brazil (1885–1900)," *Hispanic American Historical Review* 69 (1989): 91–115.

7. See Richard Drayton, *Nature's Government: Science, Imperial Britain, and the "Improvement" of the World* (New Haven: Yale University Press, 2000); and Richard Grove, *Green Imperialism: Colonial Expansion, Tropical Island Edens, and the Origins of Environmentalism, 1600–1860* (Cambridge: Cambridge University Press, 1995). Many of the major debates in the history of science and imperialism are outlined in Paolo Palladino and Michael Worboys, "Science and Imperialism," *Isis* 84 (1993): 91–102; and Lewis Pyenson, "Cultural Imperialism and the Exact Sciences Revisited," *Isis* 84 (1993): 103–108.

8. For new insights on the cultural history of U.S.–Latin American relations, see Joseph, LeGrand, and Salvatore, *Close Encounters of Empire;* Louis A. Pérez, *On Becoming Cuban: Identity, Nationality, and Culture* (Chapel Hill: University of North Carolina Press, 1999); and Thomas F. O'Brien, *The Revolutionary Mission: American Enterprise in Latin America, 1900–1945* (Cambridge: Cambridge University Press, 1996). These scientific institutions are "contact zones," analytically similar to the region Catherine LeGrand describes in "Living in Macondo: Economy and Culture in a United Fruit Company Banana Enclave in Colombia," in Joseph, LeGrand, and Salvatore, *Close Encounters of Empire,* 333–368.

I briefly discuss the idea of creole science in "Creole Science in Costa Rica," *Endeavour* 23 (1999): 118–120. For examples of other works that take the approach I describe here as "creole science," see Hebe M. C. Vessuri, "Foreign Scientists, the Rockefeller Foundation, and the Origins of Agricultural Science in Venezuela," *Minerva* 23 (Autumn 1994): 267–296; and Palmer, "Central American Encounters with Rockefeller Public Health." Even when formal bonds of empire existed, imperial interests did not alway dominate. See William Kelleher Storey's excellent study of sugar scientists in the British colony of Mauritius, *Science and Power in Colonial Mauritius* (Rochester: University of Rochester Press, 1997).

Venezuelan scholars have produced a substantial body of literature that explores the history of science in Latin America from a national perspective. See, for example, Marcel Roche, ed., *Perfil de la ciencia en Venezuela,* 2 vols. (Caracas: Fundación Polar, 1996), and Hebe M. C. Vessuri, *Las instituciones científicas en la historia de la ciencia en Venezuela* (Caracas: Fondo Editorial Acta Científica Venezolana, 1991).

9. Recently historians have published pathbreaking studies on the environmental history of the export boom. See Warren Dean's *Brazil and the Struggle for Rubber: A Study in Environmental History* (Cambridge: Cambridge University Press, 1987) and "The Green Wave of Coffee." On the banana industry in Central America, see Soluri,

"People, Plants, and Pathogens," and "Landscape and Livelihood"; and Steve Marquardt, "'Green Havoc': Panama Disease, Environmental Change, and Labor Process in the Central American Banana Industry," *American Historical Review* 106 (2001): 49–80. On the environmental history of Cuba during the early years of the export boom, see Reinaldo Funes Monzote, "Los conflictos por el aceso a la madera en la Habana: Hacendados vs. marina (1774–1815)," in *Diez miradas de historia de Cuba,* edited by José Antonio Piqueras (Castellón: Universidad Jaume I, 1998), 67–90.

10. Roseberry, introduction to *Coffee, Society, and Power in Latin America.* Vincent Peloso and Barbara Tenenbaum, introduction to *Liberals, Politics, and Power: State Formation in Nineteenth-Century Latin America,* edited by Vincent Peloso and Barbara Tenenbaum (Athens: University of Georgia Press, 1996), 6–7. Frank R. Safford, "Politics, Ideology, and Society," in Bethell, *Spanish America after Independence,* esp. 85–86. Clark, *The Redemptive Work.*

11. For an annotated list of Latin American floras, see S. F. Blake and Alice C. Atwood, *Geographical Guide to Floras of the World,* United States Department of Agriculture, Miscellaneous Publication No. 401 (Washington, D.C.: GPO, 1942), 224–261; on constructing representations of Latin America, see Ricardo D. Salvatore, "The Enterprise of Knowledge: Representational Machines of Informal Empire," in Gilbert, LeGrand, and Salvatore, *Close Encounters of Empire,* 69–104. On changing trends in botany and natural history, see Peter J. Bowler, *The Norton History of the Environmental Sciences* (New York: W. W. Norton, 1992), chap. 8. On the role of science in imagining the modern nation, see Benedict Anderson, *Imagined Communities: Reflections on the Origin and Spread of Nationalism,* rev. and expanded ed. (London: Verso, 1991); and James C. Scott, *Seeing Like a State: How Certain Schemes to Improve the Human Condition Have Failed* (New Haven: Yale University Press, 1998).

12. On "modern" landscapes in Latin America, see Soluri, "Landscape and Livelihood." On the environmental impact of forest clearances in nineteenth-century Brazil, see Stanley Stein, *Vassouras: A Brazilian Coffee County* (Cambridge, Mass.: Harvard University Press, 1957). For a firsthand account of recent forest clearances in Costa Rica, see Darryl Cole-Christensen, *A Place in the Rain Forest: Settling the Costa Rican Frontier* (Austin: University of Texas Press, 1997).

CHAPTER 1

1. Gonzalo Fernández de Oviedo y Valdés, *History of the Indies* (1541), cited in Paul Allen, *The Rain Forests of Golfo Dulce* (Gainesville: University of Florida Press, 1956), xi.

2. These three factors are adapted from J. H. Galloway, "Tradition and Innovation in the American Sugar Industry, c. 1500–1800: An Explanation," *Annals of the Association of American Geographers* 75 (1985): 334–351. On the role of maps, censuses, museums, and the state, see Benedict Anderson, *Imagined Communities: Reflections on the Origin and Spread of Nationalism,* rev. and expanded ed. (London: Verso, 1991), chap. 10; and James C. Scott, *Seeing Like a State: How Certain Schemes to Improve the Human Condition Have Failed* (New Haven: Yale University Press, 1998), esp. chap. 1.

3. James Lockhart and Stuart B. Schwartz, *Early Latin America: A History of Colonial Spanish America and Brazil* (Cambridge: Cambridge University Press, 1983), 341–

344. Sophie D. Coe and Michael D. Coe, *The True History of Chocolate* (London: Thames and Hudson, 1996), 189–193. J. L. Salcedo-Bastardo, *Historia fundamental de Venezuela*, 10th ed. (Caracas: Universidad Central de Venezuela, Ediciones de la Biblioteca, 1993), 133–140; Louis A. Pérez, *Cuba: Between Reform and Revolution*, Latin American Histories (New York: Oxford University Press, 1988), 60–61; Hugh Thomas, *Cuba, or, The Pursuit of Freedom* (New York: Da Capo Press, 1998), chaps. 4, 5.

4. Manuel Lucena Giraldo, *Laboratorio tropical: La expedición de límites al Orinoco, 1750–1767* (Caracas: Monte Avila Editores, 1993); Francisco Javier Puerto Sarmiento, *La ilusión quebrada: Botánica, sanidad, y política científica en la España ilustrada* (Madrid: CSIC, 1988).

5. Arthur Robert Steele, *Flowers for the King: The Expedition of Ruíz and Pavón and the Flora of Peru* (Durham: Duke University Press, 1964); Lilia Díaz, "El Jardín Botánico de Nueva España y la obra de Sessé según documentos mexicanos," *Historia Mexicana* 27 (July–September 1977): 49–78; Patricia Aceves Pastrana, "Las políticas botánicas metropolitanas en los virreynatos de la Nueva España y del Perú," in *Mundalización de la ciencia y cultura nacional*, edited by A. Lafuente, A. Elena, and M. L. Ortega (Madrid: Doce Calles, 1993), 287–298; and F. J. Puerto Sarmiento and A. González Bueno, "Política científica y expediciones botánicas en el programa colonial español ilustrado," in Lafuente, Elena, and Ortega, *Mundalización de la ciencia*, 331–340.

In 1928, for example, the Colombian congress passed a bill to "obtain originals or copies of the iconography and other materials of the Botanical Expedition of Bogotá, which are found in [the] Madrid [Botanical Garden]." They sent the botanist Enrique Pérez Arbeláez to Madrid to review the collections that same year. Enrique Pérez Arbeláez, "La expedición botánica colombiana," *Boletín de Agricultura* (Bogotá) 3 (June 1930): 528–537. Some of the collections were not published until the 1950s. For example, volumes 3 and 4 of the eighteenth-century *Flora of Peru* were finally published in 1957 and 1958. On these delays, and the weakness of Spanish botany in the early nineteenth century, see Jean-Pierre Clement, "De los nombres de plantas," *Revista de Indias* 47 (1987): 501–512. This entire issue (vol. 47, no. 180) of the *Revista de Indias* is devoted to the eighteenth-century scientific expeditions to the Americas.

6. Manuel Lucena Giraldo, "Los experimentos agrícolas en la Guayana española," in Lafuente, Elena, and Ortega, *Mundalización de la ciencia y cultura nacional*, 251–258; Yajaira Freites, "De la colonia a la república oligárquica (1498–1870)," in *Perfil de la ciencia en Venezuela*, edited by Marcel Roche (Caracas: Fundación Polar, 1996), 1: 49–50. On the Intendencia, the Consulado, and reforms in late-eighteenth-century Venezuela, see John V. Lombardi, *Venezuela: The Search for Order, the Dream of Progress* (Oxford: Oxford University Press, 1982), 104–115.

7. Yajaira Freites, "El problema del saber entre hacendados y comerciantes ilustrados en la provincia de Caracas-Venezuela (1793–1810)," *Dynamis* 17 (1997): 165–191; Pedro Grases, ed., *Memoria sobre el café y el cacao* (1809; reprint, Caracas: Academia Nacional de la Historia, 1983).

8. Susan Faye Cannon describes the "Humboldtean sciences" in *Science and Culture: The Early Victorian Period* (New York: Dawson and Science History Publications, 1978), chap. 3; Peter J. Bowler gives a general overview of Humboldt's influence on the environmental sciences in *The Norton History of the Environmental Sciences* (New York: W. W. Norton, 1992). Janet Browne discusses Humboldt, plants, and nations in *The*

Secular Ark: Studies in the History of Biogeography (New Haven: Yale University Press, 1983), chap. 2.

9. Thomas F. Glick, "Science and Independence in Latin America (with Special Reference to New Granada)," *Hispanic American Historical Review* 71 (1991): 307–334. See also David Wade Chambers, "Period and Process in Colonial and National Science," in *Scientific Colonialism: A Cross-Cultural Comparison*, edited by Nathan Reingold and Marc Rothenberg (Washington, D.C.: Smithsonian Institution Press, 1987); and José Luis Peset, *Ciencia y libertad: El papel del científico ante la Independencia americana* (Madrid: CSIC, 1987). On Spain, see Juan Vernet Gines, *Historia de la ciencia española* (Madrid: Instituto de España, 1975), 220–221.

10. Tulio Halperín Donghi, "Economy and Society," in *Spanish America after Independence, c. 1820 – c. 1870*, edited by Leslie Bethell (Cambridge: Cambridge University Press, 1987), 1–47. See also Tulio Halperín Donghi, *The Contemporary History of Latin America* (Durham: Duke University Press, 1993), 87.

11. Robert Jones Shafer, *The Economic Societies in the Spanish World, 1763–1821* (Syracuse: Syracuse University Press, 1958), 247, 311; Pedro Grases, ed., *Sociedad Económica de Amigos del País, memorias y estudios* (Caracas: Banco Central de Venezuela, 1958).

12. Grases, *Memorias de la Sociedad Económica*, 64, 66. For a similar case from North America, see Suzanne Zeller, *Inventing Canada: Early Victorian Science and the Idea of a Transcontinental Nation* (Toronto: University of Toronto Press, 1987).

13. Yolanda Texera Arnal, *La exploración botánica en Venezuela, 1754–1950* (Caracas: Fondo Editorial Acta Científica Venezolana, 1991), 41–42; Freites, "De la colonia a la república oligárquica," 1:74–76.

14. José Alvarez Conde, *Historia de la botánica en Cuba* (Havana: Publicaciones de la Junta Nacional de Arqueología y Etnología, 1958), 64–66, 74–92; Hermano León, *Flora de Cuba* (Havana: Cultural, 1946), 15.

15. Ramón de la Sagra, *Flora cubana* (Paris, 1863), reprinted in Alvarez Conde, *Historia de la botánica en Cuba*, 80.

16. For a vivid account of Darwin's years in South America, see Janet Browne, *Voyaging*, vol. 1 of *Charles Darwin: A Biography* (Princeton: Princeton University Press, 1995).

17. Thomas Belt, *The Naturalist in Nicaragua* (1874; reprint, Chicago: University of Chicago Press, 1985); W. B. Hemsley, *Biologia Centrali-Americana* (London, 1879–1888); Ignatius Urban, *Symbolae Antillanae* (Berlin, 1898–1928).

18. For a general overview of the period, see the introduction to *The Second Conquest of Latin America: Coffee, Henequen, and Oil during the Export Boom, 1850–1930*, edited by Steven C. Topik and Allen Wells (Austin: University of Texas Press, 1998).

19. For a broad structural account of the age of "outward-looking nationalism," see Claudio Veliz, *The Centralist Tradition of Latin America* (Princeton: Princeton University Press, 1980). For fine-grained analyses of nineteenth-century ideas of development that discuss the role of science and technology in some detail, see Frank R. Safford, *The Ideal of the Practical: Colombia's Struggle to Form a Technical Elite* (Austin: University of Texas Press, 1976); and Paul Gootenberg, *Imagining Development: Economic Ideas in Peru's "Fictitious Prosperity" of Guano, 1840–1880* (Berkeley: University of California Press, 1993).

20. Data on Cuban sugar production from Appendix 13 of Thomas, *Cuba, or, The Pursuit of Freedom*, 1574–1578. Data on land use in Puerto Rico is from James L. Dietz, *Economic History of Puerto Rico: Institutional Change and Capitalist Development* (Princeton: Princeton University Press, 1986), 19–20, table 1.3. On Central America, see Ciro Cardoso, "The Liberal Era, c. 1870–1930," in *Central America since Independence*, edited by Leslie Bethell (Cambridge: Cambridge University Press, 1991), 37–67.

21. Victor Bulmer-Thomas, *The Economic History of Latin America since Independence* (Cambridge: Cambridge University Press, 1994), 68–72; Thomas, *Cuba, or, The Pursuit of Freedom*, 316–338, 1574.

22. I give a more detailed account of the environmental history of tropical Latin American crop diseases in chapter 4. For a classic overview of crop diseases, see E. C. Large, *The Advance of the Fungi* (London: Jonathan Cape, 1940). Although Large's dramatic title is reminiscent of a B movie, the book is an elegant and serious study of the history of mycology. For more recent studies of plant diseases and plant pathology, see Gail L. Schumann, *Plant Diseases: Their Biology and Social Impact* (St. Paul, Minn.: American Phytopathological Society, 1991); and George Agrios, *Plant Pathology*, 4th ed. (San Diego: Academic Press, 1997). On the *alhorra*, see Robert J. Ferry, "Encomienda, African Slavery, and Agriculture in Seventeenth-Century Caracas," *Hispanic American Historical Review* 61 (1981): 624–625.

23. On Brazil, see Stanley J. Stein, *Vassouras: A Brazilian Coffee County, 1850–1900* (1958; reprint, Princeton: Princeton University Press, 1985), esp. chaps. 9, 11; and Warren Dean, *With Broadax and Firebrand: The Destruction of the Brazilian Atlantic Forest* (Berkeley: University of California Press, 1995), chap. 8. On the closing agricultural frontiers, see Bulmer-Thomas, *The Economic History of Latin America*, 71; and Cardoso, "The Liberal Period," 46–47.

24. David Ruiz Chastaing Z., "El afán de la modernidad: La agricultura en el pensamiento económico venezolano del siglo XIX," *Boletín de la Academia Nacional de la Historia* 81 (1998): 27–49; Thomas, *Cuba, or, The Pursuit of Freedom*, 186; Cardoso, "The Liberal Era," 47–48.

25. Alvaro Reynoso, *Ensayo sobre la caña de azúcar*, 4th ed., rev. and enl. (Havana: Talleres Tipográficos de "El magazine de la raza," 1925). Reynoso's experience is similar to that of the Austrian agronomist Whilhelm Dafert in São Paulo, Brazil. See Warren Dean, "The Green Wave of Coffee: Beginnings of Agricultural Research in Brazil (1885–1900)," *Hispanic American Historical Review* 69 (1989): 91–115.

26. Reynoso, *Ensayo sobre la caña de azúcar*; Alan Dye, *Cuban Sugar in the Age of Mass Production: Technology and the Economics of the Sugar Central, 1899–1929* (Stanford: Stanford University Press, 1998), chap. 8; Fe Iglesias García, "Changes in Cane Cultivation in Cuba, 1860–1900," *Social and Economic Studies* 37 (1988): 341–363.

27. Lawrence Busch and Carolyn Sachs, "The Agricultural Sciences and the Modern World System," in *Science and Agricultural Development*, edited by Lawrence Busch (Totowa, N.J.: Allanheld, Osmun, 1981), 132–138, table 6.1.

28. Busch and Sachs, "The Agricultural Sciences and the Modern World," 133–137. José Ramón Abad, *Puerto Rico en la Feria-Exposición de Ponce en 1882* (Ponce: Establecimiento Tipográfico "El Comercio," 1885), 201–202. Edmundo D. Colón, *Datos sobre la agricultura en Puerto Rico antes de 1898* (San Juan: Tipográfico Cantero, Fernández & Co., 1930), 122–125.

CHAPTER 2

1. Ricardo D. Salvatore describes the three-step process of collection, classification, and representation in "The Enterprise of Knowledge: Representational Machines of Informal Empire," in *Close Encounters of Empire: Writing the Cultural History of U.S.–Latin American Relations,* edited by Gilbert M. Joseph, Catherine C. LeGrand, and Ricardo D. Salvatore (Durham: Duke University Press, 1998), 69–104.

2. Most of these floras are listed in S. F. Blake and Alice C. Atwood, *Geographical Guide to Floras of the World,* United States Department of Agriculture, Miscellaneous Publication No. 401 (Washington, D.C.: GPO, 1942). On the commodities boom and export-led growth, see Victor Bulmer-Thomas, *The Economic History of Latin America since Independence* (Cambridge: Cambridge University Press, 1994); and Steven Topik and Allen Wells, *The Second Conquest of Latin America: Coffee, Henequen, and Oil during the Export Boom, 1850–1930* (Austin: University of Texas Press, 1998).

3. For a more comprehensive list of the essential elements of a flora, see Blake and Atwood, *Geographical Guide to Floras of the World,* 8–9. On science, nature, and nation, see James C. Scott's "Taming Nature, an Agriculture of Legibility and Sensibility," chap. 8 of his *Seeing Like a State: How Certain Schemes to Improve the Human Condition Have Failed* (New Haven: Yale University Press, 1998). On the role of surveys in imagining the nation, see Benedict Anderson, *Imagined Communities: Reflections on the Origin and Spread of Nationalism,* rev. and expanded ed. (London: Verso, 1991), chap. 10. On state building in Latin America, see David A. Brading, "Nationalism and State-building in Latin American History," *Ibero-Amerikanisches Archiv* 20 (1994): 83–108. Natural history surveys played a similar role in nation building in North America. See Suzanne Zeller's superb work, *Inventing Canada: Early Victorian Science and the Idea of a Transcontinental Nation* (Toronto: University of Toronto Press, 1987); and Erik Kaufmann, "Naturalizing the Nation: The Rise of Naturalistic Nationalism in the United States and Canada," *Comparative Studies in Society and History* 40 (1998): 666–695.

4. Hector Pérez-Brignoli, *A Brief History of Central America* (Berkeley: University of California Press, 1989), 91–92; L. D. Gómez and J. M. Savage, "Searchers on That Rich Coast: Costa Rican Field Biology, 1400–1980," in *Costa Rican Natural History,* edited by Daniel H. Janzen (Chicago: University of Chicago Press, 1983), 1–11; Marshall Eakin, "The Origins of Modern Science in Costa Rica: The Instituto Físico-Geográfico Nacional, 1887–1904," *Latin American Research Review* 34 (1999): 123–150; Stuart McCook, "Creole Science in Costa Rica," *Endeavour* 23 (1999): 118–120; Sterling Evans, *The Green Republic: A Conservation History of Costa Rica* (Austin: University of Texas Press, 1999), chap. 1.

5. For a nuanced discussion of the role of foreign resident scientists in Latin America, see Hebe M. C. Vessuri, "Foreign Scientists, the Rockefeller Foundation, and the Origins of Agricultural Science in Venezuela," *Minerva* 23 (Autumn 1994): 267–296.

6. Henri Pittier, *Ensayo sobre las plantas usuales de Costa Rica* (Washington, D.C.: H. L. and J. B. McQueen, 1908), 1–11; Eakin, "Origins of Science in Costa Rica," 136–138.

7. Henri Pittier, *Primitiae Florae Costaricensis,* vol. 2, pt. 1 (San José: Tipografía Nacional, 1897), 5–6. Originally published in *Anales del Instituto Físico-Geográfico Nacional* 8 (1895).

8. Luis D. Gómez P., "Contribuciones a la Pteridología Costarricense XI: Hermann Christ, su vida, obra, e influencia en la botánica nacional," *Brenesia* 12–13 (1977): 25–79.

9. Carlos Wercklé, *La subregión fitogeográfica costarricense* (San José, C.R.: Sociedad Nacional de Agricultura, 1909), 16, 5. See also Luis Diego Gómez P., "Contribuciones a la Pteridología Costarricense XII: Carlos Wercklé," *Brenesia* 14–15 (1978): 361–393.

10. Eakin, "Origins of Science in Costa Rica," 135, 138.

11. Pittier, *Plantas usuales de Costa Rica*, 9.

12. Pittier, *Plantas usuales de Costa Rica*, 72, 168.

13. Pittier, *Plantas usuales de Costa Rica*, 55–59.

14. Pittier, "Apuntes sobre identificación de productos naturales y organización de museos en la América tropical," *Boletín Comercial e Industrial del Ministerio de Relaciones Exteriores de Venezuela* 5 (30 September 1924): 273.

15. Eakin, "Origins of Modern Science in Costa Rica," 135–136, 143–147. See also McCook, "Creole Science in Costa Rica."

16. Historians of Venezuela have had a long fascination with the Gómez regime. See Emilio Pacheco, *De Castro a López Contreras: Proceso social de la Venezuela contemporanea (contribución a su estudio en los años 1900–1941)* (Caracas: Editorial Domingo Fuentes, 1984); Manuel Caballero, *Gómez, el tirano liberal (vida y muerte del siglo XIX)* (Caracas: Monte Avila Editores and Banco Maracaibo, 1993). For a general discussion of science during the Gómez dictatorship, see Yajaira Freites, "La ciencia en la época del gomecismo," *Quipu* 4 (May–August 1987): 213–251. This essay has been extensively revised and updated in her essay "Auge y caída de la ciencia nacional: La época del gomecismo (1908–1935)," in *Perfil de la ciencia en Venezuela*, edited by Marcel Roche (Caracas: Fundación Polar, 1996), 1:153–198.

17. Yolanda Texera Arnal, *Exploración botánica en Venezuela, 1754–1950* (Caracas: Fondo Editorial Acta Científica Venezolana, 1991), chap. 4.
The best work on the history of botany in Venezuela is Texera Arnal's *Exploración botánica en Venezuela*. Chapters 1–3 cover the period before 1900. See also Yolanda Texera Arnal, "Testigos de historia: Viajeros y naturalistas en Venezuela durante el siglo XIX," *Anuario de Estudios Americanos* 51 (1994): 189–198; and Yolanda Texera Arnal, "El discubrimiento del trópico: La expedición del Williams College a Venezuela en 1867," *Asclepio* 46 (1994): 197–217. For an early review of the history of botanical exploration in Venezuela, see Henri Pittier, "Investigación de la flora de Venezuela y estado actual de nuestros conocimientos acerca de ella," in his *Manual de las plantas usuales de Venezuela* (Caracas, 1926; 3d printing, with additional essays, Caracas: Fundación Eugenio Mendoza, 1978).

18. Pittier to Maxon, 17 November 1920; Pittier to Maxon, 17 January 1921, Record Unit 223, United States National Museum, Division of Plants, 1899–1947, Records, Box 8 (hereafter cited as Division of Plants Records), Smithsonian Institution Archives, Washington, D.C. (hereafter SIA).

19. Pittier, "Apuntes sobre identificación de productos naturales y organización de museos en la América tropical," 273–280.

20. Like Pittier, many scientists in Latin America feared that their labors might be lost. See, for example, Susan Sheets-Pyenson's descriptions of the Argentinian natural

history museums in Buenos Aires and La Plata in *Cathedrals of Science: The Development of Colonial Natural History Museums during the Late Nineteenth Century* (Kingston and Montreal: McGill-Queen's University Press, 1988).

21. Henri Pittier, "Botánicos nacionales," *Boletín Científico y Técnico del Museo Comercial de Venezuela* 1 (1927): 46–47.

22. Henri Pittier, *Exploraciones, botánicas y otras, en la cuenca de Maracaibo* (1922), reprinted in *Trabajos escogidos* (Caracas: Ministerio de Agricultura y Cría, 1947), 46–47; Pittier to Maxon, 31 March 1922, SIA, Record Unit 305, Registrar, 1834–1958, Box 443 (hereafter Smithsonian Registrar); 25 December 1922, Smithsonian Registrar; 19 October 1922, 7 November 1922, 7 December 1922 (Division of Plants Records).

23. Henry A. Gleason, "The Scientific Work of Nathaniel Lord Britton," *Proceedings of the American Philosophical Society* 104 (1960): 222. For a brief biography of Britton with a comprehensive bibliography of his publications, see E. D. Merrill, "Biographical Memoir of Nathaniel Lord Britton, 1859–1934," *Biographical Memoirs of the National Academy of Sciences* 19 (1938): 147–202. The competition for Venezuelan plants is described in detail in the correspondence between Henry Pittier and the Smithsonian curator W. R. Maxon in the Henri Pittier Collection, Archives of the Botanical Garden of Caracas.

24. Texera Arnal, *Exploración botánica en Venezuela*, 146–150. For a contemporary Venezuelan vision of the growing role of the United States in Venezuela, see Alberto Adriani, "Capital estadounidense en América Latina," in *Labor Venezolanista*, 2d ed. (Caracas: Tip. Garrido, 1946), 155–160.

25. Texera Arnal, *Exploración botánica en Venezuela*, chap. 1; Pittier to Maxon, 28 May 1921; Maxon to Pittier, 17 June 1921, Division of Plants Records, SIA; Pittier to Rose, 18 December 1925, Pittier Papers, Jardín Botánico de Caracas, Venezuela (hereafter PP-JBC).

26. Gleason, "The Scientific Work of Nathaniel Lord Britton," 208–215.

27. Pittier to Maxon, 22 September 1920, Division of Plants Records, SIA; Henri Pittier, preface to the *Manual de las plantas usuales de Venezuela* (Caracas, 1926), xiii.

28. Pittier to Maxon, 28 May 1921; Maxon to Pittier, 17 June 1921, Division of Plants Records, SIA; Pittier to Rose, 18 December 1925, PP-JBC.

29. Pittier to Gil Borges, 19 June 1925, PP-JBC.

30. Many of these articles have been reproduced in Yolanda Texera, ed., *La modernización difícil: Henri Pittier en Venezuela, 1920–1950* (Caracas: Fundación Polar, 1998).

31. Henri Pittier, *Esbozo de las formaciones vegetales de Venezuela con una breve reseña de los productos naturales y agrícolas* (Caracas: Litografía El Comercio, 1920), reprinted in Texera Arnal, *La modernización difícil*. Pittier to Maxon, 22 September 1920; Pittier to Maxon, 31 October 1920, Division of Plants Records, SIA.

32. Pittier to Gil Borges, 19 June 1925, PP-JBC.

33. Alamo to Pittier, 10 September 1925; Alamo to Pittier, 28 September 1925, PP-JBC.

34. Pittier, *Manual de plantas usuales de Venezuela*, xiii.

35. Lisandro Alvarado, prologue to the *Manual de las plantas usuales de Venezuela*, x–xi.

36. Pittier, *Manual de las plantas usuales de Venezuela*, s.v. "Café," "Caña de azúcar."

37. Pittier to Gil Borges, 7 March 1927, PP-JBC.

38. On Gómez's lack of interest in export agriculture, see William Roseberry, *Coffee and Capitalism in the Venezuelan Andes* (Texas: University of Texas Press, 1983).

39. On the connections between the agricultural export economy and the fate of scientific institutions in Costa Rica, see Eakin, "The Origins of Modern Science in Costa Rica." On the decline of the sciences in Venezuela during the 1920s, see Freites, "Auge y caída de la ciencia nacional," 178–181.

CHAPTER 3

1. On the United States as a model for modernization in Cuba, see Louis A. Pérez's eloquent *On Becoming Cuban: Identity, Nationality, and Culture* (Chapel Hill: University of North Carolina Press, 1999). The United States also played a similar role in Puerto Rico, although U.S. interests arguably were more directly involved in shaping Puerto Rican's economy and public institutions. For a comparative case of how U.S. models of research and development became creolized elsewhere in the Spanish Caribbean, see Steven Palmer, "Central American Encounters with Rockefeller Public Health," in *Close Encounters of Empire: Writing the Cultural History of U.S.–Latin American Relations,* edited by Gilbert M. Joseph, Catherine C. LeGrand, and Ricardo D. Salvatore (Durham: Duke University Press, 1998), 311–332.

2. Louis A. Pérez, *Cuba under the Platt Amendment, 1902–1934* (Pittsburgh: University of Pittsburgh Press, 1986), 62–72.

3. Franklin S. Earle, *Primer informe anual de la Estación Central Agronómica de Cuba, 1 de Abril 1904–30 de Junio 1905* (Havana: Imprenta "Universal," 1906), 5; Rafael Martínez Viera, *70 años de la Estación Experimental Agronómica de Santiago de las Vegas* (Havana: Academia de Ciencias de Cuba, 1977), 7–19; Louis A. Pérez, *Cuba: Between Reform and Revolution,* Latin American Histories (New York: Oxford University Press, 1988), 189–195.

4. Earle, *Primer informe,* 8–11.

5. Earle, *Primer informe,* 20, 32; Franklin S. Earle, "Botany at the Cuban Experiment Station," *Science* 20 (30 September 1904), 444–445.

6. Estación Central Agronómica, *Second Report* (30 June 1905–11 January 1909) (English ed.) (pt. 1), 18–20.

7. Earle, *Primer informe,* 12–13.

8. Estación Experimental Agronómica, *Tercer informe anual* (Febrero de 1909–30 de Julio de 1914 (Havana, 1915); Pérez, *Cuba under the Platt Amendment,* 89–94.

9. Estación Experimental Agronómica, *Tercer informe anual;* Martínez Viera, *70 años de la Estación Experimental,* 10–13; F. S. Earle, "Science and Politics in Cuba," *Science,* n.s. 29 (26 March 1909), 501; Pérez, *Cuba under the Platt Amendment,* 123–125; 125–128; 139–143.

10. Estación Experimental Agronómica, *Tercer informe anual;* Martínez Viera, *70 años de la Estación Experimental,* 10–13.

11. Cuba, Presidente [1909–1913], *Memoria de la Administración del Presidente de la República de Cuba, Mayor General José Miguel Gómez, durante el periodo comprendiendo entre el 1 de enero y el 31 de diciembre de 1912* (hereafter *Memoria del Presidente*)

(Havana, 1913), 333–345; Cuba, Presidente [1913–1921], *Memoria del Presidente* (Havana, 1915), 419–425, 442–448.

12. The exact date of Sánchez Agromonte's charge to Calvino is unclear, but it probably dates to sometime in 1917. Mario Calvino to Secretary of Agriculture and Commerce, 2 January 1919; reprinted in Estación Experimental Agronómica, *Informe de 1917–1918 de la Estación Experimental Agronómica* (Havana, 1919), 3.

13. Estación Experimental Agronómica, *Informe de 1917–1918*, 25–28.

14. Estación Experimental Agronómica, *Informe de 1917–1918*, 30–31.

15. Mario Calvino to Secretary of Agriculture and Commerce, 2 January 1919, 3–5; See also Martínez Viera, *70 años de la Estación Experimental*, 26.

16. Tirso Sáenz and Emilio G. Capote, *Ciencia y tecnología en Cuba: Antecedentes y desarrollo* (Havana: Editorial de Ciencias Sociales, 1989).

17. Leland Hamilton Jenks, *Our Cuban Colony: A Study in Sugar*, Studies in American Imperialism (New York: Vanguard Press, 1928), chap. 3, esp. 34–35.

18. Edwin F. Atkins, *Sixty Years in Cuba: Reminiscences of Edwin F. Atkins* (Cambridge, Mass.: Riverside Press, 1926), 67, 88.

19. Atkins, *Sixty Years in Cuba*, 331; Robert Grey, *Report of the Harvard Botanical Gardens, Soledad Estate, Cienfuegos, Cuba (Atkins Foundation), 1900–1926* (Cambridge, Mass.: Harvard University Press, 1927), 7–8.

20. There are several sources for the history of the garden at Soledad, most of which are vague on how the station came into existence. The best account is that of Grey, in *Report of the Harvard Botanical Gardens*, 3–14. Three other useful, although superficial, sources are David Fairchild, "The Soledad Garden and Arboretum: The Harvard Biological Institute in Cuba (Atkins Foundation) on Soledad Estate," *Journal of Heredity* 15 (1924): 451–461; Thomas Barbour, "The Harvard Garden in Cuba," *Bulletin of the Pan American Union* 70 (August 1936): 631–638; and Modesto Martínez, "The Botanical Garden of the University of Harvard," Botanic Garden in Cuba, Director's Correspondence, Harvard University Archives, Pusey Library, Cambridge, Mass. Permission courtesy the Harvard University Archives. Passing references to the garden can also be found in Atkins, *Sixty Years in Cuba*; Oakes Ames, in *Harvard University Annual Report* (1906): 230–234; Oakes Ames, *Jottings of a Harvard Botanist, 1874–1950* (Cambridge, Mass.: Botanical Museum of Harvard University, 1979), and Thomas Barbour, *A Naturalist in Cuba* (Boston: Little, Brown, 1945), 83.

21. Grey, *Report*, 3–6.

22. Grey, *Report*, 9.

23. Grey, *Report*, 10–11.

24. Ames to Hunnewell, 9 December 1919, folder 367, A. Lawrence Lowell Presidential Records, 1919–1922, Harvard University Archives, Pusey Library, Cambridge, Mass.

25. Atkins, *Sixty Years in Cuba*, 332.

26. Atkins, *Sixty Years in Cuba*, 332; Barbour, "The Harvard Garden in Cuba," 632–633.

27. Barbour, "The Harvard Garden in Cuba," 632–633.

28. Barbour, *A Naturalist in Cuba*, 89; Barbour, "The Harvard Garden in Cuba," 632–633; Memorandum to the Harvard Committee in Charge of the Botanic Garden and Laboratory at Soledad, 3/2/25, manuscripts folder, Director's Correspondence, Botanic Garden in Cuba, Harvard University Archives.

29. "Tropical Plant Research Foundation," *Bulletin of the Pan American Union* 59 (January 1925): 33; F. S. Earle, "An Institution for Tropical Research," *Science*, n.s. 52 (15 October 1920): 363–365; Fernandus Payne, "A History of the National Research Council 1919–1933: VII. Division of Biology and Agriculture," *Science*, n.s. 78 (4 August 1933): 93–95.

30. "Tropical Plant Research Foundation," 35–37.

31. "Tropical Plant Research Foundation," 35–37.

32. W. A. Orton, "Report on Work for the Cuban Sugar Club for the Fiscal Year Ending June 30, 1925," file "Statements, Memoranda, and Correspondence," Tropical Plant Research Foundation Collection, New York Botanical Garden, Bronx, N.Y.

33. "The Tropical Plant Research Foundation," *Bulletin of the Pan American Union* 61 (December 1927): 1230.

34. W. A. Orton, "Memorandum to the Harvard Committee in Charge of the Botanic Garden and Laboratory at Soledad," 3/2/25, Folder 'manuscripts,' Director's Correspondence, "Botanic Garden in Cuba," Harvard University Archives.

35. D. L. Van Dine, "The Harvard Seedlings," Tropical Plant Research Foundation Collection, New York Botanical Garden.

36. On the role of Cuban professional and technical staff at U.S.-owned sugar mills, see Pérez, *On Becoming Cuban*, 232–233.

37. W. A. Orton, introduction to F. S. Earle, *Sugar Cane Varieties in Cuba*, Foundation Information Letters, no. 6 (Washington, D.C.: Tropical Plant Research Foundation, 1925). A copy of this letter can be found in the Archives of the New York Botanical Garden, under the heading "Tropical Plant Research Foundation," folder "Statements, Memoranda, and Correspondence." For the Puerto Rican case, see Laird W. Bergad, "Agrarian History of Puerto Rico, 1870–1930," *Latin American Research Review* 13 (1978): 80.

38. Tropical Plant Research Foundation, *Plan of Work on Moth Stalkborer*, Foundation Information Letters, no. 10 (Washington, D.C.: Tropical Plant Research Foundation, 1926) and *Plan of Work on Sugar Cane Mosaic*, Foundation Information Letters, no. 11 (Washington, D.C.: Tropical Plant Research Foundation, 1926).

39. Richard A. Overfield, "The Agricultural Experiment Station and Americanization: The Hawaiian Experience, 1900–1910," *Agricultural History* 60 (Spring 1986): 256–260. Emily S. Rosenberg, *Spreading the American Dream: American Economic and Cultural Expansion, 1890–1945* (New York: Hill and Wang, 1982), 38–48.

40. James Wilson, "Report of the Secretary," *Yearbook of the United States Department of Agriculture* (hereafter *USDA Yearbook*), 1899 (Washington, D.C.: GPO, 1899), 3.

41. Roy Stone, "Agriculture in Puerto Rico," *USDA Yearbook*, 1898 (Washington, D.C.: GPO, 1898), 512. For other early government reports on Puerto Rico, see also *Congressional Record*, 70th Cong., 1st sess., vol. 69, no. 97; Henry K. Carroll, *Report on the Island of Porto Rico* (Washington, D.C.: GPO, 1899).

42. Stone, "Agriculture in Puerto Rico," 512–513.

43. Seaman A. Knapp, *Agricultural Resources and Capabilities of Puerto Rico*, House of Representatives, 56th Cong., 2d sess., 1900, vol. 43, no. 4117, Doc. No. 171, 2–3.

44. Knapp, *Agricultural Resources and Capabilities of Puerto Rico*, 30–32.

45. Knapp, *Agricultural Resources and Capabilities of Puerto Rico*, 30–32.

46. Richard A. Overfield, "Science Follows the Flag: The Office of Experiment Stations and American Expansion," *Agricultural History* 64 (Spring 1990): 31–34; Overfield, "The Agricultural Experiment Station and Americanization."

47. Frank D. Gardner, *La Estación de Experimentos Agriculturales de Puerto Rico, su establecimiento, sitio, y propósito*, Estación de Experimentos Agriculturales de Puerto Rico Bulletin no. 1 (1903), 10; Porto Rico Agricultural Experiment Station, *Annual Report* (1902), 331–333.

48. Gardner, *La Estación de Experimentos*, 13–14.

49. *USDA Yearbook* (1905), 116.

50. Edmundo D. Colón, *La gestión agrícola después de 1898* (San Juan, 1948), 107.

51. Colón, *La gestión agrícola*, 110.

52. PRAES, *Annual Report* (1902), 355; *Annual Report* (1906), 5; *Annual Report* (1909), 8.

53. PRAES, *Annual Report* (1915), 9.

54. PRAES, *Annual Report* (1922), 2–3.

55. See the *USDA Yearbook* (1908): 137–138; (1909): 140; (1910): 145; (1911): 141; PRAES, *Annual Report* (1905), 8–9.

56. *USDA Yearbook* (1912): 105, 219–220; PRAES, *Annual Report* (1907), 10–11; *Annual Report* (1920).

57. PRAES, *Annual Report* (1902), 354–355

58. PRAES, *Annual Report* (1905), 8, 9–10.

59. PRAES, *Annual Report* (1908), 10–12; *Annual Report* (1910), 8.

60. PRAES, *Annual Report* (1919), 5–7.

61. PRAES, *Annual Report* (1921), 1–2; *Annual Report* (1924), 2–3.

62. *Report of the Porto Rico Agricultural Experiment Station* (Washington, D.C.: GPO, 1923), 3.

63. Melville Thurston Cook and José I. Otero, *History of the First Quarter of a Century of the Agricultural Experiment Station at Río Piedras, Puerto Rico*, University of Puerto Rico Agricultural Experiment Station Bulletin 44 (Río Piedras: Bureau of Supplies, Printing and Transportation, 1937), 4–6, 13–15, 58; Rafael Sacarello, "La historia del Departamento de Agricultura y Comercio," *Revista de Agricultura de Puerto Rico* (October–December 1941), 501.

64. "Report of the Commissioner of Agriculture and Labor," Appendix 9 of *Report of the Governor of Porto Rico to the Secretary of War, 1919* (Washington, D.C.: GPO, 1919), 685; Cook and Otero, *History of the Experiment Station at Río Piedras*, 3–5.

65. "Report of the Commissioner of Agriculture and Labor," *Report of the Governor, 1921* (1922), 472.

66. Victor S. Clark, ed., *Porto Rico and Its Problems* (Washington, D.C.: Brookings Institution, 1930), 481.

67. "Report of the Commissioner of Agriculture and Labor," in *Report of the Governor of Puerto Rico to the Secretary of War* (Washington, D.C.: GPO, 1917), 545–549 (hereafter *Report of the Governor*); "Report of the Commissioner of Agriculture and Labor," *Report of the Governor* (1919), 698; "Report of the Commissioner of Agriculture and Labor," *Report of the Governor, 1923* (1924), 212. For a more detailed discussion of the struggle against the "mottling" disease, see chap. 4.

68. Cook and Otero, *History of the Experiment Station,* 23.

69. "Report of the Commissioner of Agriculture and Labor," *Report of the Governor, 1922* (1923), 456–457.

70. "Report of the Commissioner of Agriculture and Labor," *Report of the Governor, 1924* (1925), 586.

71. Sacarello, "La historia del Departamento de Agricultura y Comercio," 501–505.

CHAPTER 4

1. W. V. Tower, "Report of the Director," *Annual Report of the Director of the Insular Experiment Station of Porto Rico, 1916–1917* (San Juan, 1917), 9 (hereafter *Ann. Rep. Ins. Exp. Stn., 1916–1917*).

2. John A. Stevenson, "La enfermedad nueva de la caña," *Revista de Agricultura de Puerto Rico* 1 (April–May 1918): 18.

3. John A. Stevenson, "An Epiphytotic of Cane Disease in Puerto Rico," *Phytopathology* 7 (1917): 419.

4. John A. Stevenson, "The 'Mottling' Disease of Cane," *Ann. Rep. Ins. Expt. Stn., 1916–1917,* 40–41, 63–65.

5. George N. Agrios, *Plant Pathology,* 4th ed. (San Diego: Academic Press, 1997), 45; 153–158. See also Frederick L. Wellman, *Tropical American Plant Disease (Neotropical Phytopathology Problems)* (Metuchen, N.J.: Scarecrow Press, 1972).

6. E. C. Large, *The Advance of the Fungi* (London: Jonathan Cape, 1940), 240. Emphasis in the original.

7. This notion of the social construction of susceptibility (or vulnerability) draws on recent literature on the anthropology of disasters. See Anthony Oliver-Smith and Susanna Hoffman, eds., *The Angry Earth: Disaster in Anthropological Perspective* (New York: Routledge, 1999). On the interaction between global economic forces and local agricultural environments in the late twentieth century, see Lawrence S. Grossman, *The Political Ecology of Bananas: Peasants, Contract Farming, and Agrarian Change in the Eastern Caribbean* (Chapel Hill: University of North Carolina Press, 1998).

8. G. C. Stevenson, *Genetics and Breeding of Sugar Cane* (London: Longmans, 1965), 41; Franklin Earle, *Sugar Cane and Its Culture* (New York: John Wiley, 1928), 3–4; Manuel Moreno Fraginals, *El ingenio: Complejo económico social cubano del azúcar* (Havana: Editorial de Ciencias Sociales, 1978), 2:178.

9. Cesar Ayala, *The American Sugar Kingdom: The Plantation Economy of the Spanish Caribbean, 1898–1934* (Chapel Hill: University of North Carolina Press, 1999), 137–138; J. H. Galloway, *The Sugar Cane Industry: An Historical Geography from Its Origins to 1914* (Cambridge: Cambridge University Press, 1989), chap. 6; J. H. Galloway, "Tradition and Innovation in the American Sugar Industry, ca. 1500–1800: An Explanation," *Annals of the American Association of Geographers* 75 (1985): 334–351.

10. Stevenson, *Genetics and Breeding of Sugar Cane,* 13–14; Carlos Grivot Grand Court, Agustín Stahl, and José Julian Acosta, *Información sobre las diversas clases de caña sacarina introducidas en Puerto Rico* (Mayagüez, 1878), reprinted in *Boletín Historico de Puerto Rico* 8 (1921): 56–63; Jonathan D. Sauer, *Historical Geography of Crop Plants, a Select Roster* (Boca Raton, Fla.: CRC Press, 1993), 243; Earle, *Sugar Cane and*

Its Culture, 5. For a detailed study of sugarcane agriculture in a colonial context, see William Kelleher Storey, *Science and Power in Colonial Mauritius* (Rochester: University of Rochester Press, 1997).

11. Galloway, *The Sugar Cane Industry*, 96; Moreno Fraginals, *El ingenio*, 1:178; Francisco A. Scarano, *Sugar and Slavery in Puerto Rico: The Plantation Economy of Ponce, 1800–1850* (Madison: University of Wisconsin Press, 1984), 103; Franklin S. Earle, "Sugar Cane Varieties of Porto Rico, II," *Journal of the Department of Agriculture of Puerto Rico* 5 (July 1921): 7.

12. Galloway, *The Sugar Cane Industry*, 102.

13. Data on agricultural yields of Cuban sugar is taken from Ayala, *American Sugar Kingdom*, 137–138.

14. Quoted in Edmundo D. Colón's *Datos sobre la agricultura de Puerto Rico antes de 1898* (San Juan: Tipográfico Cantero, Fernández & Co., 1930), 203. On interpretations of the degeneration of sugar, see Melville Thurston Cook, *The Diseases of Tropical Plants* (London: Macmillan, 1913), 5–9.

15. Earle, "Sugar-Cane Varieties, II," 6–8.

16. A. C. Barnes, *The Sugar Cane*, 2d ed. (Aylesbury: Leonard Hill Books, 1974), 34–37.

17. Barnes, *The Sugar Cane*, 306; Galloway, *The Sugar Cane Industry*, 141; Stevenson, *Genetics and Breeding of Sugar Cane*, 18, 42;

18. Stevenson, *Genetics and Breeding of Sugar Cane*, 42–43; Moreno Fraginals, *El ingenio*, 1:179; Earle, "Sugar Cane Varieties, II," 8; Earle, *Sugar Cane and Its Culture*, 63–65.

19. Earle, *Sugar Cane and Its Culture*, 6, 7.

20. Claude W. Edgerton, *Sugarcane and Its Diseases* (Baton Rouge: Louisiana State University Press, 1955), 159–166; Stevenson, *Genetics and Breeding of Sugar Cane*, 48; Barnes, *The Sugar Cane*, 325.

21. J. H. Galloway, "Botany in the Service of Empire: The Barbados Cane-breeding Program and the Revival of the Caribbean Sugar Industry, 1880s–1930s," *Annals of the Association of American Geographers* 86 (1996): 682–708; Stevenson, *Genetics and Breeding of Sugar Cane*, chap. 2; Earle, *Sugar Cane and Its Culture*, 11. C. J. J. van Hall, "On Agricultural Research and Extension Work in the Netherland's Indies," in *Science in the Netherlands East Indies*, edited by L. M. R. Rutten (Amsterdam: Koninklijke Academie van Wetenshappen, 1930); E. W. Brandes and G. B. Sartoris, "Sugarcane: Its Origin and Improvement," *USDA Yearbook of Agriculture* (Washington, D.C.: GPO, 1936), 561–623.

22. Galloway, "Botany in the Service of Empire," 692–695. For descriptions of sugar research in Hawaii and Louisiana, see John W. Vandercook, *King Cane: The Story of Sugar in Hawaii* (New York: Harper & Brothers, 1939), esp. chap. 11; and John Alfred Heitmann, *The Modernization of the Louisiana Sugar Industry, 1830–1910* (Baton Rouge: Louisiana State University Press, 1987). Hybrids produced at the Java station were given the prefix P.O.J. (*Proef-Station Oost-Java*). Other common prefixes for hybrid canes were B.H. (Barbados Hybrid); S.C. (Santa Cruz, Virgin Islands); H (Hawaii); and D (Demerara, British Guyana).

23. "Report of the Commissioner of Agriculture and Labor," *Report of the Governor of Porto Rico, 1917* (Washington, D.C., 1917), 546.

24. Stevenson, "La enfermedad nueva de la caña," 21.

25. Stevenson, "La enfermedad nueva de la caña," 22–23.

26. Melville Thurston Cook, "Franklin Sumner Earle," *Revista de Agricultura de Puerto Rico* 23 (July 1929): 4; *American Men of Science*, 7th ed., s.v. "Matz, Julius"; Julius Matz, "Últimos desarrollos en la patología de la caña de azúcar," in *Varios trabajos (presentados en la réunion de productores y profesionales azucareros celebrada en Río Piedras el 17 de noviembre de 1920)*, Estación Experimental Insular Circular, no. 33 (San Juan: Negociado de Materiales, Imprenta, y Transporte, 1920), 17.

27. Edgerton, *Sugarcane and Its Diseases*, 176–192; Stevenson, *Genetics and Breeding of Sugar Cane*, 43, 144–146.

28. Edgerton, *Sugarcane and Its Diseases*, 176–192; Stevenson, *Genetics and Breeding of Sugar Cane*, 145. On the spatial division of Puerto Rican–owned and U.S.-owned sugar *centrales* in Puerto Rico, see Ayala, *American Sugar Kingdom*, 221–227.

29. Cook, "Franklin Sumner Earle," 4; Matz, "La patología de la caña de azúcar," 17.

30. *American Men of Science*, 7th ed., s.v. "Brandes, E. W."; E. W. Brandes, "Artificial and Insect Transmission of Sugar-Cane Mosaic," *Journal of Agricultural Research* 19 (May 1920): 131–138.

31. Carlos E. Chardón and Rafael A. Veve, "Sobre la transmisión del matizado de la caña por medio de insectos," *Revista de Agricultura de Puerto Rico* 9 (August 1922): 9–11.

32. Cited in C. E. Chardón and R. A. Veve, "The Transmission of Sugar-Cane Mosaic by *Aphis maidis* under Field Conditions in Porto Rico," *Phytopathology* 13 (1923): 25.

33. *American Men of Science*, s.v. "Chardón, Dr. Carlos E." At the time, Chardón was barely twenty-three years old, with a brand-new M.S. in mycology from Cornell.

34. Chardón and Veve, "Transmisión del matizado," 11–13.

35. Chardón and Veve, "Transmision del matizado," 13–14.

36. Carlos E. Chardón, "The Varietal Revolution in Porto Rico," *Journal of the Department of Agriculture of Porto Rico* 11 (July 1927): 16; Earle, *Sugar Cane and Its Culture*, 121; Stevenson, *Genetics and Breeding of Sugar Cane*, 27–29. The Uba cane was also widely planted in Natal, South Africa.

37. Cook, "Franklin Sumner Earle," 4; *American Men of Science*, s.v. "Rosenfeld, Arthur Hinton," and "Cook, Melville Thurston."

38. Arthur H. Rosenfeld, "Informe anual del tecnólogo especial para cañas, año fiscal 1923–1924," *Informe Anual de la Estación Experimental Insular* (1923–1924): 74–75; Stevenson, *Genetics and Breeding of Sugar Cane*, 25–27, 48–50.

39. Report of the Director, *Annual Report of the Insular Experiment Station* (1923–1924), 19–22; Earle, *Sugar Cane and Its Culture*, 54–55.

40. Earle, *Sugar Cane and Its Culture*, 101–103.

41. "Report of the Commissioner of Agriculture and Labor" (1921), 485.

42. "Report of the Commissioner of Agriculture and Labor" (1922), 460.

43. "Report of the Commissioner of Agriculture and Labor" (1922), 470.

44. Earle, *Sugar Cane and Its Culture*, 9.

45. Arthur H. Rosenfeld, "Aspecto beneficioso del matizado de la caña de azúcar," *Revista de Agricultura de Puerto Rico* 12 (January 1924): 7–8.

46. Chardón, "The Varietal Revolution in Porto Rico," 31–41.

47. Chardón, "The Varietal Revolution in Porto Rico," 9.

48. Chardón, "The Varietal Revolution in Porto Rico," 24. Emphasis in the original.

49. Alan Dye, *Cuban Sugar in the Age of Mass Production: Technology and the Economics of the Sugar Central, 1899–1929* (Stanford: Stanford University Press, 1998), chap. 8; Galloway, *The Sugar Cane Industry*, 93, 100, 101, 213, 228. On declining agricultural yields, see Ayala, *American Sugar Kingdom*, 137–141.

50. Stephen C. Bruner, *La enfermedad del mosaico de la caña de azúcar*, Estación Experimental Agronómica Santiago de las Vegas Circular no. 60 (December 1923), reprinted in *80 años de la Estación Experimental Agronómica de Santiago de las Vegas*, ed. Companioni Concepción et al. (Havana: Editorial Científico-Tecnica, 1984), 102. Ayala, *American Sugar Kindgom*, 232–234.

51. Thomas F. O'Brien, *The Revolutionary Mission: American Enterprise in Latin America, 1900–1945* (Cambridge: Cambridge University Press, 1996): 213–223; Ayala, *American Sugar Kingdom*, 232–234; Edward M. East and William H. Weston, Jr., *A Report on the Sugar Cane Mosaic Situation in February 1924 at Soledad, Cuba*, Contributions from the Harvard Institute for Tropical Biology and Medicine, no. 1 (Cambridge, 1925), 6.

52. East and Weston, *Report on the Sugar Cane Mosaic*, 4–5, 7.

53. Bruner, "La enfermedad del mosaico," 102–105; S. C. Bruner, "Departamento de Fitopatología y Entomología," *Memoria General, Secretaria de Agricultura, Comercio, y Trabajo* (1925–1928), 305–306.

54. Stephen C. Bruner, *Sobre el daño que ocasiona el "mosaico" a la caña de azúcar*, Estación Experimental Agronómica Santiago de las Vegas Circular no. 61 (Havana, 1925), reprinted in Companioni Concepción et al., *80 años de la Estación Experimental Agronómica*, 129.

55. James A. Faris, *Some Serious Sugar-Cane Diseases Not Known to Occur in Cuba*, Tropical Plant Research Foundation Bulletin no. 4 (Washington, D.C., 1926), 3–5.

56. Bruner, "La enfermedad del mosaico," 112–113.

57. Chardón, "Report of the Commissioner of Agriculture and Labor" (1925), 504.

58. R. Menéndez Ramos, "Experiences with Sugar Cane Varieties in Oriente, 1923–1927," *Asociación de Técnicos Azucareros de Cuba. Memoria de la Primera Conferencia Anual.* (December 1927): 254.

59. Menéndez Ramos, "Experiences with Sugar Cane Varieties in Oriente," 222.

60. Menéndez Ramos, "Experiences with Sugar Cane Varieties in Oriente," 250–252.

61. James A. Faris, *The Utilization of Varieties in the Field Control of Sugar Cane Mosaic and Root Diseases in Cuba (A Preliminary Report)*, Tropical Plant Research Foundation Scientific Contributions, no. 20 (Washington, D.C., 1931), 63.

62. This form of contract between the mill and the *colono* is detailed in Ayala, *American Sugar Kingdom*, 132–133. On the rationalization of the Cuban sugar industry, see O'Brien, *The Revolutionary Mission*, 213–223. A. C. Barnes briefly discusses the persistence of Crystalina in Cuba in *The Sugar Cane*, 122.

63. On the role of the South American leaf blight in preventing the development of rubber plantations in Brazil, see Warren Dean, *Brazil and the Struggle for Rubber: A Study in Environmental History* (Cambridge: Cambridge University Press, 1989). On the role of disease in the collapse of Ecuador's cacao industry, see Guillermo Arosemena Arosemena, *El fruto de los dioses* (Guayaquil: Editorial Graba, 1991), 305–321; and

Manuel Chiriboga, *Jornaleros y gran proprietarios en 135 años de exportación cacaotera (1790–1925)* (Quito: Consejo Provincial de Pichincha, 1980), 391–416.

CHAPTER 5

1. Carlos E. Chardón, "Graduate School of Tropical Agriculture," *Porto Rico Progress,* 29 December 1927, 10.

2. Chardón, "Graduate School of Tropical Agriculture," 7.

3. Herbert Hice Whetzel to Alfred Mann, 14 September 1924, and Mann to Whetzel, 25 October 1924, folder Belten & Mann, H. H. Whetzel Papers (Collection 21/29/45), Cornell University Archives (hereafter cited as Whetzel MSS).

4. Chardón, "Graduate School of Tropical Agriculture," 10–11.

5. Chardón, "Graduate School of Tropical Agriculture," 5–6. On "dollar diplomacy" and Harding and Coolidge's visions of the role of the United States abroad, see Emily S. Rosenberg's *Spreading the American Dream: American Economic and Cultural Expansion, 1890–1945* (New York: Hill and Wang, 1982), chap. 8.

6. For a brief overview, see Edith M. Irvine-Rivera, "School of Tropical Medicine, University of Porto Rico," *Bulletin of the Pan American Union* 61 (1927): 164–167. Bailey Ashford gives a more detailed and personal account of the school in his autobiography, *A Soldier in Science* (New York: William Morrow, 1934), 355–381.

7. Chardón, "Graduate School of Tropical Agriculture," 11.

8. Chardón, "Graduate School of Tropical Agriculture," pt. 2, *Porto Rico Progress,* 5 January 1928, 7.

9. Chardón, "Graduate School of Tropical Agriculture," pt. 2, 10; Jones to Chardón, 23 April 1928, Carlos E. Chardón Papers, in the possession of Carlos E. Chardón, Jr., San Juan, Puerto Rico (hereafter Chardón Papers).

10. Chardón to Mann, 13 June 1928, Chardón Papers.

11. Marco Palacios, *Coffee in Colombia, 1850–1970: An Economic, Social, and Political History* (Cambridge: Cambridge University Press, 1980), 207; David Bushnell, *The Making of Modern Colombia: A Nation in Spite of Itself* (Berkeley: University of California Press, 1993), 169–174; Charles W. Bergquist, *Coffee and Conflict in Colombia, 1886–1910* (Durham: Duke University Press, 1978), 247–262; Catherine C. LeGrand, *Frontier Expansion and Peasant Protest in Colombia, 1850–1930* (Albuquerque: University of New Mexico Press, 1986); James J. Parsons, *Antioqueño Colonization in Western Colombia,* rev. ed. (Berkeley: University of California Press, 1968).

12. Malcom Deas, "Colombia, Ecuador, and Venezuela, c. 1880–1930," in *Cambridge History of Latin America,* edited by Leslie Bethell (Cambridge: Cambridge University Press, 1986), 5:644–663; Bergquist, *Coffee and Conflict in Colombia,* 257.

13. Jesús Bejarano A., *Economía y poder: La SAC y el desarrollo agropecuaro colombiano, 1871–1984* (Bogotá: SAC, Fondo Editorial CEREC, 1985), 149–150. "Las Sociedades de Agricultores," *Boletín de Agricultura* (Bogotá) 1 (January 1928): 439–445.

14. Frank R. Safford, *The Ideal of the Practical: Colombia's Struggle to Form a Technical Elite* (Austin: University of Texas Press, 1976), 200–201; Pamela Murray, *Dreams of Development: Colombia's National School of Mines and Its Engineers, 1887–1970* (Tus-

caloosa: University of Alabama Press, 1998); Alberto Mayor Mora, *Etica, trabajo, y productividad en Antioquia* (Bogotá: Ediciones Tercer Mundo, 1984).

15. Safford, *The Ideal of the Practical,* 13. Carlos E. Chardón, *Informe sobre la reorganización de la Escuela Superior de Agricultura y Medicina Veterinaria* (Medellín: Department of Antioquia, 1926), 10–13. "Sociedad Antioqueña de Agricultores," *Revista Nacional de Agricultura* 21 (November–December 1925): 129–130.

16. Chardón, *La reorganización de la Escuela Superior,* 8, 16–19; 35–53.

17. Chardón, *La reorganización de la Escuela Superior,* 3, 4; "Las sociedades de agricultores," 441.

18. On tensions between planters and governments, see Michael F. Jiménez, "At the Banquet of Civilization: The Limits of Planter Hegemony in Early-Twentieth-Century Colombia," in *Coffee, Society, and Power in Latin America,* edited by William Roseberry, Lowell Gudmundson, and Mario Samper Kutschbach (Baltimore: Johns Hopkins University Press, 1995). Agudelo to Chardón, 19 April 1928; Toro to Chardón, 17 August 1928; Chardón to Toro, Monzón, and Mattei, 11 April 1927, Chardón Papers.

19. Chardón to Toro, Monzón, and Mattei, 11 April 1927, Chardón Papers. Emphasis in original.

20. Chardón, *La reorganización de la Escuela Superior,* 9.

21. Agudelo to Chardón, 21 February 1928, Chardón Papers.

22. Toro to Chardón, 9 November 1928, Chardón Papers. On the figures for secondary school attendance in Colombia, see Murray, *Dreams of Development,* 64.

23. Rafael A. Toro, "La Escuela de Agricultura y el Plan "Chardón," *La Defensa* (Medellín), 16 November 1928.

24. Chardón to Restrepo, 25 September 1929; Restrepo to Chardón 5 October 1929; Chardón to Robledo, 29 June 1929, Secretaria de Agricultura y Fomento to Carlos Chardón, 30 January 1930, Chardón Papers.

25. "La producción nacional," *Boletín de Agricultura* 1 (January 1928): 389–391.

26. Chardón to Toro, 18 June 1928, Chardón Papers. Eduardo Mejía Prado, "Carlos Durán Castro: Gestor del desarrollo agropecuario del Valle del Cauca," *Revista Credencial Historia* no. 92 (August 1997) http://bochica.banrep.gov.co/blaavirtual/credencial/9203.htm.

27. Chardón to Farrand, 13 June 1928, Chardón Papers; Carlos E. Chardón, *Reconocimiento Agro-Pecuario del Valle del Cauca. Informe emitido por la Misión Agrícola Puertorriqueña, dirigida por el Hon. Carlos E. Chardón, y presentado al Gobernador del Departamento del Valle en Colombia* (San Juan, 1930), 7. The mission consisted of five Puerto Rican scientists, four of whom had been trained in the United States. The three plant scientists (including Chardón) had degrees from Cornell, and the veterinarian had a degree from the University of Pennsylvania.

28. Chardón, *Reconocimiento del Valle del Cauca,* 8–13, 335–336.

29. Chardón to Whetzel, 15 June 1929 and 26 June 1929, Chardón Papers.

30. Bejarano A., *Economía y poder,* 143–164.

31. Bejarano A., *Economía y poder,* 143–164.

32. Bejarano A., *Economía y poder,* 154–158. The Venezuelan economist Alberto Adriani was a perceptive analyst of Colombia's agriculture during the 1920s. See his es-

says "La valorización del café," and "Sobre el porvenir de la industria cafetera," in his *Labor venezolanista,* 2d ed. (Caracas: Tip. Garrido, 1946).

33. Chardón to Robledo, 26 June 1929, Chardón Papers.

34. Chardón to Kern, 30 June 1929; Carlos E. Chardón, "Orientaciones a seguir en los trabajos agrícolas de Colombia," *Revista de Agricultura de Puerto Rico* 23 (August 1929): 49–50. On SAC and its attempts (frequently unsuccessful) to remain separate from Colombian politics, see Bejarano A., *Economía y poder,* 150–164. On the tensions between agricultural scientists, farmers, and politicians in the United States, see Deborah Fitzgerald, *The Business of Breeding: Hybrid Corn in Illinois, 1890–1940* (Ithaca: Cornell University Press, 1990); and Alan I. Marcus, *Agricultural Science and the Quest for Legitimacy: Farmers, Agricultural Colleges, and Experiment Stations, 1870–1890* (Ames: Iowa State University Press, 1985).

35. Chardón, "Los trabajos agrícolas de Colombia," 50–53.

36. Chardón, "Los trabajos agrícolas de Colombia," 94; Bejarano, *Economía y poder,* 154; "Apuntaciones sobre las enfermedades de las plantas cultivadas," *Boletín de Agricultura* 3 (July 1929): 3–7.

37. "Tropical Plant Research Foundation," *Bulletin of the Pan American Union* 59 (January 1925), 33–37; Chardón to Whetzel, 29 June 1929; Chardón to Montalvo, 24 September 1929, Chardón Papers.

38. Tropical Plant Research Foundation, "Preliminary Outline of a Memorandum of Agreement Between the Government of Colombia and the Tropical Plant Research Foundation," typescript, with annotations by Chardón. 17 August 1929, Chardón Papers.

39. Chardón to Montalvo, 24 September 1929; Chardón to Toro, 10 January 1929; Toro to Chardón, 23 January 1929; Chardón to Gil Borges, 27 March 1929, Chardón Papers.

40. "The President Elect of Colombia, Dr. Enrique Olaya Herrera," *Bulletin of the Pan American Union* 64 (April 1930): 325–329. Molina Garces to Chardón, 19 February 1930, Chardón Papers.

41. Paul W. Drake, *The Money Doctor in the Andes: The Kemmerer Missions, 1923–1933* (Durham: Duke University Press, 1989), 60–73.

42. Chardón to Jones, 3 March 1930; Chardón to Ospina Pérez, 28 May 1930, Chardón Papers. Bushnell, *The Making of Modern Colombia,* 181–185.

CHAPTER 6

1. Victor Bulmer-Thomas, *The Economic History of Latin America since Independence* (Cambridge: Cambridge University Press, 1994), 194–237; Commission on Cuban Affairs, *Problems of the New Cuba* (New York: Foreign Policy Association, 1935), 238, 251.

2. Christopher Abel, "Colombia, 1930–1958," in *The Cambridge History of Latin America,* edited by Leslie Bethell (Cambridge: Cambridge University Press, 1984), 8:592–596; Molina Garces to Chardón, 16 January 1930, Chardón Papers. Chardón to Olaya Herrera, 14 October 1929; Secretary of Agriculture and Development (Medellín) to Chardón, 30 January 1930; Chardón to Molina Garces, 25 February 1930, Chardón Papers.

3. Rowe to Chardón, 10 January 1930; Jones to Chardón, 22 November 1930; Jones to Chardón, 30 April 1931, Chardón Papers.

4. Christopher E. London, "Class Relations and Capitalist Development: Subsumption in the Colombian Coffee Industry, 1928–1992," *Journal of Peasant Studies* 24 (July 1997): 269–295; Mariano Ospina Pérez, *Manual del cafetero colombiano* (Bogotá: Federación Nacional de Cafeteros, 1932); Alberto Adriani, "La organización de la industria cafetera colombiana," *Labor venezolanista,* 2d ed. (Caracas: Tip. Garrido, 1946), 298–308.

5. Yajaira Freites, "Auge y caída de la ciencia nacional: La época del gomecismo (1908–1935)," in *Perfil de la ciencia en Venezuela,* edited by Marcel Roche (Caracas: Fundación Polar, 1996), 2:186–188; Yolanda Texera Arnal, *La modernización difícil: Henri Pittier en Venezuela, 1920–1950* (Caracas: Fundación Polar, 1998), 35–39. Pittier's reports are also reprinted in this volume.

6. J. Valerio to P. Standley, 29 May 1936; J. Valerio to P. Standley, 29 June 1934, v. 35 folio 130; J. Valerio to C.R. Secretary of Education, 7 July 1936, vol. 45, fol. 212–213, all in Correspondencia General, vol. 45, fol. 47–48, Archivo del Museo Nacional de Costa Rica. Paul Standley, *Flora of Costa Rica* (Chicago: Field Museum of Natural History, 1937–1940); and Stuart McCook, "Creole Science in Costa Rica," *Endeavour* 23 (1999): 118–120.

7. James L. Dietz, *Economic History of Puerto Rico: Institutional Change and Capitalist Development* (Princeton: Princeton University Press, 1986), 135–143. Chardón to Farrand, 26 October 1929; Farrand to Chardón, 29 January 1930, Chardón Papers.

8. Commission on Cuban Affairs, *Problems of the New Cuba,* 1–23.

9. Rafael Martínez Viera, *70 años de la Estación Experimental Agronómica de Santiago de las Vegas* (Havana: Academia de Ciencias de Cuba, 1977), 52–60.

10. Thomas Barbour, *A Naturalist in Cuba* (Boston: Little, Brown, 1945), 94–97; Thomas Barbour, "The Harvard Garden in Cuba," *Bulletin of the Pan American Union* 70 (August 1936): 631–638.

11. Barbour, *A Naturalist in Cuba,* 94–97; Barbour, "The Harvard Garden in Cuba," 631–638; Thrall to Lowell, 13 June 1932, Lowell Presidential Records, 1930–1933, UAI 5.160, Harvard University Archives, Cambridge, Mass.

12. On the economic effects of the depression in Latin America, see Bulmer-Thomas, *The Economic History of Latin America since Independence,* chap. 7; and Steven C. Topik and Allen Wells's epilogue to *The Second Conquest of Latin America: Coffee, Henequen, and Oil during the Export Boom, 1850–1930* (Austin: University of Texas Press, 1998), 227–236.

13. Arthur M. Hyde, "Speech of the Secretary of Agriculture to the Inter-American Conference on Agriculture," *Report of the Delegates of the United States to the Inter-American Conference on Agriculture* (Washington, D.C.: GPO, 1930), 99–100.

14. Chardón to Mann, 20 November 1930; Chardón to Jones, 21 March 1931; Chardón to Jones, 22 April 1931, Chardón Papers. Melville Thurston Cook and José I. Otero, *History of the First Quarter of a Century of the Agricultural Experiment Station at Río Piedras, Puerto Rico,* University of Puerto Rico Agricultural Experiment Station Bulletin 44 (San Juan: Bureau of Printing, Supplies, and Transportation, 1937), 7–8.

15. Puerto Rico Policy Commission, *Report of the Puerto Rico Policy Commission*

(Chardón Report) (Washington, D.C., 1934); Dietz, *Economic History of Puerto Rico*, 149–154.

16. Dietz, *Economic History of Puerto*, 154–158, 169–170.

17. Rexford Guy Tugwell, *The Stricken Land: The Story of Puerto Rico* (Garden City, N.Y.: Doubleday, 1947), 49–56.

18. *Report of the Puerto Rico Agricultural Experiment Station* (1935), 1; and (1939), 1–2; Dietz, *Economic History of Puerto Rico*, 174.

19. Raymond Leslie Buell et al., *Problems of the New Cuba: Report of the Commission on Cuban Affairs* (New York: Foreign Policy Association, 1935), 492.

20. Buell et al., *Problems of the New Cuba*, 493–494.

21. Martínez Viera, *70 años de la Estación Experimental Agronómica*, 60–85.

22. Walsingham to Barbour, 31 August 1933; Walsingham to Barbour, 20 September 1933, Director's Correspondence, Botanic Garden.

23. Hugh Thomas, *Cuba, or, The Pursuit of Freedom* (New York: Da Capo, 1998), 650–657; Louis A. Pérez, *Cuba: Between Reform and Revolution* (New York: Oxford University Press, 1988), 266–275; Robert M. Grey to Thomas Barbour, December 6, 1934. Botanic Garden in Cuba, Director's Correspondence, Harvard University Archives.

24. "The Atkins Institution of the Arnold Arboretum," *Journal of the Arnold Arboretum* 20 (1939): 458; Barbour to Lowell, 29 December 1931; Buell et al., *Problems of the New Cuba*, 464.

25. Jesús A. Bejarano A., "Las ciencias agropecuarias y la revolución agrícola," in his *Ensayos de historia agraria colombiana* (Bogotá: Fondo Editorial CEREC, 1987), 186–189; Catherine C. LeGrand, *Frontier Expansion and Peasant Protest in Colombia, 1850–1930* (Albuquerque: University of New Mexico Press, 1986), chap. 7; Eduardo Mejía Prado, "Carlos Durán Castro: Gestor del desarrollo agropecuario del Valle del Cauca," *Revista Credencial Historia* no. 92 (August 1997) http://bochica.banrep.gov.co/blaavirtual/credencial/9203.htm.

26. Carlos Durán Castro, "La agricultura nacional entra en una nueva etapa," *Boletín de Agricultura* 6 (March–May 1933): 177–180.

27. Ministerio de la Economía Nacional de Colombia, *Informe Anual de la Estación Agrícola Experimental de Palmira* (Bogotá: Imprenta Nacional, 1941).

28. Abel, "Colombia," 596–597; on the implication of López Pumarejo's reforms for technical education in Colombia, see Pamela Murray, *Dreams of Development: Colombia's National School of Mines and Its Engineers, 1887–1970* (Tuscaloosa: University of Alabama Press, 1998), 38–42. Bejarano, "Las ciencias agropecuarias y la revolución agrícola," 192.

29. See the volume on science in and after the Febuary Program, Yajaira Freites and Yolanda Texera Arnal, eds., *Tiempos de cambio: La ciencia en Venezuela, 1936–1948* (Caracas: Fondo Editorial Acta Científica Venezolana, 1992).

30. Henri Pittier, *Manual de las plantas usuales de Costa Rica* (Caracas: Litografía del Comercio, 1926), 1.

31. Standley, *Flora of Costa Rica*, 23; Skutch to Maxon, 12 September 1935. Record Unit 223, Box 10, Smithsonian Institution Archives, Washington, D.C.; Manuel Valerio to the Secretary of Public Education, 14 May 1934. Signatura 3559, Libro de Correspondencia, Secretario de Educación Pública, Archivo Nacional de Costa Rica, San José, Costa Rica.

BIBLIOGRAPHY

UNPUBLISHED SOURCES

Manuscripts

Archivo Nacional de Costa Rica, San José, Costa Rica.
    Libros de Correspondencia, Secretaría de Educación Pública.
Archivo del Museo Nacional de Costa Rica.
    Correspondencia General.
Botanical Gardens of Caracas (Jardín Botánico de Caracas).
    Pittier, Henri, Papers.
Cornell University Archives.
    Whetzel, Herbert Hice, Papers.
Family of Carlos E. Chardón, San Juan, Puerto Rico.
    Chardón, Carlos, Papers.
Harvard University Archives, Cambridge, Massachusetts.
    Botanic Garden in Cuba, Director's Correspondence. UAV 231.5.
    Lowell, A. Lawrence. Lowell Presidential Records. UAI 5.160.
New York Botanical Garden, Bronx, New York.
    Tropical Plant Research Foundation Collection.
Smithsonian Institution Archives, Washington, D.C.
    Smithsonian Institution. Department of Botany, 1918–1949. Record Unit 226.
    Smithsonian Institution. Division of Grasses, 1884, 1899–1963. Record Unit 229.
    Smithsonian Institution. Registrar, 1834–1958. Record Unit 305.
    United States National Museum. Division of Plants, 1899–1947. Record Unit 223.
    United States National Museum. Permanent Administrative Files, 1877–1975. Record Unit 192, Box 187.

Dissertations

Soluri, John. "Landscape and Livelihood: An Agroecological History of Export Banana Growing in Honduras, 1870–1975." Ph.D. dissertation, University of Michigan, 1998.

PUBLISHED SOURCES

Abad, José Ramon. *Puerto Rico en la Feria-Exposición de Ponce en 1882.* Ponce, P.R.: Establecimiento Tipográfico "El Comercio," 1885.

Abel, Christopher. "Colombia, 1930–1958." In *The Cambridge History of Latin America,* edited by Leslie Bethell, 8:592–596. Cambridge: Cambridge University Press, 1984.

Aceves Pastrana, Patricia. "Las políticas botánicas metropolitanas en los virreynatos de la Nueva España y del Perú." In *Mundalización de la ciencia y cultura nacional,* edited by A. Lafuente, A. Elena, and M. L. Ortega, 187–198. Madrid: Doce Calles, 1993.

Adams, Frederick Upham. *Conquest of the Tropics: The Story of the Creative Enterprises Conducted by the United Fruit Company.* Garden City, N.Y.: Doubleday, Page, 1914.

Adas, Michael. *Machines as the Measure of Men: Science, Technology, and Ideologies of Western Dominance.* Cornell Studies in Comparative History. Ithaca: Cornell University Press, 1989.

Adler, Emmanuel. *The Power of Ideology: The Quest for Technological Autonomy in Argentina and Brazil.* Berkeley: University of California Press, 1987.

Adler Lomnitz, Larissa, and Leticia Mayer. "Veterinary Medicine and Animal Husbandry in Mexico: From Empiricism to Science and Technology." *Minerva* 32 (Summer 1994): 144–157.

Adriani, Alberto. *Alberto Adriani, "Estímulo de la Juventud." Labor Venezolanista,* 2d ed., augmented and edited by R. A. Rondon Marquez. Caracas: Tip. Garrido, 1946.

———. "The Inter-American Conference on Agriculture." *Bulletin of the Pan American Union* 64 (January 1930): 149–155.

———. "La organización de la industria cafetera colombiana." In Adriani, *Labor venezolanista,* 2d ed., 198–308. Caracas: Tip. Garrido, 1946.

———. "La próxima conferencia agrícola panamericana." *Boletín de la Cámara de Comercio de Caracas* (March 1930): 4759–4762.

———. "Sobre el porvenir de la industria cafetera." In Adriani, *Labor venezolanista,* 2d ed. Caracas: Tip. Garrido, 1946.

———. "La valorización del café." In Adriani, *Labor venezolanista,* 2d. ed. Caracas, 1946.

"La agricultura." *Boletín de la Cámara de Comercio de Caracas* (October 1927): 3849–3851.

"Agricultura Experimental." *Boletín de la Cámara de Comercio de Caracas* (February 1927): 3610–3611.

"Agricultural Education and Experiments in Colombia." *Bulletin of the Pan American Union* 68 (February 1934): 146–150.

"Agricultural Experimentation in Peru." *Bulletin of the Pan American Union* 67 (October 1933): 819–821.

Agriculture in Venezuela. American Agriculture Series. Washington, D.C.: Pan American Union, Division of Agricultural Cooperation, 1947.

Agrios, George. *Plant Pathology.* 4th ed. San Diego: Academic Press, 1997.

Aguilera, M., V. Rodríguez Lemoine, and L. Yero. *La participación de la comunidad científica frente a las alternativas de desarrollo.* Caracas: Asociación Venezolana para el Avance de la Ciencia, 1982.

Ainsworth, G. C. *Introduction to the History of Plant Pathology.* Cambridge: Cambridge University Press, 1981.

Albert, Bill, and Adrian Graves, eds. *Crisis and Change in the International Sugar Economy, 1860–1914.* Norwich and Edinburgh: ISC Press, 1984.

Allen, David Elliston. *The Naturalist in Britain: A Social History.* London: Allen Lane, 1976.

Allen, Paul. *The Rain Forests of Golfo Dulce.* Gainesville: University of Florida Press, 1956.

Alvarez Conde, José. *Historia de la botánica en Cuba.* Havana: Publicaciones de la Junta Nacional de Arqueología y Etnología, 1958.

Alvarez Díaz, José R. *A Study on Cuba.* Coral Gables: University of Miami, 1965.

Ames, Oakes. *Jottings of a Harvard Botanist, 1874–1950.* Cambridge, Mass.: Botanical Museum of Harvard University, 1979.

Anderson, Benedict. *Imagined Communities: Reflections on the Origin and Spread of Nationalism.* Rev. and expanded ed. London: Verso, 1991.

Ardao, Alicia. *El café y las ciudades en los Andes venezolanos, 1870–1930.* Caracas: Academia Nacional de la Historia, 1984.

Arellano Moreno, Antonio. *Orígenes de la economía venezolana.* Colección Ciencias Económicas. Caracas: Universidad Central de Venezuela, 1982.

Arends, Tulio. *Ciencia y tecnología en la época de Simón Bolívar.* Caracas: Fondo Editorial Acta Científica Venezolana, 1986.

Arosemena Arosemena, Guillermo. *El fruto de los dioses.* Vol. 1. Guayaquil: Editorial Graba, 1991.

Ascanio Evanoff, Carlos E. *Biología del café.* Caracas: Universidad Central de Venezuela, 1994.

Ascanio R., Consuelo. "Consideraciones sobre la situación del café venezolano entre 1908 y 1935." *Tierra Firme* 3 (1985): 613–628.

Ashford, Bailey. *A Soldier in Science.* New York: William Morrow, 1934.

"Aterrizajes: El nuevo rector de la Universidad." *Indice* 2 (November 1930): 315.

Atkins, Edwin F. *Sixty Years in Cuba: Reminiscences of Edwin F. Atkins.* Cambridge, Mass.: Riverside Press, 1926.

"The Atkins Institution of the Arnold Arboretum." *Journal of the Arnold Arboretum* 20 (1939): 457–458.

Atwood, Wallace W. "The Seventh American Scientific Congress." *Bulletin of the Pan American Union* 69 (November 1935): 815–822.

Ayala, Cesar. *The American Sugar Kingdom: The Plantation Economy of the Spanish Caribbean, 1898–1934.* Chapel Hill: University of North Carolina Press, 1999.

Azcarte Luxan, Isabel, and Luis Maldonado Polo. "La plaga de la langosta y el tizón del trigo en la España ilustrada." *Llull* 15 (1992): 309–330.

Bagué, Jaime. "Puerto Rico: An Interesting Experiment." *Bulletin of the Pan American Union* 58 (1924): 662–675.

Balderrama, Rafael. *Ciencia y política agroalimentaria: La experiencia venezolana de los últimos sesenta años.* Caracas: Universidad Central de Venezuela and Fondo Editorial Acta Científica Venezolana, 1993.

Barbour, Thomas. "The Harvard Garden in Cuba." *Bulletin of the Pan American Union* 70 (August 1936): 631–638.

———. *A Naturalist in Cuba.* Boston: Little, Brown, 1945.

Barker, E. Eugene. "Relación entre el cruzamiento de plantas y la agricultura." *Revista de Agricultura de Puerto Rico* 5 (July 1920): 4–12.

Barnes, A. C. *The Sugar Cane*. 2d ed. Aylesbury: Leonard Hill Books, 1974.

Barrett, O. W. "La agricultura y el proveimiento del mundo." *Revista de Agricultura de Puerto Rico* 16 (March 1926): 135–141; 16 (April 1926): 186–193.

Basalla, George. "The Spread of Western Science: A Three-Stage Model Describes the Introduction of Modern Science into Any Non-European Nation." *Science* 156 (5 May 1967): 611–622.

Bauer, Arnold. "Modernizing Landlords and Constructive Peasants: In the Mexican Countryside." *Mexican Studies/Estudios Mexicanos* 14 (Winter 1998): 191–212.

Bejarano A., Jesús Antonio. "Las ciencias agropecuarias y la revolución agrícola." In Bejarano, *Ensayos de historia agraria colombiana*, 186–189. Bogotá: Fondo Editorial CEREC, 1987.

———. *Ensayos de historia agraria colombiana*. Bogotá: Fondo Editorial CEREC, 1987.

Bell, P. L. *Venezuela: A Commercial and Industrial Handbook with a Chapter on the Dutch West Indies*. U.S. Department of Commerce, Bureau of Foreign and Domestic Commerce, Special Agents Series, no. 212. Washington, D.C.: GPO, 1922.

Belt, Thomas. *The Naturalist in Nicaragua*. 1874. Reprint, Chicago: University of Chicago Press, 1985.

Bennett, Hugh H., and Robert V. Allison. *The Soils of Cuba*. Washington, D.C.: Tropical Plant Research Foundation, 1928.

Bergad, Laird W. "Agrarian History of Puerto Rico, 1870–1930." *Latin American Research Review* 13 (1978): 63–94.

Bergquist, Charles W. *Coffee and Conflict in Colombia, 1886–1910*. Durham: Duke University Press, 1978.

Blake, S. F., and Alice C. Atwood. *Geographical Guide to Floras of the World*. United States Department of Agriculture, Miscellaneous Publication No. 401. Washington, D.C.: GPO, 1942.

Blume, Helmut. *Geography of Sugar Cane: Environmental, Structural, and Economic Aspects of Cane Sugar Production*. Berlin: Verlag Dr. Albert Bartens, 1985.

Bowler, Peter J. *The Norton History of the Environmental Sciences*. New York: W. W. Norton, 1992.

Box, Harold E. *Notas sobre dos insectos perjudiciales a las matas de café en Venezuela*. Translated by Luis Catoni Alvarado, with revisions by Henri Pittier. Caracas: Empresa el Cojo, 1927.

Brading, David A. "Nationalism and State-building in Latin American History." *Ibero-Amerikanisches Archiv* 20 (1994): 83–108.

Brandes, E. W. "Artificial and Insect Transmission of Sugar-Cane Mosaic." *Journal of Agricultural Research* 19 (May 1920): 131–138.

Brandes, E. W., and G. B. Sartoris. "Sugarcane: Its Origin and Improvement." *U.S.D.A. Yearbook of Agriculture*. Washington, D.C.: GPO, 1936.

Braudel, Fernand. *Capitalism and Material Life, 1400–1800*. London: Wiedenfeld and Nicholson, 1973.

Bravo, José Oscar. "Estudio del aumento de producción de azúcar en Puerto Rico." *Revista de Agricultura de Puerto Rico* 23 (July 1929): 28–36.

Bressman, Earl N. "Inauguration of the Inter-American Institute of Agricultural Sciences." *Bulletin of the Pan American Union* 77 (June 1943): 326–332.

Brockway, Lucile. "Plant Imperialism." *History Today* 33 (July 1983): 31–36.

———. "Plant Science and Colonial Expansion: The Botanical Chess Game." In *Seeds and Sovereignty: The Use and Control of Plant Genetic Resources,* edited by Jack R. Kloppenburg, Jr. Durham: Duke University Press, 1988.

———. *Science and Colonial Expansion: The Role of the Royal Botanical Garden.* New York: Academic Press, 1979.

Browne, Janet. *The Secular Ark: Studies in the History of Biogeography.* New Haven: Yale University Press, 1983.

———. *Voyaging.* Vol. 1 of *Charles Darwin: A Biography.* Princeton: Princeton University Press, 1995.

Bruner, Stephen C. "Departamento de Fitopatología y Entomología." *Memoria General, Secretaria de Agricultura, Comercio, y Trabajo* (Havana, 1925–1928), 305–306.

———. *La enfermedad del mosaico de la caña de azúcar.* Estación Experimental Agronómica Santiago de las Vegas Circular, no. 60. Havana, December 1923. Reprinted in *80 años de la Estación Experimental Agronómica de Santiago de las Vegas,* edited by Companioni Concepción et al. Havana: Editorial Científico-Tecnica, 1984.

———. *Sobre el daño que ocasiona el "mosaico" a la caña de azúcar.* Estación Experimental Agronómica Santiago de las Vegas Circular, no. 61. Havana, 1925.

Buell, Raymond Leslie, et al. *Problems of the New Cuba: Report of the Commission on Cuban Affairs.* New York: Foreign Policy Association, 1935.

Bulmer-Thomas, Victor. *The Economic History of Latin America since Independence.* Cambridge: Cambridge University Press, 1994.

Burkholder, Mark A., and Lyman L. Johnson. *Colonial Latin America.* 2d ed. New York: Oxford University Press, 1994.

Bush, Lawrence, ed. *Science and Agricultural Development.* Totowa, N.J.: Allanheld, Osmun, 1981.

Bush, Lawrence, and Carolyn Sachs. "The Agricultural Sciences and the Modern World System." In *Science and Agricultural Development,* edited by Lawrence Bush. Totowa, N.J.: Allanheld, Osmun, 1981.

Bushnell, David. *The Making of Modern Colombia: A Nation in Spite of Itself.* Berkeley: University of California Press, 1993.

Bushnell, David, and Neill Macaulay. *The Emergence of Latin America in the Nineteenth Century.* New York: Oxford University Press, 1988.

C.A.B. "La situación actual en relación con el matizado en Cuba." *Revista de Agricultura de Puerto Rico* 13 (October 1924): 265–276.

Caballero, Manuel. *Gómez, el tirano liberal (vida y muerte del siglo XIX).* Caracas: Monte Avila Editores and Banco Maracaibo, 1993.

Calderón, Humberto Ruíz, Hebe M. C. Vessuri, Maria Cristina Di Prisco, Yajaira Freites, Yolanda Texera, Marcel Roche, José Avila Bello, Jacinto Convit, Ignacio Avalos, Walter Jaffé, and Julio Urbina. *La ciencia en Venezuela: Pasado, presente, y futuro.* Cuadernos Lagoven. Serie Medio Milenio. Caracas: Lagoven, 1992.

Cameron, C. R. "The Second International Coffee Conference." *Bulletin of the Pan American Union* 65 (September 1931): 901–915.

Cannon, Susan Faye. *Science and Culture: The Early Victorian Period.* New York: Dawson and Science History Publications, 1978.

Cardoso, Ciro. "The Liberal Era, c. 1870–1930." In *Central America since Independence,* edited by Leslie Bethell. Cambridge: Cambridge University Press, 1991.

Carr, Raymond. *Puerto Rico: A Colonial Experiment.* New York: Vintage Books, 1984.

Carrera Damas, Germán. *Una nación llamada Venezuela.* 4th. ed. Caracas: Monte Avila Editores, 1991.

Carroll, Henry K. *Report on the Island of Porto Rico.* Washington, D.C.: GPO, 1899.

Cartay, Rafael. *Historia económica de Venezuela, 1830–1900.* Valencia: Vadell Hermanos Editores, 1988.

Carter, Adam. "Agricultural Cooperation in the Americas." *Bulletin of the Pan American Union* 66 (April 1932): 279–287.

Carvallo, Gastón, and Josefina Ríos de Hernández. *Temas de la Venezuela agroexportadora.* Caracas: Fondo Editorial Tropykos, 1984.

Castillo, Ocarina. *Agricultura y política en Venezuela, 1948–1958.* Caracas: Universidad Central de Venezuela, 1985.

Chambers, David Wade. "Period and Process in Colonial and National Science." In *Scientific Colonialism: A Cross-Cultural Comparison,* edited by Nathan Reingold and Marc Rothenberg, 297–321. Washington, D.C.: Smithsonian Institution Press, 1987.

Chapin, Edward A. "Science Helps Save Colombian Crops: A Glimpse of Colombia's Expanding Work in Entomology." *Bulletin of the Pan American Union* 76 (July 1942): 435–439.

Chardón, Carlos E. "La agricultura necesita la ayuda de los gobiernos." *Boletín de la Cámara de Comercio de Caracas* (September 1930): 4896–4897.

———. "La aportación de las ciencias agrícolas a la industria azúcarera de Puerto Rico." *Revista de Agricultura de Puerto Rico* 25 (June 1930): 221–224.

———. "Discurso del Dr. Carlos E. Chardón en la comida ofrecida por el Colegio de Agrónomos en el Hotel Condado." *Revista de Agricultura de Puerto Rico* 33 (October–December 1941): 542–546.

———. *Discurso inaugural del rector Carlos E. Chardón, 20 de mayo de 1931.* Río Piedras: Universidad de Puerto Rico, 1931.

———. "Experimentos sobre matizado en la central Cambalache." *Revista de Agricultura de Puerto Rico* 13 (October 1924): 205–218.

———. "Graduate School of Tropical Agriculture." *Porto Rico Progress* (29 December 1927): 5–7, 10–11; (5 January 1928): 7, 10.

———. *Informe sobre la reorganización de la Escuela Superior de Agricultura y Medicina Veterinaria.* Medellín: Departamento de Antioquia, 1926.

———. "Life Zones in the Andes of Venezuela." *Bulletin of the Pan American Union* 67 (August 1933): 620–633.

———. "Mis impresiones de una visita al ingenio 'San Luis' en Santo Domingo." *Revista de Agricultura de Puerto Rico* 13 (October 1924): 251–254.

———. "La misión agrícola de Puerto Rico en Colombia." *Revista de Agricultura de Puerto Rico* 23 (November 1929): 173–189.

———. "La misión agrícola de Puerto Rico en Colombia." *Boletín de la Cámara de Comercio de Caracas* (February 1930): 4670–4674.

————. *Los naturalistas en la América Latina*. Vol. 1. Ciudad Trujillo: Editorial del Caribe, 1949.

————. "Orientaciones a seguir en los trabajos agrícolas de Colombia." *Revista de Agricultura de Puerto Rico* 23 (August 1929): 49–53, 94.

————. *Reconocimiento Agro-Pecuario del Valle del Cauca. Informe emitido por la Misión Agrícola Puertorriqueña, dirigida por el Hon. Carlos E. Chardón, y presentado al Gobernador del Departamento del Valle en Colombia*. San Juan, 1930.

————. "Las tendencias universitarias del Dr. Chardón." *Boletín de la Cámara de Comercio de Caracas* (June 1931): 5197–5201.

————. "The Varietal Revolution in Porto Rico." *Journal of the Department of Agriculture of Puerto Rico* 11 (July 1927): 9–41.

————. *Viajes y naturaleza*. Caracas: Editorial Sucre, 1941.

Chardón, Carlos E., and Rafael A. Veve. "Sobre la transmisión del matizado de la caña por medio de insectos." *Revista de Agricultura de Puerto Rico* 9 (August 1922): 9–20.

————. "The Transmission of Sugar-Cane Mosaic by *Aphis maidis* under Field Conditions in Porto Rico." *Phytopathology* 13 (1923): 24–29.

Chastaing Z., David Ruíz. "El afán de la modernidad: La agricultura en el pensamiento económico venezolano del siglo XIX." *Boletín de la Academia Nacional de la Historia* 81 (1998): 27–49.

Chiriboga, Manuel. *Jornaleros y gran proprietarios en 135 años de exportación cacaotera (1790–1925)*. Quito: Consejo Provincial de Pichincha, 1980.

Cittadino, Eugene. *Nature as the Laboratory: Darwinian Plant Ecology in the German Empire, 1880–1900*. Cambridge: Cambridge University Press, 1990.

Clark, A. Kim. *The Redemptive Work: Railway and Nation in Ecuador, 1895–1930*. Wilmington, Del.: Scholarly Resources, 1998.

Clark, Victor S., ed. *Porto Rico and Its Problems*. Washington, D.C.: Brookings Institution, 1930.

Clement, Jean-Pierre. "De los nombres de plantas." *Revista de Indias* 47 (1987): 501–512.

Codazzi, Augustín. *Resumen de la geografía de Venezuela*. Caracas: Biblioteca Venezolana de Cultura, 1940.

Coe, Sophie D., and Michael D. Coe. *The True History of Chocolate*. London: Thames and Hudson, 1996.

"Coffee and the Bogotá Conference." *Bulletin of the Pan American Union* 71 (January 1937): 39–45.

Cole-Christensen, Darryl. *A Place in the Rain Forest: Settling the Costa Rican Frontier*. Austin: University of Texas Press, 1997.

Coll y Toste, Cayetano. *Colón en Puerto Rico: Disquisiciónes histórico-filológicas*. Barcelona: Artes Gráficas Medinaceli, 1971.

Colom, José L. "The First Inter-American Conference on Agriculture." *Bulletin of the Pan American Union* 64 (November 1930): 1081–1093.

————. "How Colombia Is Improving Agricultural Production." *Bulletin of the Pan American Union* 68 (January 1934): 51–59.

————. "Pan American Cooperation in Agriculture." *Bulletin of the Pan American Union* 75 (June 1941): 330–336.

————. "The Third Inter-American Conference on Agriculture." *Bulletin of the Pan American Union* 79 (December 1945): 704–707.

Colón, Edmundo D. *Datos sobre la agricultura en Puerto Rico antes de 1898.* San Juan: Tipográfico Cantero, Fernández, 1930.

————. *La gestión agrícola después de 1898.* San Juan, 1948.

Commission on Cuban Affairs. *Problems of the New Cuba.* New York: Foreign Policy Association, 1935.

"Conferencia Interamericana sobre Agricultura, Selvicultura, e Industria Animal." *Boletín de la Cámara de Comercio de Caracas* (April 1930): 4739–4740.

Cook, Melville Thurston. *The Diseases of Tropical Plants.* London: Macmillan, 1913.

————. "El dominio del matizado de la caña de azúcar." *Revista de Agricultura de Puerto Rico* 14 (January 1925): 7–9.

————. "Estudios sobre la causa del matizado." *Revista de Agricultura de Puerto Rico* 13 (December 1924): 373–376.

————. "Franklin Summer Earle." *Revista de Agricultura de Puerto Rico* 23 (July 1929): 4.

————. "Producción de azúcar y enfermedades de la caña." *Revista de Agricultura de Puerto Rico* 15 (December 1925): 273–276.

————. "La situación actual en enfermedades de la caña de azúcar en Puerto Rico." *Revista de Agricultura de Puerto Rico* 25 (June 1930): 227–231.

Cook, Melville Thurston, and José I. Otero. *History of the First Quarter of a Century of the Agricultural Experiment Station at Río Piedras, Puerto Rico.* University of Puerto Rico Agricultural Experiment Station Bulletin, no. 44. San Juan: Bureau of Supplies, Printing, and Transportation, 1937.

Cook, O. F. "The Debt of Agriculture to Tropical America." *Bulletin of the Pan American Union* 64 (September 1930): 874–887.

Cook, O. F., and G. N. Collins. *Economic Plants of Puerto Rico.* Contributions from the United States National Herbarium, no. 8. Washington, D.C.: GPO, 1903–1905.

Coons, G. H. "Progress in Plant Pathology: Control of Disease by Resistant Varieties." *Phytopathology* 27 (1937): 621–632.

Corbitt, D. C. "La introducción en Cuba de la caña de Otahiti, el árbol del pan, el mango y otras plantas." *Revista Bimestre Cuba* 47 (May–June 1941): 360–366.

Correa, M. P. *Flora do Brazil: Algunas plantas uteis, suas aplicaçoes e distribuçao geographica.* Rio de Janeiro, 1909.

Crema, Edoardo. "El mesianismo científico en Venezuela." *Revista Nacional de Cultura* 41 (1943): 80–103.

Cronon, William. *Changes in the Land: Indians, Colonists, and the Ecology of New England.* New York: Hill and Wang, 1983.

————. *Nature's Metropolis: Chicago and the Great West.* New York: W. W. Norton, 1991.

————. "A Place for Stories: Nature, History, and Narrative." *Journal of American History* 97 (March 1992): 1347–1376.

————. "The Uses of Environmental History." *Environmental History Review* 17 (Fall 1993): 1–22.

Crosby, Alfred W. *The Columbian Exchange: Biological and Cultural Consequences of 1492.* Westport, Conn.: Greenwood, 1972.

———. *Ecological Imperialism: The Biological Expansion of Europe, 900–1900.* Cambridge: Cambridge University Press, 1986.

———. *Germs, Seeds, and Animals: Studies in Ecological History.* Armonk, N.Y.: M. E. Sharpe, 1994.

———. "The Past and Present of Environmental History." *American Historical Review* 100 (October 1995): 1177–1189.

Crowther, Samuel. *The Romance and Rise of the American Tropics.* Garden City, N.Y.: Doubleday, Doran, 1929.

Cuba. Presidente. *Memoria de la Administración del Presidente de la República de Cuba.* Havana, 1912–1921.

———[1909–1913]. *Memoria de la Administración del Presidente de la República, Mayor General José Miguel Gómez, durante el periodo comprendido el 1 de enero y el 31 de diciembre de 1912.* Havana, 1913.

———[1913–1921]. *Memoria de la Administración del Presidente de la República, Mariano G. Menocal.* Havana, 1915.

Cueto, Marcos. *Excelencia científica en la periferia: Actividades científicas e investigación biomédica en el Perú, 1890–1950.* Lima: GRADE, 1989.

———. "*Indigenismo* and Rural Medicine in Peru: The Indian Sanitary Brigade and Manuel Nuñez Butrón." *Bulletin of the History of Medicine* 65 (Spring 1991): 22–41.

———. "Sanitation from Above: Yellow Fever and Foreign Intervention in Peru, 1919–1922." *Hispanic American Historical Review* 72 (1992): 1–22.

———, ed. *Missionaries of Science: The Rockefeller Foundation and Latin America.* Bloomington: Indiana University Press, 1994.

Dalton, Leornard V. *Venezuela.* London: T. Fisher Unwin, 1912.

Daly, Douglas C. "The Leaf That Launched a Thousand Ships." *Natural History* 105 (January 1996): 24–32.

Dean, Warren. *Brazil and the Struggle for Rubber: A Study in Environmental History.* Cambridge: Cambridge University Press, 1987.

———. *A botânica e a política imperial: Introdução y adaptação de plantas no Brasil colonial e imperial.* Universidade de São Paulo, Coleção Documentos, Série História das Ideologias e Mentalidades. São Paulo: Universidade de São Paulo, 1992.

———. "The Green Wave of Coffee: Beginnings of Agricultural Research in Brazil (1885–1900)." *Hispanic American Historical Review* 69 (1989): 91–115.

———. *With Broadax and Firebrand: The Destruction of the Brazilian Atlantic Forest.* Berkeley: University of California Press, 1995.

Deas, Malcom. "Colombia, Ecuador, and Venezuela, c. 1880–1930." In *Cambridge History of Latin America,* edited by Leslie Bethell, 5:644–663. Cambridge: Cambridge University Pres, 1986.

Deerr, Noel. *The History of Sugar.* Vol. 1. London: Chapman and Hall, 1949.

"The Department of Agriculture and Latin America in Cooperative Agricultural Programs." *Bulletin of the Pan American Union* 79 (July 1945): 379–382.

Di Prisco, Carlos Augusto, and Erika Wagner. *Visiones de la ciencia: Homenaje a Marcel Roche.* Caracas: Monte Avila Editores and Instituto Venezolano de Investigaciones Científicas, 1992.

Díaz, Elena, Yolanda Texera, and Hebe M. C. Vessuri, eds. *La ciencia periférica: Ciencia y sociedad en Venezuela*. Caracas: Monte Avila Editores, 1983.

Díaz, Lilia. "El Jardín Botánico de Nueva España y la obra de Sessé según documentos mexicanos." *Historia Mexicana* 27 (July–September 1977): 49–78.

Dietz, James L. *Economic History of Puerto Rico: Institutional Change and Capitalist Development*. Princeton: Princeton University Press, 1986.

Diffie, Bailey W., and Justine Whitfield Diffie. *Porto Rico: A Broken Pledge*. Studies in American Imperialism. New York: Vanguard Press, 1931.

Drake, Paul W. *The Money Doctor in the Andes: The Kemmerer Missions, 1923–1933*. Durham: Duke University Press, 1989.

Drayton, Richard. *Nature's Government: Science, Imperial Britain, and the "Improvement" of the World*. New Haven: Yale University Press, 2000.

Dunlap, Thomas R. *DDT: Scientists, Citizens, and Public Policy*. Princeton: Princeton University Press, 1981.

Dupree, A. Hunter. *Science in the Federal Government*. Baltimore: Johns Hopkins University Press.

Durán Castro, Carlos. "La agricultura nacional entra en una nueva etapa." *Boletín de Agricultura* 6 (March–May 1933): 177–180.

Dye, Alan. *Cuban Sugar in the Age of Mass Production: Technology and the Economics of the Sugar Central, 1899–1929*. Stanford: Stanford University Press, 1998.

Eakin, Marshall. "The Origins of Modern Science in Costa Rica: The Instituto Físico-Geográfico Nacional, 1887–1904." *Latin American Research Review* 34 (1999): 123–150.

Earle, Franklin S. "Botany at the Cuban Experiment Station." *Science* 20 (30 September 1904): 444–445.

———. "An Institution for Tropical Research." *Science*, n.s. 52 (15 October 1920): 363–365.

———. *Primer informe anual de la Estación Central Agronómica de Cuba, 1 de Abril 1904–30 de Junio 1905*. Havana: Imprenta "Universal," 1906.

———. "Problemas económicos de Puerto Rico." *Revista de Agricultura de Puerto Rico* 4 (1920): 10–19.

———. *Sugar Cane and Its Culture*. New York: John Wiley, 1928.

———. *Sugar Cane Varieties in Cuba*. Foundation Information Letter No. 6. Washington, D.C.: Tropical Plant Research Foundation, 1925.

———. "Sugar Cane Varieties of Porto Rico, II." *Journal of the Department of Agriculture of Puerto Rico* 5 (July 1921): 3–141.

———. "Las variedades de caña en Puerto Rico." *Varios trabajos (presentados en la reunión de productores y profesionales azucareros celebrada en Río Piedras el 17 de noviembre de 1920)*. Puerto Rico, Departamento de Agricultura y Trabajo, Estación Experimental Insular Circular, no. 33, 16–19. San Juan: Bureau of Supplies, Printing, and Transportation, 1920.

East, Edward M., and William H. Weston, Jr. *A Report on the Sugar Cane Mosaic Situation in February 1924 at Soledad, Cuba*. Contributions from the Harvard Institute for Tropical Biology and Medicine, no. 1. Cambridge, Mass., 1925.

Eastabrook, Leon N. "The World Agricultural Census in the Latin American Republics." *Bulletin of the Pan American Union* 63 (August 1929): 882–896.

Edgerton, Claude W. *Sugarcane and Its Diseases*. Baton Rouge: Louisiana State University Press, 1955.

Egerton, Frank N. "The History of Ecology: Achievements and Opportunities." *Journal of the History of Biology* 16 (Summer 1983): 259–310; 18 (Spring 1985): 103–143.

Elliott, John H. *The Old World and the New, 1492–1650*. Cambridge: Cambridge University Press, 1970.

Ellner, Steve. "Venezuelan Revisionist Political History, 1908–1958: New Motives and Criteria for Analyzing the Past." *Latin American Research Review* 30 (1995): 91–122.

"La enfermedad del mosaico de la caña de azúcar." *Revista de Agricultura de Puerto Rico* 16 (January 1926): 7–8.

Engstrand, Iris H. W. *Spanish Scientists in the New World: The Eighteenth-Century Expeditions*. Seattle: University of Washington Press, 1981.

Erlanson, Carl O. "The First South American Botanical Congress." *Bulletin of the Pan American Union* 73 (May 1939): 297–300.

Ernst, Adolfo. *La Exposición Nacional de Venezuela en 1883* in his *Obras Completas*, edited by Blas Bruni Celli. Caracas: Fundación Venezolana para la Salud y Educación, 1983.

Estación Experimental Agronómica. *Informe de 1917–1918 de la Estación Experimental Agronómica*. Havana, 1919.

———. *Second Report* (30 June 1905–1 January 1909). Havana, 1910.

———. *Tercer informe anual* (February 1909–30 July 1914). Havana, 1915.

Evans, Sterling. *The Green Republic: A Conservation History of Costa Rica*. Austin: University of Texas Press, 1999.

Fairchild, David. "The Soledad Garden and Arboretum: The Harvard Biological Institute in Cuba (Atkins Foundation) on Soledad Estate." *Journal of Heredity* 15 (1924): 451–461.

Faris, James A. *Some Serious Sugar-Cane Diseases Not Known to Occur in Cuba*. Tropical Plant Research Foundation Bulletin No. 4. Washington, D.C., 1926.

———. *The Utilization of Varieties in the Field Control of Sugar Cane Mosaic and Root Diseases in Cuba. (A Preliminary Report)*. Tropical Plant Research Foundation Scientific Contributions, no. 20. Washington, D.C.: Tropical Plant Research Foundation, 1931.

Felipe, C., T. Zambrana, R. M. Ross, C. Hernández, A. Ramírez, P. C. Martín, and M. Velásquez. *Surgimiento en Cuba de la política científica en el sector agropecuario*. Conferencias y estudios de historia y organización de la ciencia. Havana: Academia de Ciencias de Cuba, 1987.

Fernández Méndez, Eugenio, ed. *Crónicas de Puerto Rico desde la conquista hasta nuestros días (1493–1955)*. Río Piedras: University of Puerto Rico, 1976.

Ferry, Robert J. "Encomienda, African Slavery, and Agriculture in Seventeenth-Century Caracas." *Hispanic American Historical Review* 61 (1981): 609–635.

Figueroa, Carlos Arturo. "El matizado de la caña de azúcar y la producción de azúcar en Puerto Rico." *Revista de Agricultura de Puerto Rico* 5 (September 1920): 25–32.

Fitzgerald, Deborah. *The Business of Breeding: Hybrid Corn in Illinois, 1890–1940*. Ithaca and London: Cornell University Press, 1990.

———. "Exporting American Agriculture: The Rockefeller Foundation in Mexico,

1943–1953." In *Missionaries of Science: The Rockefeller Foundation in Latin America,* edited by Marcos Cueto. Bloomington: Indiana University Press, 1994.

Freites, Yajaira. "Auge y caida de la ciencia nacional: La época del gomecismo (1908–1935)." In *Perfil de la ciencia en Venezuela,* edited by Marcel Roche, 2:153–198. Caracas: Fundación Polar, 1996.

———. "La ciencia en la época del gomecismo." *Quipu* 4 (May–August 1987): 213–251.

———. "De la colonia a la república oligárquica (1498–1870)." In *Perfil de la ciencia en Venezuela,* edited by Marcel Roche, 1:25–92. Caracas: Fundación Polar, 1996.

———. "De ilustrados a profesionales: Los ingenieros venezolanos entre 1899 y 1935." *Dynamis* 12 (1992): 105–129.

———. "El problema del saber entre hacendados y comerciantes ilustrados in la provincia de Caracas-Venezuela (1793–1810)." *Dynamis* 17 (1997): 165–191.

Freites, Yajaira, and Yolanda Texera Arnal, eds. *Tiempos de cambio: La ciencia en Venezuela, 1936–1948.* Caracas: Fondo Editorial Acta Científica Venezolana, 1992.

Funes Monzote, Reinaldo. "Los conflictos por el aceso a la madera en la Habana: Hacendados vs. marina (1774–1815)." In *Diez nuevas miradas de historia de Cuba,* edited by José Antonio Piqueras, 67–90. Castellón: Universidad Jaume I, 1998.

Galloway, J. H. "Botany in the Service of Empire: The Barbados Cane-breeding Program and the Revival of the Caribbean Sugar Industry, 1880s-1930s." *Annals of the American Association of Geographers* 86 (1996): 682–708.

———. *The Sugar Cane Industry: An Historical Geography from Its Origins to 1914.* Cambridge: Cambridge University Press, 1989.

———. "Tradition and Innovation in the American Sugar Industry, ca. 1500–1800: An Explanation." *Annals of the American Association of Geographers* 75 (1985): 334–351.

García Naranjo, Nemesio. *Venezuela and Its Ruler.* Translated by Calla Wheaton Esteva. New York: Carranza, 1927.

Gardner, Frank D. *La Estación de Experimentos Agriculturales de Puerto Rico, su establecimiento, sitio, y propósito.* Estación de Experimentos Agriculturales de Puerto Rico, Boletín No. 1. Washington, D.C.: GPO, 1903.

Gayer, Arthur D., Paul T. Homan, and Earle K. James. *The Sugar Economy of Puerto Rico.* New York: Columbia University Press, 1938.

Gaztambide Arrillaga, Carlos. "In Memoriam: Dr. Carlos E. Chardón." *El Mundo* (San Juan), 17 March 1965.

Geertz, Clifford. *Agricultural Involution: The Process of Ecological Change in Indonesia.* Berkeley: University of California Press, 1966.

Gerbi, Antonello. *Nature in the New World: From Christopher Columbus to Gonzalo Fernández de Oviedo.* Translated by Jeremy Moyle. Pittsburgh: Pittsburgh University Press, 1985.

Gil-Bermejo García, Juana. *Panorama histórico de la agricultura en Puerto Rico.* Seville: Escuela de Estudios Hispano-Americanos de Sevilla, 1970.

Gines, Juan Vernet. *Historia de la ciencia española.* Madrid: Instituto de España, 1975.

Glade, William. "Latin America and the International Economy, 1870–1914." In *Latin America, Economy and Society, 1870–1930,* edited by Leslie Bethell. Cambridge: Cambridge University Press, 1989.

Gleason, Henry A. "The Scientific Work of Nathaniel Lord Britton." *Proceedings of the American Philosophical Society* 104 (1960).

Glick, Thomas F. "La ciencia latinoamericana en el siglo XX." *Arbor* 142 (June–August 1992): 233–252.

———. "Science and Independence in Latin America (with Special Reference to New Granada)." *Hispanic American Historical Review* 71 (1991): 307–334.

———. "Science and Society in Twentieth-Century Latin America." In *The Cambridge History of Latin America,* edited by Leslie Bethell. Vol. 6, pt. 1. Cambridge: Cambridge University Press, 1985.

Glick, Thomas F., and David M. Quinlan. "Félix de Azara: The Myth of the Isolated Genius in Spanish Science." *Journal of the History of Biology* 8 (1975): 67–83.

Gómez P., Luis D. "Contribuciones a la pteridología costarricense XI: Hermann Christ, su vida, obra, e influencia en la botánica nacional." *Brenesia* 12–13 (1977): 25–79.

———. "Contribuciones a la pteridología Costarricense XII: Carlos Wercklé." *Brenesia* 14–15 (1978): 361–393.

Gómez P., Luis D., and J. M. Savage. "Searchers on That Rich Coast: Costa Rican Field Biology, 1400–1980." In *Costa Rican Natural History,* edited by Daniel H. Janzen, 1–11. Chicago: University of Chicago Press, 1983.

Goodman, David C. *Power and Penury: Government, Technology, and Science in Philip II's Spain.* Cambridge: Cambridge University Press, 1988.

Gootenberg, Paul. *Imagining Development: Economic Ideas in Peru's "Fictitious Prosperity" of Guano, 1840–1880.* Berkeley: University of California Press, 1993.

Grand Court, Carlos Grivot, Agustín Stahl, and José Julian Acosta. *Información sobre las diversas clases de caña sacarina introducidas en Puerto Rico.* Mayagüez, 1878. Reprinted in *Boletín Histórico de Puerto Rico* 8 (1921): 56–63.

Grases, Pedro, ed. *Memoria sobre el café y el cacao.* 1809; reprint, Caracas: Academia Nacional de la Historia, 1983.

———. *Sociedad Económica de Amigos del País, memorias y estudios.* Caracas: Banco Central de Venezuela, 1958.

Grey, Robert. *Report of the Harvard Botanical Gardens, Soledad Estate, Cienfuegos, Cuba (Atkins Foundation), 1900–1926.* Cambridge, Mass.: Harvard University Press, 1927.

Grisanti, Carlos Felipe. "Discurso en la Cámara del Senado." 1919. Reprinted in *Los pensadores positivistas y el gomecismo,* vol. 7, edited by Ramón J. Velásquez. Caracas: Congreso de la República, 1983.

Grossman, Lawrence S. *The Political Ecology of Bananas: Peasants, Contract Farming, and Agrarian Change in the Eastern Caribbean.* Chapel Hill: University of North Carolina Press, 1998.

Grove, Richard. *Green Imperialism: Colonial Expansion, Tropical Island Edens, and the Origins of Environmentalism, 1600–1860.* Cambridge: Cambridge University Press, 1995.

Hagen, Joel B. "Ecologists and Taxonomists: Divergent Traditions in Twentieth-Century Plant Geography." *Journal of the History of Biology* 19 (Summer 1986): 197–214.

Hall, Carolyn. *El café y el desarrollo histórico-geográfico de Costa Rica.* San José: Editorial Costa Rica, 1991.

————. *Costa Rica: A Geographical Interpretation in Historical Perspective.* Boulder, Colo.: Westview, 1985.

Halperín Donghi, Tulio. *The Contemporary History of Latin America.* Durham: Duke University Press, 1993.

————. "Economy and Society." In *Spanish America after Independence, c. 1820 – c. 1870,* edited by Leslie Bethell, 1–47. Cambridge: Cambridge University Press, 1987.

Hamilton, David E. "Building the Associative State: The Department of Agriculture and American State-building." *Agricultural History* 64 (Spring 1990): 207–218.

Hamm, Margherita Arlina. *Porto Rico and the West Indies.* London: F. Tennyson Neely, 1899.

Harwich Vallenilla, Nikita. "Venezuelan Positivism and Modernity." *Hispanic American Historical Review* 70 (1990): 327–344.

Häsler, Beatrice, and Thomas W. Baumann. *Henri Pittier, 1857–1950: Leben und Werk eines Schweizer Naturforschers in den Neotropen.* Basel: Reinhardt, 2000.

Heald, Frederick Deforest. *Introduction to Plant Pathology.* 2d ed. New York: McGraw-Hill, 1943.

Heitmann, John Alfred. *The Modernization of the Louisiana Sugar Industry, 1830–1910.* Baton Rouge: Louisiana State University Press, 1987.

Hemsley, W. B. *Biologia Centrali-Americana.* London, 1879–1888.

Henao Jaramillo, Jaime. *El café en Venezuela.* Caracas: Universidad Central de Venezuela, 1982.

Hill, Arthur W. "The History and Functions of Botanic Gardens." *Annals of the Missouri Botanical Garden* 2 (1915): 185–240.

Hobhouse, Henry. *Seeds of Change: Five Plants That Transformed Mankind.* London: Sidgwick & Jackson, 1985.

Hobsbawm, Eric. *The Age of Empire: 1875–1914.* New York: Vintage Books, 1989.

Humboldt, Alexander von. *Personal Narrative of Travels to the Equinoctal Regions of the New Continent During the Years 1799–1804.* 2d ed. London: Longman, Hurst, Rees, Orme, and Brown, 1822.

Hyde, Arthur M. "Speech of the Secretary of Agriculture to the Inter-American Conference on Agriculture." In *Report of the Delegates of the United States to the Inter-American Conference on Agriculture,* 99–100. Washington, D.C.: GPO, 1930.

Iglesias García, Fe. "Changes in Cane Cultivation in Cuba, 1860–1900." *Social and Economic Studies* 37 (1988): 341–363.

————. *Del ingenio al central.* Havana: Editorial de Ciencias Sociales, 1999.

————. "Inter-American Conference on Agriculture, Forestry, and Animal Industry." *Bulletin of the Pan American Union* 63 (July 1929): 689–691.

Irvine-Rivera, Edith M. "School of Tropical Medicine, University of Porto Rico." *Bulletin of the Pan American Union* 61 (1927): 164–167.

Izard, Miguel, comp. *Series estadísticas para la historia de Venezuela.* Mérida: Universidad de los Andes, 1970.

Izquierdo, Luis A. "Treinta años: Síntesis histórica del Departamento de Agricultura y Comercio." *Almanaque Agrícola de Puerto Rico* (1947): 17–31.

Jahn, Alfredo. "Prof. Henry Pittier, esbozo biográfico." *Boletín de la Sociedad Venezolana de Ciencias Naturales* 30 (September–October 1937): 1–24.

Janzen, Daniel. "Tropical Agroecosystems." *Science* 182 (December 1973): 1212–1220.

Jenks, Leland Hamilton. *Our Cuban Colony: A Study in Sugar.* Studies in American Imperialism. New York: Vanguard Press, 1928.

Jennings, Bruce H. *Foundations of International Agricultural Research: Science and Politics in Mexican Agriculture.* Boulder, Colo.: Westview, 1988.

Jensen, James H. "Notas sobre la presente situación de las enfermedades de la caña de azúcar en Puerto Rico." *Revista de Agricultura de Puerto Rico* 28 (September 1936): 89–94.

Jiménez, Michael F. "At the Banquet of Civilization: The Limits of Planter Hegemony in Early-Twentieth-Century Colombia." In *Coffee, Society, and Power in Latin America,* edited by William Roseberry, Lowell Gudmundson, and Mario Samper Kutschbach, 262–293. Baltimore: Johns Hopkins University Press, 1995.

Johnston, John R. "Phytopathological Work in the Tropics." *Phytopathology* 6 (October 1916): 381–386.

Jones, Lewis Ralph. "William Allen Orton, 1877–1930." *Phytopathology* 21 (January 1931): 1–11.

Joseph, Gilbert M., Catherine C. LeGrand, and Ricardo D. Salvatore, eds. *Close Encounters of Empire: Writing the Cultural History of U.S.–Latin American Relations.* Durham: Duke University Press, 1998.

Juma, Calestous. *The Gene Hunters: Biotechnology and the Scramble for Seeds.* Princeton: Princeton University Press, 1989.

Kaufman, Erik. "Naturalizing the Nation: The Rise of Naturalistic Nationalism in the United States and Canada." *Comparative Studies in Society and History* 40 (1998): 666–695.

Kelbaugh, Paul R. "Pan American Cooperation in Agriculture." *Bulletin of the Pan American Union* 73 (March 1939): 160–171.

———. "Recent Trends and Events in the Agriculture of Latin America." *Bulletin of the Pan American Union* 69 (March 1935): 212–229.

Kellogg, Vernon. "On International Biology." *Bulletin of the Pan American Union* 59 (December 1925): 1209–1219.

Kern, Frank D. "Dr. Carlos E. Chardón (1897–1965)." *Mycologia* 42 (November–December 1965): 839–844.

Kern, Frank, and Herbert Hice Whetzel. "Nuestra opinión acerca de la fundación de un jardín botánico en Puerto Rico." *Revista de Agricultura de Puerto Rico* 13 (August 1924): 77–78.

Kloppenburg, Jack Ralph. *First the Seed: The Political Economy of Plant Biotechnology, 1492–2000.* Cambridge: Cambridge University Press, 1988.

———, ed. *Seeds and Sovereignty: The Use and Control of Plant Genetic Resources.* Durham: Duke University Press, 1988.

Knapp, Seaman A. *Agricultural Resources and Capabilities of Porto Rico.* 56th Cong., 2d sess., 1900, H. Doc. 171, vol. 43, serial 4117.

Knight, Franklin W. *The Caribbean: The Genesis of a Fragmented Nationalism.* 2d ed. New York: Oxford University Press, 1990.

Kricher, John C. *A Neotropical Companion: An Introduction to the Animals, Plants, and Ecosystems of the New World Tropics.* Princeton: Princeton University Press, 1989.

Lafuente, Antonio, and Jose Sala Catala. "Ciencia colonial y roles profesionales en la América española del siglo XVIII." *Quipu* 6 (September–December 1989): 387–403.

Lafuente, A., A. Elena, and M. L. Ortega, eds. *Mundalización de la ciencia y cultura nacional.* Madrid: Doce Calles, 1993.

Large, E. C. *The Advance of the Fungi.* London: Jonathan Cape, 1940.

Lasser, Tobias. "Biografía de Henri Pitter." In *Venezolanos del siglo XX,* vol. 1, edited by Pedro Grases. Caracas: Fundación Eugenio Mendoza, 1982.

Layrisse, Miguel, and Marcel Roche, eds. *La ciencia: Base de nuestro progreso.* Caracas: Ediciones IVIC, 1965.

LeGrand, Catherine C. *Frontier Expansion and Peasant Protest in Colombia, 1850–1930.* Albuquerque: University of New Mexico Press, 1986.

———. "Living in Macondo: Economy and Culture in a United Fruit Company Banana Enclave in Colombia." In *Close Encounters of Empire: Writing the Cultural History of U.S.–Latin American Relations,* edited by Gilbert M. Joseph, Catherine C. LeGrand, and Ricardo D. Salvatore, 333–368. Durham: Duke University Press, 1998.

Leon, Hermano. *Flora de Cuba.* Havana: Cultural, 1946.

Leonard, Irving A. "Science, Technology, and Hispanic America." *Michigan Quarterly Review* 2 (1963): 237–245.

Lewis, Gordon K. *Puerto Rico: Freedom and Power in the Caribbean.* New York: Monthly Review Press, 1963.

Lewis, W. Arthur. *The Evolution of the International Economic Order.* Princeton: Princeton University Press, 1978.

———. "The Export Stimulus." In *Tropical Development, 1880–1913,* edited by W. Arthur Lewis. London: George Allen & Unwin, 1970.

Lockhart, James, and Stuart B. Schwartz. *Early Latin America: A History of Colonial Spanish America and Brazil.* Cambridge: Cambridge University Press, 1983.

Lockmiller, David A. "Agriculture in Cuba during the Second United States Intervention, 1906–1909." *Agricultural History* 11 (July 1937): 181–188.

Lombardi, John V. *Venezuela: The Search for Order, the Dream of Progress.* Oxford: Oxford University Press, 1982.

London, Christopher E. "Class Relations and Capitalist Development: Subsumption in the Colombian Coffee Industry, 1928–1992." *Journal of Peasant Studies* 24 (July 1997): 269–295.

López Domínguez, Francisco A. "La Estación Experimental Insular: Ideas y procedimientos para su desarrollo." *Revista de Agricultura de Puerto Rico* 16 (February 1926): 78–90.

Lucena Giraldo, Manuel. "Los experimentos agrícolas en la Guayana española." In *Mundalización de la ciencia y cultura nacional,* edited by A. Lafuente, A. Elena, and M. L. Ortega, 251–258. Madrid: Doce Calles, 1993.

———. *Laboratorio tropical: La expedición de límites al Orinoco, 1750–1767.* Caracas: Monte Avila Editores, 1993.

MacCameron, Robert. "Environmental Change in Colonial New Mexico." *Environmental History Review* 18 (Summer 1994): 17–39.

MacLeod, Murdo J. *Spanish Central America: A Socioeconomic History, 1520–1720.* Berkeley: University of California Press, 1973.

Mackenzie, John M., ed. *Imperialism and the Natural World.* Manchester: Manchester University Press, 1990.

Maldonado, Teófilo. "El Plan Chardón: Su precursor, sus orígenes, sus alternativas, su triunfo." *Puerto Rico Ilustrado,* 2 November 1935.

Marcus, Alan I. *Agricultural Science and the Quest for Legitimacy: Farmers, Agricultural Colleges, and Experiment Stations, 1870–1890.* Ames: Iowa State University Press, 1985.

————. "The Wisdom of the Body Politic: The Changing Nature of Publicly Sponsored American Agricultural Research since the 1830s." *Agricultural History* 62 (1988): 4–26.

Marquardt, Steve. "'Green Havoc': Panama Disease, Environmental Change, and Labor Process in the Central American Banana Industry." *American Historical Review* 106 (2001): 49–80.

Martínez Mendoza, Rafael. "Informe de la Estación Experimental de Agricultura y Selvicultura, Campo Experimental de Cotiza." *Memoria del Ministerio de Fomento* (1923): 31.

Martínez Sanz, José Luis. *Relaciones científicas entre España y América.* Madrid: Editorial MAPFRE, 1992.

Martínez Viera, Rafael. *70 años de la Estación Experimental Agronómica de Santiago de las Vegas.* Havana: Academia de Ciencias de Cuba, 1977.

Martínez-Vergne, Teresita. *Capitalism in Colonial Puerto Rico: Central San Vicente in the Late Nineteenth Century.* Gainesville: University Press of Florida, 1992.

Martorell, Luis F., Alain H. Liogier, and Roy O. Woodbury. *Catálogo de los nombres vulgares y científicos de las plantas de Puerto Rico.* Río Piedras: Universidad de Puerto Rico, 1981.

Mathews, Thomas. *Puerto Rican Politics and the New Deal.* Gainesville: University Press of Florida, 1960.

Matz, Julius. "Recientes investigaciones en el estudio de la naturaleza del mosaico de la caña de azúcar y otras plantas." *Revista de Agricultura de Puerto Rico* 9 (October 1922): 9–22.

————. "Últimos desarrollos en la patología de la caña de azúcar." *Varios trabajos (presentados en la reunión de productores y profesionales azucareros celebrada en Río Piedras el 17 de noviembre de 1920).* Puerto Rico, Departamento de Agricultura y Trabajo, Estación Experimental Insular Circular, no. 33, 32–36. San Juan: Bureau of Supplies, Printing, and Transportation, 1920.

Mayor Mora, Alberto. *Etica, trabajo, y productividad en Antioquia.* Bogotá: Ediciones Tercer Mundo, 1984.

McClellan, James E. *Colonialism and Science: Saint Domingue in the Old Régime.* Baltimore: Johns Hopkins University Press, 1992.

McConnie, R. C. "Nuevas variedades de cañas de azúcar." *Revista de Agricultura de Puerto Rico* 1 (April–May 1918): 12–17.

McCook, Stuart. "Cosechas inciertas: La investigación agrícola bajo la dictadura de Juan Vicente Gómez (1908–1935)." In *Ciencia, tecnología y sociedad en América Latina,* edited by Hebe M. C. Vessuri. Caracas: ALAS/Nueva Sociedad, 1994.

————. "Creole Science in Costa Rica." *Endeavour* 23 (1999): 118–120.

————. "Promoting the 'Practical': Science and Agricultural Modernization in Puerto Rico and Colombia, 1920–1940." *Agricultural History* 75 (Winter 2001): 52–82.

Mejía Prado, Eduardo. "Carlos Durán Castro: Gestor del desarrollo agropecuario del Valle del Cauca." *Revista Credencial Historia* 92 (August 1997) http://bochica .banrep.gov.co/blaavirtual/credencial/9203.htm.

"El mejoramiento agrícola." *Boletín de la Cámara de Comercio de Caracas* (May 1927): 3704–3705.

Melville, Elinor G. K. *A Plague of Sheep: Environmental Consequences of the Conquest of Mexico.* Cambridge: Cambridge University Press, 1994.

"Memoria que la Asociación de Productores de las Cañas Dulces de Caguas, presentaron a la consideración de la Honorable Asamblea." *Revista de Agricultura de Puerto Rico* 8 (1922): 29–33.

Menéndez Ramos, Rafael. "Estudios sobre el mosaico de la caña. Movimiento del virus de la enfermedad a través del tallo en el caso de infecciones secundarias." *Revista de Agricultura de Puerto Rico* 13 (October 1924): 219–226.

———. "Experiences with Sugar Cane Varieties in Oriente, 1923–1927." *Asociación de Técnicos Azucareros de Cuba, Memoria de la Primera Conferencia Anual.* Havana, 1927.

Merrill, E. D. "Biographical Memoir of Nathaniel Lord Britton, 1859–1934." *Biographical Memoirs of the National Academy of Sciences* 19 (1938): 147–202.

Meyer, Hermann Henry Bernard. *Select List of References on Sugar, Chiefly in Its Economic Aspects.* Washington, D.C.: GPO, 1910.

Meyer, Jean. *Histoire du sucre.* Paris: Éditions Desjonquières, 1989.

Minaudier, Jean-Pierre. *Histoire de la Colombie: De la conquête à nos jours.* Collection Horizons Amériques Latines. Paris: Éditions L'Hartmann, 1992.

Minguet, Charles. "Alejandro de Humboldt y los científicos españoles e hispanoamericanos." In *Ciencia, vida, y espacio en Iberoamérica,* edited by José Luis Peset, 3:439–456. Madrid: CSIC, 1989.

———. *Hacia un interpretación de Hispanoamérica (perfiles y identidades).* Rome: Bulzoni Editore, 1987.

Mintz, Sindey. *Sweetness and Power: The Place of Sugar in Modern History.* New York: Penguin, 1985.

Moreno Fraginals, Manuel. *El ingenio: Complejo económico social cubano del azúcar.* Havana: Editorial de Ciencias Sociales, 1978.

———. *The Sugarmill: The Socioeconomic Complex of Sugar in Cuba, 1760–1860.* Translated by Cedric Belfrage. New York: Monthly Review Press, 1976.

Moscoso, R. M. *Catálogo Florae Domingensis: Catálogo de la flora dominicana.* New York: Universidad de Santo Domingo, 1943.

Muñoz Vicuña, Elías, ed. *El cacao.* Guayaquil: Universidad de Guayaquil, 1981..

Murray, Pamela. *Dreams of Development: Colombia's National School of Mines and Its Engineers, 1887–1970.* Tuscaloosa: University of Alabama Press, 1998.

———. "Engineering Development: Colombia's National School of Mines, 1887–1930." *Hispanic American Historical Review* 74 (1994): 63–82.

Nicholson, Malcom. "National Styles, Divergent Classifications: A Comparative Case Study from the History of French and American Plant Ecology." *Knowledge and Society* 8 (1989): 139–186.

Nolla, J. A. B. *Informe presentado al Dr. Alfredo Mejía, Ministro de Agricultura y Cría, relacionado con el proyecto de organización de un colegio de agricultura, una estación experimental, el servicio de fomento agrícola, y una escuela practica de agricultura* 28 (March 1937): 535–550.

Nolla, J. A. B., and Manuel V. Fernández Valiela. "Contributions to the History of Plant Pathology in South America, Central America, and Mexico." *Annual Review of Phytopathology* 14 (1976): 11–29.

Ober, Frederick A. *Puerto Rico and Its Resources.* New York: D. Appleton, 1899.

Obregón Torres, Diana. "El sentimiento de la nación en la literatura médica y naturalista de finales del siglo XIX en Colombia." *Anuario Colombiano de Historia Social y de Cultura* 16–17 (1988–1989): 141–161.

———. *Sociedades científicas en Colombia: La invención de una tradición, 1859–1936.* Bogotá: Banco de la República, 1992.

O'Brien, Thomas F. "The Revolutionary Mission: American Enterprise in Cuba." *American Historical Review* 98 (June 1993): 765–785.

———. *The Revolutionary Mission: American Enterprise in Latin America, 1900–1945.* Cambridge: Cambridge University Press, 1996.

Oliver-Smith, Anthony, and Susanna Hoffman, eds. *The Angry Earth: Disaster in Anthropological Perspective.* New York: Routledge, 1999.

Ortíz, Fernando. *Contrapunteo cubano del tabaco y el azúcar.* Biblioteca Ayacucho, no. 42. Caracas: Biblioteca Ayacucho, 1978.

Orton, W. A. "Agricultural Progress in Latin America." *Bulletin of the Pan American Union* 60 (September 1926): 894–905.

———. "Botanical Problems of American Tropical Agriculture." *Bulletin of the Torrey Botanical Club* 53 (1926): 67–75.

———. "Memoria sobre la agricultura tropical." *Boletín de la Cámara de Comercio de Caracas* (January 1931): 5013–5018.

Ospina Pérez, Mariano. *Manual del cafetero colombiano.* Bogotá: Federación Nacional de Cafeteros, 1932.

Otero, J. I., and R. A. Toro. *Catálogo de los nombres vulgares y científicos de algunas plantas puertorriqueñas.* Estación Experimental de la Universidad de Puerto Rico Bulletin 37. Río Piedras, 1931.

Overfield, Richard A. "The Agricultural Experiment Station and Americanization: The Hawaiian Experience, 1900–1910." *Agricultural History* 60 (Spring 1986): 256–266.

———. "Charles E. Bessey: The Impact of the "New" Botany on American Agriculture, 1880–1910." *Technology and Culture* 16 (1975): 162–181.

———. "Science Follows the Flag: The Office of Experiment Stations and American Expansion." *Agricultural History* 64 (Spring 1990): 31–40.

———. *Science with Practice: Charles E. Bessey and the Maturing of American Botany.* Ames: Iowa State University Press, 1993.

Pacheco, Emilio. *De Castro a López Contreras: Proceso social de la Venezuela contemporánea (contribución a su estudio en los años 1900–1941).* Caracas: Editorial Domingo Fuentes, 1984.

Palacios, Marco. *Coffee in Colombia, 1850–1970: An Economic, Social, and Political History.* Cambridge: Cambridge University Press, 1980.

Palladino, Paolo, and Michael Worboys. "Science and Imperialism." *Isis* 84 (1993): 91–102.

Palmer, Steven. "Central American Encounters with Rockefeller Public Health, 1914–1921." In *Close Encounters of Empire: Writing the Cultural History of U.S.–Latin American Relations,* edited by Gilbert M. Joseph, Catherine C. LeGrand, and Ricardo D. Salvatore, 311–332. Durham: Duke University Press, 1998.

Pan American Union. "Pan American Union Notes: The Governing Board. *Bulletin of the Pan American Union* 74 (July 1940): 536–541.

Parsons, James J. *Antioqueño Colonization in Western Colombia.* Rev. ed. Berkeley: University of California Press, 1968.

Paty, Michel. "L'histoire des sciences en Amérique Latine." *Pensée* 288–289 (1992): 21–45.

Payne, Fernandus. "A History of the National Research Council, 1919–1933. VII. Division of Biology and Agriculture." *Science,* n.s. 78 (4 August 1933): 93–95.

Pedreira, Antonio S. *Bibliografía Puertorriqueña (1493–1930).* Madrid: Hernando, 1932.

———. "En la universidad: Presentación del nuevo Canciller Don Carlos E. Chardón al Claustro de Profesores de la Universidad de Puerto Rico." *Indice* 2 (March 1931): 397.

Pelayo López, Francisco. "La expedición de Pehr Löfling al Orinoco (1754–1756)." In *La ciencia española en ultramar: Actas de la I Jornadas sobre "España y las expediciones científicas en América y Filipinas,"* edited by Alejandro R. Díez Torre et al. Madrid: Doce Calles, 1991.

Peloso, Vincent, and Barbara Tenenbaum, eds. *Liberals, Politics, and Power: State Formation in Nineteenth-Century Latin America.* Athens: University of Georgia Press, 1996.

Pérez, Louis A. *Cuba: Between Reform and Revolution.* Latin American Histories. New York: Oxford University Press, 1988.

———. *Cuba under the Platt Amendment, 1902–1934.* Pittsburgh: University of Pittsburgh Press, 1986.

———. *On Becoming Cuban: Identity, Nationality, and Culture.* Chapel Hill: University of North Carolina Press, 1999.

———. "Twenty-five Years of Cuban Historiography: Views from Abroad." *Cuban Studies* 18 (1988): 87–101.

———, ed. *Slaves, Sugar, and Colonial Society: Travel Accounts of Cuba, 1801–1899.* Wilmington, Del.: Scholarly Resources, 1992.

Pérez Arbeláez, Enrique. "La expedición botánica colombiana." *Boletín de Agricultura* (Bogotá) 3 (June 1930): 528–537.

Perloff, Harvey S. *Puerto Rico's Economic Future: A Study in Planned Development.* Chicago: University of Chicago Press, 1950.

Peset, José Luis. *Ciencia y libertad: El papel del científico ante la independencia americana.* Madrid: CSIC, 1987.

Picó, Fernando. *Amargo Café: Los pequeños y medianos caficultores de Utuado en la segunda mitad del siglo XIX.* Río Piedras: Ediciones Huracán, 1981.

Pineo, Ronn F. "Misery and Death in the Pearl of the Pacific: Health Care in Guayaquil, Ecuador, 1870–1925." *Hispanic American Historical Review* 70 (1990): 609–637.

Pino Iturrieta, Elías, ed. *Juan Vicente Gómez y su época.* 2d ed. Caracas: Monte Avila Editores, 1993.

Piñero, Eugenio. "The Cacao Economy of the Eighteenth-Century Province of Caracas and the Spanish Cacao Market." *Hispanic American Historical Review* 68 (1988): 75–97.

Pittier, Henri. "Acerca de dos contribuciones sobre el cultivo del café." *Boletín de la Cámara de Comercio de Caracas* (January 1929). Reprint. Caracas: Empresa el Cojo, 1929.

———. "Acerca del cultivo intenso del cafeto." *Boletín de la Cámara de Comercio de Caracas* (June 1931): 5163–5165.

———. "Agricultura y suelos." June 1928. Reprinted in *Indice alfabético del boletín mensual,* 243–244. Caracas: Cámara de Comercio de Caracas, 1968.

———. "Apuntes sobre identificación de productos naturales y organización de museos en la América tropical." *Boletín Comercial e Industrial del Ministerio de Relaciones Exteriores de Venezuela* 5 (30 September 1924): 273–280.

———. "Botánicos nacionales." *Boletín Científico y Técnico del Museo Comercial de Venezuela* 1 (1927): 46–47.

———. *Ensayo sobre las plantas usuales de Costa Rica.* Washington, D.C.: H. L. and J. B. McQueen, 1908.

———. *Esbozo de las formaciones vegetales de Venezuela, con una breve reseña de los productos naturales y agrícolas.* Caracas, Litografía del Comercio, 1920.

———. "El estudio de los productos forestales en Venezuela." *Boletín Científico y Técnico del Museo Comercial de Venezuela* 1 (January 1927): 3–33.

———. *Exploraciones, botánicas y otras, en la cuenca de Maracaibo.* Caracas: Tipografía Mercantil, 1923.

———. "Informe del Director de la Estación Experimental de Agricultura y Selvicultura." *Memoria del Ministerio de Fomento* (1918): 165–183.

———. *Manual de las plantas usuales de Venezuela.* Caracas: Litografía del Comercio, 1926.

———. *La mesa de Guanipa: Ensayo de fitogeografía.* Caracas: Tipografía Garrido, 1942.

———. "The Middle American Species of the Genus *Inga.*" *Journal of the Department of Agriculture of Porto Rico* 13 (October 1929): 117–173.

———. "Notas acerca del cultivo del café." *Cultura Venezolana* 13 (1930): 373–381.

———. *Notas sobre agricultura en Puerto Rico.* Caracas: Empresa el Cojo, 1928.

———. *Primitiae Florae Costaricensis.* San José: Tipografía Nacional, 1897.

———. "El problema del cacao." October 1934. Reprinted in *Indice alfabético del boletín mensual,* 252–258. Caracas: Cámara de Comercio de Caracas, 1968.

———. "Sobre cooperación en la producción agrícola." *Boletín Comercial e Industrial del Ministerio de Relaciones Exteriores de Venezuela* 2 (30 September 1921): 597–601.

———. *Trabajos escogidos.* Caracas: Ministerio de Agricultura y Cría, 1947.

———. "Una grave amenaza (la escoba de bruja del cacao)." June 1930. Reprinted in *Indice alfabético del boletín mensual,* 260–261. Caracas: Cámara de Comercio de Caracas, 1968.

Plaza, Elena. *José Gil Fortúl (1861–1943): Los nuevos caminos de la razón.* Caracas: Academia Nacional de la Historia, 1988.

Plucknett, Donald L., Nigel J. H. Smith, J. T. Williams, and N. Murthi Anishetty. *Gene Banks and the World's Food.* Princeton: Princeton University Press, 1987.

Poleo Pérez, Luisa M. *Rafael Villavicencio: Del postivisimo al espiritualismo.* Caracas: Academia Nacional de la Historia, 1986.

Popenoe, Wilson. "The Development of Inter-American Cooperation in Agriculture." *Bulletin of the Pan American Union* 80 (July 1946): 361–374.

"The President Elect of Colombia, Dr. Enrique Olaya Herrera." *Bulletin of the Pan American Union* 64 (April 1930): 325–329.

"La producción nacional." *Boletín de Agricultura* 1 (January 1928): 389–391.

Puerto Rico. Governor. *Report of the Governor of Porto Rico to the Secretary of War.* Washington, D.C.: GPO, 1899–1932.

———. Insular Experiment Station. *Annual Report of the Director of the Insular Experiment Station of Puerto Rico.* San Juan, 1918–1932.

Puerto Sarmiento, Francisco Javier. *La ilusión quebrada: Botánica, sanidad, y política científica en la España Ilustrada.* Madrid: CSIC, 1988.

Puerto Sarmiento, F. J., and A. González Bueno. "Política científica y expediciones botánicas en el programa colonial español ilustrado." In *Mundalización de la ciencia y cultura nacional,* edited by A. Lafuente, A. Elena, and M. L. Ortega, 287–298. Madrid: Doce Calles, 1993.

Pyenson, Lewis. "Cultural Imperialism and the Exact Sciences Revisited." *Isis* 84 (1993): 103–108.

———. "Science and Imperialism." In *Companion to the History of Modern Science,* edited by R. C. Olby, G. N. Cantor, J. R. R. Christie, and M. J. S. Hodge, 920–933. London: Routledge, 1990.

Ramos Mattei, Andres A. "The Growth of the Puerto Rican Sugar Industry under North American Domination, 1899–1910." In *Crisis and Change in the International Sugar Economy, 1860–1914,* edited by Bill Albert and Adrian Graves. Norwich and Edinburgh: ISC Press, 1984.

Randall, Stephen J., and Graeme S. Mount. *The Caribbean Basin: An International History.* London: Routledge, 1998.

Reingold, Nathan. "American Indifference to Basic Research." In *Science, American Style,* edited by Nathan Reingold. New Brunswick: Rutgers University Press, 1991.

Reingold, Nathan, and Marc Rothenberg, eds. *Scientific Colonialism: A Cross-Cultural Comparison.* Washington, D.C.: Smithsonian Institution Press, 1987.

Report of the Delegates of the United States of America to the Inter-American Conference on Agriculture. Washington, D.C.: GPO, 1930.

Report of the Puerto Rico Policy Commission (Chardón Report). San Juan, 1934.

Reynoso, Alvaro. *Ensayo sobre la caña de azúcar.* 4th ed. rev. and enl. Havana: Talleres Tipográficos de "El magazine de la raza," 1925.

———. *Selección de textos.* Edited by Francisco Díaz Barreiro. Havana: Editorial de Ciencias Sociales, 1984.

Richardson, Bonham C. *The Caribbean in the Wider World, 1492–1992: A Regional Geography.* Cambridge: Cambridge University Press, 1992.

Richardson Kuntz, Pedro. "Notas al margen de nuestra labor experimental en caña de azúcar." *Revista de Agricultura de Puerto Rico* 23 (September 1929): 99–100, 130.

———. "Notas sobre el cultivo de la caña de azúcar en Puerto Rico." *Revista de Agricultura de Puerto Rico* 9 (September 1922): 21–23.

Ríos de Hernández, Josefina, and Gaston Carvallo. *Análisis histórico de la organización del espacio en Venezuela.* Caracas: Universidad Central de Venezuela, 1990.

Ríos de Hernández, Josefina, and Nelson Prato. *Las transformaciones de la agricultura venezolana: De la agroexportación a la agroindustria.* Caracas: Fondo Editorial Tropykos–CENDES, 1990.

Rivera, Eugenio M. "Informe preliminar sobre algunas variedades de caña en la isla de Cuba." *Revista de Agricultura de Puerto Rico* 13 (October 1924): 227–235.

Roche, Marcel. "Science in Spanish and Spanish American Civilization." In *Civilization and Science, in Conflict or Collaboration?* 143–160. Amsterdam: ASP, 1971.

———. *Perfil de la ciencia en Venezuela.* 2 vols. Caracas: Fondo Editorial Acta Científica Venezolana, 1987.

———, ed. *La ciencia: Base de nuestro progreso. Fundamentos para la creación de un Consejo Nacional de Investigaciones Científicas y Tecnológicas en Venezuela.* Caracas: Ediciones IVIC, 1965.

Rodríguez, José Angel. *Los paisages geohistóricos cañeros en Venezuela.* Caracas: Academia Nacional de la Historia, 1986.

Roseberry, William. *Coffee and Capitalism in the Venezuelan Andes.* Austin: University of Texas Press, 1983.

Roseberry, William, Lowell Gudmundson, and Mario Samper Kutschbach, eds. *Coffee, Society, and Power in Latin America.* Baltimore: Johns Hopkins University Press, 1995.

Rosenberg, Emily S. *Spreading the American Dream: American Economic and Cultural Expansion, 1890–1945.* New York: Hill and Wang, 1982.

Rosenfeld, Arthur H. "Aspecto beneficioso del matizado de la caña de azúcar." *Revista de Agricultura de Puerto Rico* 12 (January 1924): 7–14.

———. "La causa del matizado: Un paso hacia la solución de este misterio." *Revista de Agricultura de Puerto Rico* 13 (September 1924): 145–148.

———. "Informe anual del tecnólogo especial para cañas, año fiscal 1923–1924." *Informe anual de la Estación Experimental Insular* (1923–1924): 69–76.

Rossiter, Margaret W. *The Emergence of Agricultural Science: Justus Liebig and the Americans, 1840–1880.* New Haven: Yale University Press, 1975.

Rothe, Werner A. "Informe . . . acerca de los trabajos practicados en el Campo Experimental de Maracay, durante el año de 1924." *Memoria del Ministerio de Fomento* 2 (1925): 187.

Rowe, L. S. "The Inter-American Conference on Agriculture, Forestry, and Animal Industry: Greetings to the Delegates." *Bulletin of the Pan American Union* 64 (September 1930): 873.

Ruiz Calderón, Humberto, et al., eds. *La ciencia en Venezuela: Pasado, presente, y futuro.* Caracas: Cuadernos Lagoven, 1992.

Rutten, L. M. R., ed. *Science in the Netherlands East Indies.* Amsterdam: Royal Academy of Sciences, 1929.

Sacarello, Rafael. "La historia del Departamento de Agricultura y Comercio." *Revista de Agricultura de Puerto Rico* (October–December 1941): 501–509.

Sáenz, Tirso, and Emilio G. Capote. *Ciencia y tecnología en Cuba: Antecedentes y desarrollo.* Havana: Editorial de Ciencias Sociales, 1989.

Safford, Frank R. "Acerca de la incorporación de las ciencias naturales en la periferia: El caso de Colombia en el siglo XIX." *Quipu* 2 (September–December 1985): 423–435.

————. *The Ideal of the Practical: Colombia's Struggle to Form a Technical Elite.* Austin: University of Texas Press, 1976.

————. "Politics, Ideology, and Society." In *Spanish America after Independence, c. 1820–c.1870,* edited by Leslie Bethell, 48–122. Cambridge: Cambridge University Press, 1987.

Sagasti, Francisco R. "La política científica y tecnológica en el nuevo entorno de América Latina." *Comercio Exterior (Mexico)* 42 (November 1992): 991–994.

————. "Underdevelopment, Science and Technology: The Point of View of the Underdeveloped Countries." *Science Studies* 3 (1973): 47–59.

Salcedo-Bastardo, J. L. *Historia fundamental de Venezuela.* 10th ed. Caracas: Universidad Central de Venezuela, Ediciones de la Biblioteca, 1993.

Sale, Kirkpatrick. *The Conquest of Paradise: Christopher Columbus and the Columbian Legacy.* New York: Alfred A. Knopf, 1990.

Salvatore, Ricardo D. "The Enterprise of Knowledge: Representational Machines of Informal Empire." In *Close Encounters of Empire: Writing the Cultural History of U.S.–Latin American Relations,* edited by Gilbert M. Joseph, Catherine C. LeGrand, and Ricardo D. Salvatore, 69–104. Durham: Duke University Press, 1998.

Sauer, Jonathan D. *Historical Geography of Crop Plants, a Select Roster.* Boca Raton, Fla.: CRC Press, 1993.

Scarano, Francisco A. *Sugar and Slavery in Puerto Rico: The Plantation Economy of Ponce, 1800–1850.* Madison: University of Wisconsin Press, 1984.

Schedvin, C. B. "Environment, Economy, and Australian Biology, 1890–1939." *Historical Studies* 21 (1984): 11–28.

Schnakenbourg, Christian. "From the Sugar Estate to the Central Factory: The Industrial Revolution in the Caribbean, 1840–1905." In *Crisis and Change in the International Sugar Economy, 1860–1914,* edited by Bill Albert and Adrian Graves. Norwich and Edinburgh: ISC Press, 1984.

Schroeder-Guderhus, Brigitte. "Nationalism and Internationalism." In *Companion to the History of Modern Science,* edited by R. C. Olby, G. N. Cantor, J. R. R. Christie, and M. J. S. Hodge, 909–919. London: Routledge, 1990.

Schumann, Gail L. *Plant Diseases: Their Biology and Social Impact.* St. Paul: American Phytopathological Society, 1991.

Schwartzman, Simon. "Peripheral Science." *Social Studies of Science* 17 (1987): 569–573.

————. *A Space for Science: The Development of the Scientific Community in Brazil.* University Park: Pennsylvania State University Press, 1991.

Scott, James C. *Seeing Like a State: How Certain Schemes to Improve the Human Condition Have Failed.* New Haven: Yale University Press, 1998.

Scott, Rebecca J. "The Transformation of Sugar Production in Cuba after Emancipation, 1880–1900: Planters, Colonos, and Former Slaves." In *Crisis and Change in the International Sugar Economy, 1860–1914,* edited by Bill Albert and Adrian Graves. Norwich and Edinburgh: ISC Press, 1984.

Segnini, Yolanda. *La consolidación del régimen de Juan Vicente Gómez.* Caracas: Academia Nacional de la Historia, 1982.

————. "Vida intelectual y Gomecismo." In *Juan Vicente Gómez y su época,* edited by Elías Pino Iturrieta. 2d ed. Caracas: Monte Avila Editores, 1993.

Shafer, Robert Jones. *The Economic Societies in the Spanish World, 1763–1821.* Syracuse: Syracuse University Press, 1958.

Sheets-Pyenson, Susan. *Cathedrals of Science: The Development of Colonial Natural History Museums during the Late Nineteenth Century.* Kingston and Montreal: McGill-Queen's University Press, 1988.

———. "New Directions for Scientific Biography: The Case of Sir William Dawson." *History of Science* 28 (1990): 399–410.

Smith, S. Ivan. "Functional Ecology of Sugarcane in the American Tropics." *Caribbean Studies* 15 (1975): 57–77.

"Sociedad Antioqueña de Agricultores." *Revista Nacional de Agricultura* 21 (November–December 1925): 129–130.

"Las Sociedades de Agricultores." *Boletín de Agricultura* (Bogotá) 1 (January 1928): 439–445.

Solbrig, Otto T., and Dorothy J. Solbrig. *So Shall You Reap: Farming and Crops in Human Affairs.* Washington, D.C.: Island Press, 1994.

Soluri, John. "Plants, People, and Pathogens: The Eco-social Dynamics of Export Banana Production in Honduras, 1875–1950." *Hispanic American Historical Review* 80 (2000): 463–501.

Stahl, Augustín. *Estudios sobre la flora de Puerto Rico.* 2d ed. San Juan de Puerto Rico: Publicaciones de la Federal Emergency Relief Administration, 1936.

Stakman, E. C., Richard Bradfield, and Paul C. Mangelsdorf. *Campaigns against Hunger.* Cambridge, Mass.: Belknap Press of Harvard University Press, 1967.

Standley, Paul C. *Flora of Costa Rica.* Chicago: Field Museum of Natural History, 1937–1940.

Steele, Arthur Robert. *Flowers for the King: The Expedition of Ruíz and Pavón and the Flora of Peru.* Durham: Duke University Press, 1964.

Stein, Stanley. *Vassouras: A Brazilian Coffee County.* Cambridge, Mass.: Harvard University Press, 1957.

Stein, Stanley J., and Barbara H. Stein. *The Colonial Heritage of Latin America: Essays on Economic Dependence in Perspective.* New York: Oxford University Press, 1970.

Stepan, Nancy. *Beginnings of Brazilian Science: Oswaldo Cruz, Medical Research and Policy, 1890–1920.* New York: Science History Publications, 1976.

———. *"The Hour of Eugenics": Race, Gender, and Nation in Latin America.* Ithaca: Cornell University Press, 1991.

———. "The Interplay between Socio-Economic Factors and Medical Science: Yellow Fever Research, Cuba, and the United States." *Social Studies of Science* 8 (1978): 397–423.

Stevenson, G. C. *Genetics and Breeding of Sugar Cane.* London: Longmans, 1965.

Stevenson, John A. "La enfermedad nueva de la caña." *Revista de Agricultura de Puerto Rico* 1 (April–May 1918): 18–25.

———. "An Epiphytotic of Cane Disease in Puerto Rico." *Phytopathology* 7 (1917): 418–425.

———. "The 'Mottling' Disease of Cane." *Annual Report of the Insular Experiment Station of Puerto Rico, 1916–1917,* 40–41. San Juan, 1917.

Stone, Roy. "Agriculture in Puerto Rico." *Yearbook of the United States Department of Agriculture.* Washington, D.C.: GPO, 1898.

Storey, William Kelleher. *Science and Power in Colonial Mauritius*. Rochester: University of Rochester Press, 1997.

Street, Donald R. "Spanish Antecedents to the Hatch Act Experiment System and Land Grant Education." *Agricultural History* 62 (1988): 27–40.

Street, James H. "Overcoming Technological Dependence in Latin America." In *Readings in Latin American History*. Vol. 2, *The Modern Experience*, edited by John J. Johnson, Peter J. Bakewell, and Meredith D. Dodge, 419–435. Durham: Duke University Press, 1985.

Suárez, M. M., R. Torrealba, and H. Vessuri, eds. *Cambio social y urbanización en Venezuela*. Caracas: Monte Avila Editores, 1983.

Szinetar Gabaldón, Miguel. "La primera estación agrícola experimental de plantas y semillas de Venezuela." *Quipu* 8 (May–August 1991): 235–253.

———. "Progreso, ciencia, y técnica en el proyecto 'nacional' de Alberto Adriani." In *Ciencia, tecnología, y sociedad en América Latina*, edited by Hebe M. C. Vessuri. Caracas: Nueva Sociedad, 1994.

Tamayo, Francisco. *El hombre frente a la naturaleza*. Caracas: Monte Avila, 1993.

———. *Imagen y huella de Henri Pittier*. Caracas: Publicaciones Intevep, 1987.

Taylor, James David. "'Base Commoditie': Natural Resource and Natural History in Smith's *The Generall Historie*." *Environmental History Review* 17 (Winter 1993): 73–89.

Tello, Jaime. *Historia natural de Caracas*. Caracas: Ediciones del Concejo Municipal del Distrito Federal, 1968.

Tercero, Dorothy M. "Second Inter-American Conference of Agriculture." *Bulletin of the Pan American Union* 76 (December 1942): 668–671.

Texera Arnal, Yolanda. "El discubrimiento del trópico: La expedición de Williams College a Venezuela en 1867." *Asclepio* 46 (1994): 197–217.

———. *Exploración botánica en Venezuela, 1754–1950*. Caracas: Fondo Editorial Acta Científica Venezolana, 1991.

———. *La modernización difícil: Henri Pittier en Venezuela, 1920–1950*. Caracas: Fundación Polar, 1998.

———. "Testigos de historia: Viajeros y naturalistas en Venezuela durante el siglo XIX." *Anuario de Estudios Americanos* 51 (1994): 189–198.

"Third Inter-American Conference on Agriculture." *Bulletin of the Pan American Union* 79 (May 1945): 281–282.

Thomas, Hugh. *Cuba, or, The Pursuit of Freedom*. New York: Da Capo, 1998.

Thorp, Rosemary. "Latin America and the International Economy from the First World War to the Depression." In *Latin America, Economy and Society, 1870–1930*, edited by Leslie Bethell. Cambridge: Cambridge University Press, 1989.

Tío, Aurelio. *Dr. Diego Alvarez Chanca: Estudio biográfico*. Puerto Rico, 1966.

Topik, Steven C., and Allen Wells. "Introduction: Latin America's Response to the Export Boom." In *The Second Conquest of Latin America: Coffee, Henequen, and Oil during the Export Boom, 1850–1930*, edited by Steven C. Topik and Allen Wells, 1–36. Austin: University of Texas Press, 1998.

———, eds. *The Second Conquest of Latin America: Coffee, Henequen, and Oil during the Export Boom, 1850–1930*. Austin: University of Texas Press, 1998.

Toro, Rafael A. "La Escuela de Agricultura y el Plan "Chardón." *La Defensa* (Medellín), 16 November 1928. Chardón Papers.

"Tropical Plant Research Foundation." *Boletín de la Cámara de Comercio de Caracas* (July 1927): 3778.

"Tropical Plant Research Foundation." *Bulletin of the Pan American Union* 59 (January 1925): 33–37.

"Tropical Plant Research Foundation." *Bulletin of the Pan American Union* 61 (December 1927): 1228–1232.

Tropical Plant Research Foundation. *Plan of Work on Moth Stalkborer.* Foundation Information Letters, no. 10. Washington, D.C.: Tropical Plant Research Foundation, 1926.

———. *Plan of Work on Sugar Cane Mosaic.* Foundation Information Letters, no. 11. Washington, D.C.: Tropical Plant Research Foundation, 1926.

———. *Tropical Plant Research Foundation: Its Objects, Organization, Personnel and Publications.* Washington, D.C.: Tropical Plant Research Foundation, 1927.

Tucker, Richard P. *Insatiable Appetite: The United States and the Ecological Degradation of the Tropical World.* Berkeley: University of California Press, 2000.

Tugwell, Rexford Guy. *The Stricken Land: The Story of Puerto Rico.* New York: Doubleday, 1947.

Urban, Ignatius. "Apuntes históricos de las investigaciones botánicas de la isla." *Revista de Agricultura de Puerto Rico* 12 (February 1924): 97–107.

———. *Symbolae Antillanae.* Berlin, 1898–1928.

Vandercook, John W. *King Cane: The Story of Sugar in Hawaii.* New York: Harper & Brothers, 1939.

van Hall, C. J. J. "On Agricultural Research and Extension Work in the Netherland's Indies." In *Science in the Netherlands East Indies,* edited by L. M. R. Rutten. Amsterdam: Koninklijke Academie van Wetenshappen, 1930.

Vasey, Daniel E. *An Ecological History of Agriculture, 10,000 B.C.–A.D. 10,000.* Ames: Iowa State University Press, 1992.

Veliz, Claudio. *The Centralist Tradition of Latin America.* Princeton: Princeton University Press, 1980.

Veloz, Ramón. *Economía y finanzas de Venezuela desde 1830 hasta 1944.* Caracas: Impresores Unidos, 1945.

Veloz Goiticoa, Nicolas. *Venezuela: Geographical Sketch, Natural Resources, Laws, Economic Conditions, Actual Development, Prospects of Future Growth.* Washington, D.C.: International Bureau of the American Republics, GPO, 1904.

Verdoorn, Frans. "Plant Science Institutions, Stations, Museums, Gardens, Societies, and Commissions in Central and South America." In *Plants and Plant Science in Latin America,* edited by Frans Verdoorn, 337–349. Waltham, Mass.: Chronica Botanica, 1945.

———, ed. *Plants and Plant Science in Latin America.* Waltham, Mass.: Chronica Botanica, 1945.

Verrill, Alpheus Hyatt. *Porto Rico Past and Present, and Santo Domingo of To-Day.* New York: Dodd, Mead, 1914.

Vessuri, Hebe M. C. "Foreign Scientists, the Rockefeller Foundation, and the Origins of Agricultural Science in Venezuela." *Minerva* 23 (Autumn 1994): 267–296.

———. "Intercambios internacionales y estilos nacionales periféricos: Aspectos de la mundalización de la ciencia." In *Mundalización de la ciencia y cultura nacional,* edited by A. Lafuente, A. Elena, and M. L. Ortega. Madrid: Doce Calles, 1993.

———. "The Search for a Scientific Community in Venezuela: From Isolation to Applied Research." *Minerva* 23 (1984): 196–235.

———. "Technological Change and the Social Organization of Agricultural Production." *Current Anthropology* 21 (June 1980): 315–327.

———. "Universalismo y nacionalismo en la ciencia moderna: Una aproximación desde el caso venezolano." *Quipu* 8 (May–August 1991): 255–271.

———. "The Universities, Scientific Research and the National Interest in Latin America." *Minerva* 24 (1986): 1–38.

———, ed. *Ciencia académica en la Venezuela moderna: Historia reciente y perspectivas de las disciplinas científicas.* Caracas: Fondo Editorial Acta Científica Venezolana, 1984.

———. *Las instituciones científicas en la historia de la ciencia en Venezuela.* Caracas: Fondo Editorial Acta Científica Venezolana, 1987.

Vitale, Luis. "Ciencia y ambiente." *Nueva Sociedad* 51 (November–December 1980): 59–68.

Walker, Kathleen. "The Inter-American Institute of Agriculture." *Bulletin of the Pan American Union* 81 (May–June 1947): 321–326.

Wallace, Henry A. "Inter-American Agricultural Cooperation." *Bulletin of the Pan American Union* 74 (April 1940): 265–276.

Weinberg, Gregorio. "Sobre la historia de la tradición científica latinoamericana." *Interciencia* 3 (March–April 1978): 72–77.

Wellman, Frederick L. *Tropical American Plant Disease (Neotropical Phytopathology Problems).* Metuchen, N.J.: Scarecrow Press, 1972.

Wercklé, Carlos. *La subregión fitogeográfica costarricense.* San José: Sociedad Nacional de Agricultura, 1909.

Whorton, James. *Before Silent Spring: Pesticides and Public Health in Pre-DDT America.* Princeton: Princeton University Press, 1974.

Wickizer, V. D. *The World's Coffee Economy with Special Reference to Control Schemes.* Stanford: Food Research Institute, 1943.

Wilgus, A. Curtis, ed. *The Caribbean at Mid-Century.* Gainesville: University Press of Florida, 1951.

———, ed. *The Caribbean: Venezuelan Development, a Case History.* Gainesville: University Press of Florida, 1963.

Wilson, Charles Morrow. "The School of Pan American Agriculture: New Center for Tropical Agriculture in the Honduras." *Bulletin of the Pan American Union* 78 (April 1944): 210–217.

———, ed. *New Crops for the New World.* New York: Macmillan, 1945.

Wionczek, Miguel. "Ciencia y tecnología y relaciones de dependencia in América Latina." *Revista de Economía Latinoamericana* 54 (1978): 91–105.

Worcester, Donald E., and Wendell G. Schaeffer. *The Growth and Culture of Latin America.* New York: Oxford University Press, 1971.

Worster, Donald. *The Dust Bowl: The Southern Plains in the 1930s.* Oxford: Oxford University Press, 1979.

———. "Nature and the Disorder of History." *Environmental History Review* 18 (Summer 1994): 1–15.

———. *Nature's Economy: A History of Ecological Ideas.* 2d ed. Cambridge: Cambridge University Press, 1994.

———. "Transformations of the Earth: Toward an Agroecological Perspective in History." *Journal of American History* (March 1990): 1087–1106.

Zeller, Suzanne. *Inventing Canada: Early Victorian Science and the Idea of a Transcontinental Nation.* Toronto: University of Toronto Press, 1987.

INDEX

Lightning Source UK Ltd.
Milton Keynes UK
UKHW010221280121
377819UK00001B/39